To Bobby –
Happy Father's Day

Love,
mom

THE
MATCH

Also by Mark Frost

The Greatest Game Ever Played
The Grand Slam
The Second Objective
Game Six

THE
MATCH

The Day the Game of Golf Changed Forever

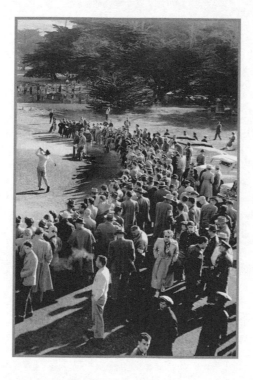

MARK FROST

NEW YORK   BOSTON

Hachette Books
Hachette Book Group
1290 Avenue of the Americas
New York, NY 10104
www.HachetteBookGroup.com

Printed in the United States of America

LSC-C

Originally published in hardcover by Hyperion.
First Hachette Books hardcover edition: May 2015

20 19 18

Hachette Books is a division of Hachette Book Group, Inc.
The Hachette Books name and logo are trademarks of Hachette Book Group, Inc.

The publisher is not responsible for websites (or their content) that are not owned by the publisher.

Library of Congress Cataloging-in-Publication Data
    The match : the day the game of golf changed forever / Mark Frost. — 1st ed.
        p. cm.
    ISBN: 978-1-4013-0278-8
    1. Golf—California—Pebble Beach—History. 2. Lowery, Eddie. I. Title.
    GV983.P43F76 2007
    796.352'660979476—dc22   2007023325

Design by James Sinclair

For Kenny, Lord Byron, the Hawk, and Ol' Harv

CONTENTS

THE
MATCH

PROLOGUE

Monterey, California, August 1945

A fter finishing his second round of the day, a fourteen-year-old caddie wanders down to the sixteenth tee at Cypress Point Golf Club. The son of a fishing net twine salesman, he reads golf magazines while he waits for his father to finish his sales calls at the canneries in nearby Monterey before driving them back to their modest home in the Mission District of San Francisco. The young man is a loner by default, socially traumatized by merciless teenage peers because of a persistent, debilitating stutter. Since taking up golf for its solitary virtues and rigors, he has made this isolated vantage point overlooking the Pacific his favorite refuge from the harsh realities of his life. Gazing out along the stark, forbidding shoreline and across at the green of the par three sixteenth—a two-hundred-and-twenty-yard carry over a turbulent cove, the most spectacular golf hole in the world—Kenny Venturi dreams of one day competing there against his heroes, Byron Nelson and Ben Hogan, at the game's highest level.

Texas, 1927

A fifteen-year-old caddie makes the day-long trip from his home outside Fort Worth to Dallas, to watch his professional idol, the peerless Sir Walter Hagen, play in the semifinals of the Tenth Annual PGA Championship at Cedar Crest Country Club. Hagen trails by one when they reach the final hole, and the young caddie notices him squinting and shading his eyes as he lines up his shot from the eighteenth fairway, so the lad offers him his baseball cap to keep the sun from his eyes. The elegant populist Hagen, who has made an extravagant living by playing to the gallery, gallantly accepts the boy's offer, makes a great show of setting the tattered cap on his luxurious, brilliantined black scalp, and drills his five iron to eight feet from the flag, then graciously returns the cap with a bow to the boy that draws sustained applause for both of them. The caddie, John Byron Nelson, Jr., is thrilled when Hagen sinks the putt for birdie, ties his match, wins it on the first extra hole, and the next day goes on to win his fourth PGA Championship in a row, and his fifth overall.

Four months later, at Glen Garden Country Club outside Fort Worth, Byron Nelson faces off against another fifteen-year-old in the finals of the club's annual Caddie Championship. Byron, a few months older and a head taller, is the clear favorite, admired equally by the members and his peers for his native kindness and sunny good nature. The son of rural, Christian, second-generation cotton farmers, he shines with the clean, upright virtues instilled by his loving, uncomplicated upbringing. Although he barely survived a problematic birth and suffered a near fatal bout of typhoid fever at eleven, Byron has grown strong and hardy through his years of outdoor manual labor and become a gifted athlete. Blessed with great natural balance, and guided by a dog-eared copy of Harry Vardon's instruction book on golf, during his three years in the Glen Garden caddie yard he has begun to develop a powerful, rhythmic, and dependable swing.

His opponent that day, a solemn, grim-faced young man, is slight and smaller in stature, but his outsized hands, inherited from his beloved blacksmith father, are those of a hardened adult. His face already looks as careworn and weathered as that of a man in his twenties. He is Byron's temperamental opposite in every regard— guarded, pessimistic, introverted—and has come by it the hard way, through misfortune. By all accounts Ben Hogan had lived an idyllic country childhood similar to Byron's, until it was shattered six years earlier in a moment of unspeakable tragedy that he and his family will keep a closeted secret until the end of their days. From that terrible divide young Hogan's life descended into an ordeal of urban poverty and child labor that damaged and darkened what had been until that moment a carefree, innocent spirit. Since securing his first job as a caddie three years earlier, Hogan has only recently begun to play the game himself and for the first time glimpsed a path that could lead him out of his nightmarish existence. His perilous, fifteen-year journey of deliverance is only just beginning, and anything from assured; he will have to carve and claw his way out of the deep hole into which life has dropped him, a club in his hands as his only tool.

Their nine-hole caddie championship match ends in a tie when Nelson sinks a thirty-foot putt on the last green, just as he'd watched his idol Walter Hagen do at the recent PGA Championship. Urged by the members to settle the matter in a play-off, Ben wins their first extra hole. Under the impression that they were playing sudden death, Ben is puzzled when his competitor and their gallery hurry on to the next tee without congratulations or comment; only then does he realize he didn't know, or wasn't told, that they are engaged in a nine-hole play-off. Emotionally crushed, Ben quickly gives back his advantage, and Byron has a chance to win at the final hole if he can sink another thirty-footer. As he stands over that putt, Byron tells himself: "This putt is for the U.S. Open." Tracking straight and sure, in it falls to win the match. Both boys are handed a new iron from the pro shop as their prize, which, each lacking the one the other received, they promptly trade with each other.

The victorious, outgoing Byron follows the members who've witnessed their battle into the clubhouse for a Christmas dinner with all the trimmings. The winner in more ways than one, Byron learns he will also be awarded a junior membership and full playing privileges at the club, assuring him regular access to the golf course, exactly the break his developing skills need to realize his dream of becoming a champion golfer. On this night, Byron's future success in the game he's grown to love seems all but guaranteed. Within three years he will be confident enough to step onto the game's national stage.

There will be no holiday dinner or extended club privileges for the runner-up, but then he has never known anything other than the short end of a bargain. For starters, he was born left-handed into a right-handed world and is still struggling to play golf from that unfamiliar side. Nor will he be ready anytime soon to compete as a professional; any chance he has to arrive at that distant station will come only through relentless hard work and ruthless self-discipline. To the end of his days he will never find satisfaction or consolation in finishing second, at anything.

As twilight fades, young Ben Hogan grips his new five iron and heads back to the practice range alone.

Pinehurst, North Carolina, 1948

On a whim, and at the last minute, a twenty-two-year-old economics major named Edward Harvie Ward drives down to Pinehurst from the University of North Carolina in Chapel Hill to enter the North & South Amateur Championship. Played on Donald Ross's famed Number Two Course, this match play tournament is considered second in importance only to the USGA National Amateur and for nearly fifty years has drawn an equally accomplished field. Although Harvie, as he's been known all his life, plays on the Tar Heels' collegiate team, and qualified for the National Amateur the year before, the native North Carolinian anticipates an early exit; he's brought along only a toothbrush and the white Oxford shirt and crimson cashmere sweater on his back.

Popular at Chapel Hill, but a nonchalant student at best, he set out to study medicine, backtracked to pharmacy, and retreated once again to a general business degree. Your college years, Harvie had decided, are supposed to be fun, so why ruin them with study and scholarship? His higher education has already been interrupted by World War Two and two years in the army; he describes his role in uniform as "keeping the Nazis out of Kansas," where he played a lot of golf while amusing his senior officers. Equally liked by men and women, Harvie is already both a man's man and a notorious ladies' man. He's musical, a good singer and a great dancer, a teller of tales, always good for a laugh, the center of the room at every party. Blessed with movie star looks, an abundance of charm, and a devil-may-care personality that already reflects his roguish indifference to nine-to-five conformity, Harvie exudes the confident aura of a big man on campus for whom greatness seems a foregone conclusion, despite his, to date, conspicuous lack of accomplishment.

With a hint that might be about to change, Harvie shoots 74 in Monday's qualifying round, good for fourth place in the field, to reach the match play segment of the North & South. While that qualifying round is still being played, news reaches the clubhouse that Donald Ross has died in a local Pinehurst hospital at the age of seventy-five. Born in Dornoch on the northern coast of Scotland, Ross learned his craft at St. Andrews as an apprentice to the

Methuselah of golf, Old Tom Morris, and after making the crossing as a young man became the most prolific architect in early American golf history. His professional association with Pinehurst, where he built his masterpiece, began in 1901, and Ross had worked and made his home there ever since. He would craft over two hundred courses around the country, among them enduring classics like Oakland Hills, Seminole, and East Lake, helping to define the standards by which all future American courses would be judged. The flag over Pinehurst's clubhouse will be lowered to half-mast for the week, and canceling the tournament is briefly considered, but it is decided that Ross would've wanted the games to continue.

In his opening match Harvie catches a serious case of the jitters on the first tee and finds himself four down after five holes, somehow pulls himself together, goes on a tear, and rallies to win on the first extra hole. To everyone's surprise but his own, Harvie reels off a string of four more victories through the week that propel him into the semifinals of the North & South. Every evening, after winning that day's match, he dutifully phones the university's assistant athletic director, the man who gave him permission to enter the tournament. After receiving the go-ahead to extend his stay another day—avoiding classes doesn't exactly qualify as a hardship for Harvie—he washes out his socks, shirt, and underwear in the sink of his cheap motel room and, instead of heading out for his customary evening of extracurricular amusements, tries to get some sleep.

In the semifinals Harvie faces a rising star and Atlantic Coast Conference rival from Wake Forest's golf team, a strapping Pennsylvanian sophomore named Arnold Palmer, and bests him handily, 5 & 4. When news of Harvie's victory filters back to Chapel Hill, his fraternity brothers from Zeta Psi dragoon busloads of UNC coeds and convoy down to Pinehurst to cheer him on in the finals. His sister and parents, owners of two drugstores in his hometown of Tarboro, North Carolina, also drive in for the match. They're successful, upward-striving, middle-class people, proud that they were able to send their adored younger son to private prep school, prouder still that his dedication to their favorite sport has brought Harvie to the cusp of such an achievement. (Given Harvie's lifelong lack of interest in academics, and work in general, they're thrilled he's on the cusp of anything.) As an added incentive, at dinner the night they arrive, his pharmacist father promises to buy Harvie a used car if he can come out on top.

The odds are stacked impressively against him. Harvie's opponent that day is not only the best amateur player in the world; Frank Stranahan is in the middle of the most dominant international run by a nonprofessional since the heyday of Bobby Jones. Runner-up at both the 1947 Masters and British Open—and the reigning British, Canadian, Mexican, and Brazilian amateur champion—Stranahan has been close to unbeatable for over a year. He is also one of the most eccentric and peculiar characters to ever materialize in the genteel history of the gentleman's game.

Frank is twenty-five, the favorite son of Robert Stranahan, the man who created one of the key components of the automobile revolution, Champion Sparkplugs, based in Toledo, Ohio. Bankrolled by his multimillionaire father, Stranahan grew up with the entitlements of a feudal prince, free to pursue his early passion for golf without ever stressing about a paycheck. Tall, tan, and ruggedly handsome, he is known as "Muscles" on the golf circuit, for his zealous obsession with weight lifting, health food, and physical fitness. Suffice it to say that in the era of the double martini, grilled T-bone, and Baked Alaska, Stranahan's cult of the body is slightly ahead of his time. His favorite prank is to carry the suitcases loaded with his 356 pounds of traveling free weights into a hotel lobby, set them down to check in, then collapse with laughter when a bellboy falls on his face trying to lift them. With a thirst for publicity and a propensity for lecturing anyone who'll listen on his quasi-religious devotion to physical culture—all the while boasting about its beneficial effects on his length off the tee—the self-absorbed Frank Stranahan comes as close as anyone in American sports to the stereotype of the spoiled rich kid.

A few years earlier, after becoming club champion while still in his teens at his home course—Inverness in Ohio, a Donald Ross design—Stranahan regularly challenged the club's resident professional to a match. The pro had given up trying to teach Frank two years earlier because he refused to listen to a single suggestion, a failure he was then compelled to justify to the boy's meddling father. A number of run-ins followed as the headstrong youngster continually challenged or ignored the club's rules and the basic etiquette of the game, trying the patience of every employee in the place, particularly the head professional. When Frank finally tried to provoke the pro out of the shop by suggesting the man was afraid to be shown up by a teenager, that pro, the reigning U.S. Open champion and a gentleman who was very slow to anger—but heaven help you if he got there—by the name of Byron Nelson, finally reached his limit. So the day came in 1940 when Byron accepted Frank's challenge, and then upped the ante on him, offering to play against both young Stranahan and two of his cronies, both single-digit junior players, in a best-ball match. His ball against all three of theirs. Word spread quickly of the challenge and a sizeable crowd gathered to watch.

Byron shot a course record 63 that day, dusted the floor with Stranahan and his two buddies, and as he delicately put it afterward, "Frankie never bothered me again."

Since Stranahan burst onto the international golf scene in 1947, blue collar sports reporters have made dependable sport of taking him to task for his egotistical excesses. Frank often provokes their barbs, for instance when he is photographed showing off that week working out with his customized barbells in front of Pinehurst's Carolina Hotel. In spite of the personal antipathy he inspires, all the experts and reporters on hand, and Stranahan himself in a typically unguarded moment, have predicted that he will crush his unheralded younger opponent in the North-South finals. Stranahan has taken his blue steel self-assurance one step further, renting the ballroom of the Carolina Hotel the night of the championship round and booking in a band for his anticipated victory party.

When the two men tee it up that Saturday morning at Pinehurst Number Two, few people in town aside from his parents are rooting for Frank Stranahan to attend his party. Harvie's introduction is cheered by the boisterous collegiate crowd, close to three thousand of them, most under the impression that golf and football share not only a grass playing field but spectator etiquette. As the round progresses, they go berserk every time Harvie gets his ball airborne, and boo every swing Stranahan makes.

With that home court advantage, and for the first time all week wearing fresh clothes brought down by his roommate, Harvie Ward proves that the cool confidence he exhibits off the course is no act. Although constantly out-driven by his brawny opponent, Harvie's fairway woods are flawless and his touch around Number Two's treacherous crowned greens is as soft and silky as a cat's whisker. Using a rusty old hickory-shafted derelict putter he found at his home club in Tarboro when he took up the game eight years earlier, he sinks twelve putts of ten feet or more during their first round. As they walk off to break for lunch, exasperated at Harvie's uncanny ability to erase his power advantage by sinking another long putt, Stranahan complains frostily:

"If you couldn't putt you wouldn't even be in the game."

Harvie smiles, knowing at that moment he has his man beat, and replies: "Well, Frank, last I checked putting is *part* of the game."

Never trailing all day, Harvie ices the fearsome Stranahan when he sinks a three-footer on the final hole to win the North & South Amateur one up. Stranahan takes it manfully, shakes his hand, and drives off with his parents in their chauffeured Cadillac, stopping at the hotel to cancel their ballroom rental. The jubilant Tar Heel gallery hoists Harvie onto their shoulders, parading their native son hero off the eighteenth green toward the historic Pinehurst club-house. Harvie has to hurry back to Chapel Hill that night in order to return to class the next day, but an impromptu victory party at a local bar takes place for him in absentia. When a young local who looks a little like Harvie wanders in and is mistaken for him, despite his protests, which quickly subside once he realizes how spectacularly the error works in his favor, the substitute victor is celebrated until the wee hours. Displaying impeccable manners, the man promptly writes Harvie a thank-you note.

As he always suspected he would, Harvie likes the view from the top of the heap. Propelled by his unlikely victory, the following spring in his senior year he will go on to win the 1949 NCAA Collegiate Championship, qualify for the National Amateur, and make his first appearance at the Masters. His future as one of the greatest amateurs in history, perhaps even the heir apparent to Bob Jones, appears as inevitable as income tax.

For the next nine years—but then, tragically, no longer—he will fulfill that promise.

Their paths will soon cross repeatedly. Four men from two different generations, united by a complex web of personal and professional relationships. Vastly different personalities, but all brothers under the skin, shaped and distilled by the difficult, disciplined game they share. The single perfect day that will ultimately bring them all together falls into place casually but with the stubborn inevitability of fate. Few people heard about it at the time, and none of the headline makers involved immediately regarded the event or its outcome as in any way remarkable, but it has since accrued the weight and character of myth. There will be no newsreel or television cameras on hand to record the remarkable events of that day. No one appears to have preserved it with even a single photograph that survives. Newspaper accounts mentioned it only in passing, it appears no reporters actually witnessed any part of their encounter.

In spite of which, over the years this one casual game has become the sport's great suburban legend, as captivating and elusive as Brigadoon. Looking back from a future vantage point, in addition to its human dimensions, a broader significance that no one at the time could have assigned to their encounter takes shape, because the sport these men played had reached an equally decisive moment. Since golf's early days at the start of the American century, the game had been dominated on the course and administered off it by the aristocratic amateurs of the United States Golf Association. They organized the first private clubs; they popularized the sport with their peers; it was their game. Between 1913 and 1933 an amateur had won the U.S. Open eight times; gentlemen amateurs were not only the game's social elite, they could also claim parity on the course itself. Golf professionals, the distinctly working class men who taught and played the game for a meager living, had struggled for decades toward social and economic equality. By the mid-1950s, only one generation removed from a time when they were not allowed to set foot into private clubhouses, a handful of top professionals—chief among them Ben Hogan, Byron Nelson, and Sam Snead—had finally broken through into broader cultural stardom and higher tax brackets. But the vast majority of the men working the pro golf circuit still faced an uneasy hand-to-mouth existence, living on the road most of the year with no guaranteed money, playing for a tiny fraction of the paychecks and none of the entitlements we so routinely see run-of-the-mill pros receive today. The gallant amateur champion who played for the love of the game—embodied by the golden memory of the immortal Bob Jones, more than twenty years after his retirement—still represented the upper class *beau ideal* of what a golfer should be.

By the second half of the 1950s, that image was about to be forever transformed by the twin arrivals of televised tournament coverage and a charismatic proletarian pro from Pennsylvania named Arnold Palmer. But in early 1956 Palmer hadn't yet made his stunning entrance, and one last young group of gifted amateurs, dedicated to the Jonesian model, had arrived with both the wherewithal to make their livings elsewhere and the talent to capture a major championship. Because these two opposing factions so seldom faced each other in competition, aside from the annual U.S. Open—where an amateur hadn't won in over twenty years—the question of which side produced the better players remained a heated and ongoing debate. Given today's standards, the answer appears laughably obvious— "amateur" is a pejorative term at best—but at that time it remained an undecided issue. The best pros of that era often went out of their way to avoid playing against the best amateurs in high-profile situations, particularly in match play—a format in which amateurs specialized and excelled—unwilling to risk the damage to their fragile pride and reputations if they should fail. So in many ways the sport had been waiting for a moment like this game was about to provide, a decisive showdown to help determine the future direction of the sport: whose game was golf going to be, the pros' or the amateurs', and which champions would each side send forward to settle the issue?

These questions would find their answers at Cypress Point, January 10, 1956. As time passed, even the participants would remember its specifics in varying ways, a vivid reminder that all of human experience is subjective, and memory is a perilously fragile vessel for collective truth. But between the facts that can be certified, the often conflicting versions each man has left us of these events, and their impact on the sport and the remarkable lives that would intersect at this crossroads, there is more than enough lore to tell the tale. Ask anyone well versed in the history of the game about it and they will smile and shake their heads in wonder.

The Match. Ah yes, The Match.

The Clambake

It never would have happened without Bing Crosby. By definition popular culture lives only in the present, desperately seeking currency and the fickle attentions of youth, without a thought to the past. But the twenty-first century's entertainment empire rests on a handful of original foundations that still stand, and for every one of them Harry Lillis "Bing" Crosby helped lay the bricks. Here are the improbable facts:

Bing Crosby sang most of the classic American standards first, popularizing the work of every important composer from Gershwin to Cole Porter, principal inspiration for every big voice that followed him, from Sinatra to Elvis. He delivered more hit records than any artist before or since—sixteen charted songs per year for two and a half decades—and to this day, at over seventeen hundred hours, his silvery baritone remains the most recorded voice in human history. He was the first white singing star to incorporate African-American idioms into his work, and in their collaborative recordings he helped bring artists like Louis Armstrong and the Mills Brothers into the mainstream.

For twelve years during radio's heyday Crosby starred in *Kraft Mu-*

sic Hall, the most popular weekly show in history, and turned CBS into a national network. Bing also appeared in seventy-nine movies over a forty-year career, in every genre from musicals to light comedy to serious drama. He performed four songs that won Oscars, won one himself for Best Actor, was the number one box-office star for five years running, and remained a top attraction for over two decades. Alongside partner Bob Hope in their immensely popular Road pictures, and in every other arena he conquered, Bing Crosby embodied the whole idea of "cool" before cool was cool.

In 1937, scaling the peak of his stardom, Bing had another idea. A friendly golf tournament, to help out the lads on the struggling professional tour. A casual event at the start of the year to bridge a gap in the PGA's West Coast winter schedule, and partner the pros with his golf-crazed show business buddies for a thirty-six-hole, better-ball affair. A perfect excuse to throw a nonstop party—a stag weekend at the beach near the racetrack Bing had a financial stake in at Del Mar—and while they were having fun, why not raise a few bucks for charity? Bing took up the game of golf seriously while still a youngster in Spokane, Washington. Once a star, he played it religiously—considering golf a stress reliever and social activity, he organized his film schedule around his tee times—and expertly; Crosby carried a single-digit handicap his entire life, won his club championship at Lakeside Golf Club five times, and qualified for both the U.S. and British Amateur.

On opening day of the first Crosby Amateur-Pro, a monsoon blew in off the Pacific, the round was canceled, but no one missed a beat. Bing tossed some steaks on the grill and sang a few tunes on his own patio, which was just off the back nine. Mixed drinks flowed like the Ganges. Waves of aspiring actresses, unbidden, materialized like woodland nymphs. When the sun came out the following day, a rough-edged, smooth-swinging rookie pro who'd recently emerged from the West Virginia hills named Samuel Jackson Snead stepped up to win both the abbreviated tournament and the Pro-Am, then refused Bing's personal check for $732, preferring to take his prize money in cash, no offense to Mr. Crosby. The twenty-five-year-old Snead explained, in his back country banjo twang, that he didn't put much stock in bank accounts. He was still carrying around the bankroll from his first professional victory in Oakland only two weeks earlier.

Born the same year as Nelson and Hogan, in 1912, the youngest of five brothers from an Appalachian coal mining county, Sam Snead grew up around a swank resort called the Homestead Hotel in Hot Springs, Virginia, where his father worked as a handyman. Without much formal education, the Snead family tree was crowded with musicians, eccentric inventors, and gifted athletes, qualities that all found their way into Sam's supremely natural game. A tall, lanky, and almost freakishly strong physical specimen, he was the most gifted natural athlete to ever seriously pursue golf. Sam excelled at every sport he tried, but grew up caddying and fell in love with the game at the Homestead's home course—an early Donald Ross design—and landed his first job as a professional at the Greenbrier, a rival resort in neighboring West Virginia. He emerged from these mountain retreats a few years later onto golf's national stage, his greatness fully formed, as a kind of prodigal Forrest Gump.

Sam would go on to win three more times after the inaugural Crosby that season, the tour's second leading money winner in 1937, the strongest debut in PGA history. Over a career that spanned the next four decades the Slammer would capture seven majors and win more tournaments all over the world—135 is the consensus figure—than anyone else in golf's long history. His fluid, powerhouse swing remains one of the game's gold standards. Sam may have drawled like a hillbilly, but he dressed like a big city bon vivant, and under all that molasses and sassafras he was lot cagier than he liked to let on. Coming of age around a high-end resort, Sam had catered to the whims of the wealthy all his life; he would forever resent their class advantages, but he also studied their every move to his advantage, and as an emerging talent benefited enormously from their patronage. Once he hit the big time, his calculated but colorful image as a coarse, cracker-barrel country boy provided irresistible copy that made him an immediate favorite with the sporting press; public fascination would quickly follow.

Along with the entrance of Sam Snead, another legend was born that week. The first edition of what quickly became known as "The Clambake"—for the final night's seaside blowout, although no one remembers clams on the menu—turned into such big fun for all involved Bing decided to make it an annual affair. No one had ever put together anything like it before, but it was a surefire recipe: pro athletes, Hollywood stars, a sprinkling of corporate potentates, add copious amounts of alcohol and mix vigorously. Almost without trying—but then such an integral part of his genius was that he never *looked* like he was trying—the King of Pop Culture had invented the celebrity pro-am. Already an established star on the PGA Tour, Byron Nelson showed up for the second Clambake in 1938. So did his twenty-five-year-old traveling companion, Ben Hogan, struggling to make ends meet in his third dogged attempt to hack it as a touring pro. On the amateur side the wisecracking thirty-four-year-old vaudevillian and Broadway headliner who'd just moved to Hollywood to try his luck in films and radio, Leslie "Bob" Hope, made his first appearance, cementing a friendship with Bing that was about to pay off like the Irish Sweepstakes.

Sam Snead, now a national sports icon known as "Slammin' Sammy," successfully defended his title that year. The courtly Byron Nelson finished out of the money—paired with Johnny "Tarzan" Weissmuller—but he and Bing hit it off so well that Byron became a Clambake regular. Byron renewed his acquaintance that week with another amateur, a wealthy car dealer from the Bay Area named Eddie Lowery, who would soon play a pivotal role in every aspect of his life. Hard luck Ben Hogan finished eighth in 1938 and took home $75, barely covering expenses. On the verge of selling his car for a train ticket home to Fort Worth and abandoning golf for the oil business, Hogan managed to hang on through the West Coast swing and cash a few small checks. The following year he inched up to sixth, to win $112. In 1940—painfully slow progress—Hogan finished fourth and won $225, but had yet to win his first PGA Tournament.

In 1942 World War Two dimmed the lights of Crosby's annual bash and all the major golf championships, and altered every other form of American entertainment. Bing threw himself into the civilian war effort, performing for front-line troops all over Europe while leading the domestic war bond drive, appearing in countless charity golf exhibitions with Byron Nelson and Bob Hope. For his efforts the Armed Forces named Crosby the one celebrity who had done the most for GI morale. When civilian life resumed at war's end, Bing decided to revive his Clambake, a few hours up the coast, on the Monterey Peninsula, where he'd purchased a new home. He also suggested the novel notion of playing his tournament on three remarkable courses in the area: the Monterey Peninsula Country Club, Cypress Point Golf Club, and Pebble Beach. The PGA had never heard of such a thing and threatened to withhold its support. Bing told them he'd be perfectly happy to proceed without their sanction and pay the purse from his own pocket; from the legendarily tightfisted Crosby this was a threat difficult to ignore. (Dean Martin used to say of him: "Don't you worry about old Bing. He's got about twenty million . . . on him.") And so, played over three courses, the resurrected Bing Crosby Pro-Am resumed in 1948 as an official PGA Tour stop.

For a generation that had saved the free world and borne witness to the horrors of war, the Clambake satisfied perfectly their postwar hunger for grown-up celebrity hijinks. The general who led that war effort, Dwight Eisenhower, had won the White House and faced almost certain reelection in the fall of 1956. He had also become the first chief executive to unashamedly profess his love for the sport of golf, and insisted on playing it as a prerogative of office. Millions around the country followed suit; golf and the national mood were, at long last, in perfect synch, the country's future stretching out ahead like a pristine fairway. These were the headiest years of America's expansion after two long decades of depression and war. The shadows cast by the threats of the Communist cold war abroad and McCarthyism at home could not dampen a collective instinct for a recuperative period of smooth sailing, and the cultural and generational upheaval hinted at by the recent arrival of rock and roll into the mainstream seemed worlds away. The three television networks that ruled the airwaves were dominated by depictions of conventional middle-class families like the Nelsons and the Cleavers, suggesting a social complacency devoid of dysfunction. With television eroding the motion picture's grip on American audiences, bland wide-screen spectacles like *Around the World in Eighty Days* and *The Ten Commandments* dominated the box office. Jack Kerouac's *On the Road*, the first anthem of the coming counterculture, was a year away from finding a publisher, while racy revelations of cracks underlying the placid façade of small-town life in *Peyton Place* stormed to the top of best-seller lists.

With Bing Crosby as its reassuring public face, the Clambake's attendance and reputation grew every year, and the advent of national network coverage—along with The Masters, it was the first tournament to be extensively telecast—would soon turn it into a midwinter cultural institution. A chance to watch their favorite entertainers shank golf balls into the Pacific proved irresistible to the public. Bing used to hand out commemorative, handcrafted ceramic fifths of bourbon, whiskey, and brandy—one a day to every participant—so a good percentage were either still lubricated from the night before when they reached the tee, or replastered by the time they finished. The nonstop bacchanal that went on behind the scenes was less suitable for broadcast, but when the curtain between entertainer and audience dropped in that era, it stayed down. The few journalists lucky enough to be invited maintained a strict code of silence;

they wouldn't dream of telling tales out of school, and there were plenty. Comedy, tragedy, drama, liquor, and sex—the Clambake offered everything to its privileged participants except a good night's sleep.

Some old-timers, even Bing himself in private, wistfully regretted that the tournament never recaptured the warmth and intimacy of the early prewar sessions, but every January hundreds of stars and titans of industry sweated out whether Bing's handwritten invitation would show up in their mailbox. His annually revised list of 168 invitees became one of the most closely guarded secrets in Hollywood. Outrageous acts of supplication—one involving skywriting—were offered by big shots dying to get in. In the mid-1950s, in order to avoid these shows of unseemly desperation, Bing bought a house in a remote area of Baja Mexico and repaired there every year after Christmas to relax on his fishing boat, away from the telephones, and compose his list in peace.

At the Clambake Bing's rule was absolute. All the amateurs' homegrown handicaps were tossed to the curb; Bing assessed each man's game and without discussion personally dispensed the strokes they were granted. Sandbaggers were persona non grata; run afoul of Bing's old-school idea of fair play, and you'd earn banishment for life. His pairings were as carefully crafted as seating arrangements at a White House state dinner. Bing always took his pick of playing partners, but never rigged the game, only once coming within five shots of winning his own pro-am. By the mid-1950s, as Bing passed his own half-century mark, his game began to falter, while the responsibilities of running the show grew ever more pressing. He decided the time had come to step offstage, but not before he gave it one last shot as a participant. For his swan song in 1956, Bing decided to recruit as his partner the toughest competitor the game had produced in a quarter of a century. Four-time U.S. Open champion—the man now universally known as the Hawk—Ben Hogan. The defending champion from 1955's Crosby Pro-Am that year was Ben's old caddie-yard running mate, Byron Nelson. Now forty-four years old and nine years retired from the PGA Tour, living as a gentleman cattle rancher in Fort Worth, Lord Byron made the Clambake one of his only regular appearances on the pro circuit.

Byron's amateur playing partner, and his closest friend, was that car dealer tycoon he'd met at the '38 Clambake, Eddie Lowery. A member of the USGA's Executive Committee, Lowery had a legitimate claim as one of the founding fathers of American golf. He had been present at its birth, as Francis Ouimet's ten-year-old caddie at the 1913 U.S. Open, where Ouimet's upset victory over the English greats Vardon and Ray put their sport on America's front pages. The first American-born player to ever win a U.S. Open, Ouimet ushered in the era of the great gentlemen amateurs with his win, and lifted Eddie Lowery out of poverty and obscurity into an unlikely fame that would lead to tremendous worldly success. In love with the spotlight ever since—which seldom burned brighter than at the Clambake— the ferociously competitive Lowery had every intention of successfully defending his Pro-Am title with Byron in 1956. But as he drove down the coast to Monterey for that year's Crosby, Eddie Lowery had no idea that he was about to bear witness to the last shining hour of the American gentleman amateur, and had already set into motion events that would lead to that player's decline.

Coleman's Cocktail Party

The rituals and revels of the Clambake began, as they did every year, on Tuesday night, January 10, 1956. VIPs rolled into Monterey that day from all over the map, and for the next seven days this hamlet by the sea transformed into the center of high society in North America. Moguls who didn't own a mansion on the Peninsula rented palatial estates for the week, flew in their staffs, and stocked enough provisions to retake Normandy. Most of the PGA Tour players who came to play the tournament bunked at the old Pine Inn in Carmel or a hotel in Monterey called the Casa Munras. At dozens of parties up and down the Seventeen Mile Drive, on that Tuesday evening friendships and rivalries formed or rekindled in anticipation of the coming competition.

Bing Crosby always hosted a low-key affair at his own house just off the thirteenth green at Pebble Beach, but by 1956 the A-list event had become the annual cocktail party at George Coleman's house. George Coleman was an American original from an Oklahoma mining clan. His father and uncle had taken part in the epic turn-of-the-century land claim, racing a team of horses into the newly opened territory to lay down stakes on a swatch of its northeast corner that held massive lead and zinc deposits. The yields from the five resulting mines were so rich that for a time the Colemans controlled the world market in both minerals. An only child, George grew up on the family's vast prairie spread outside Miami, Oklahoma. When he took an interest in golf as a young boy, his father built him a nine-hole course on the property. While eighteen and still a freshman at the University of Oklahoma, George married a sixteen-year-old Oklahoma beauty, Elizabeth Fullerton. He took over the family concern at twenty-one after his father died, and diversified into banking, cattle ranching, and wildcat oil drilling. One of his earliest investments was a little company that turned into Pennzoil; Coleman's Midas touch continued with nearly every bet he placed from that point forward. A lifelong friend described George as "a man who owned five percent of everything."

As their fortune grew, the Colemans entertained lavishly at homes they owned in Colorado, Palm Beach, New York City, and Northern Italy, charter members of what soon came to be known as the "jet set." George did the flying himself. An accomplished pilot since high school, during World War Two Coleman trained nearly five hundred navy pilots at the Spartan School of Aeronautics in Oklahoma. He was equally at home on the water, where he set world records as a competitive hydroplane pilot, anticipated the postwar boating craze, and invested early in Chris-Craft Industries. His love of baseball led to partial ownership of the Detroit Tigers. As part of the first generation to grow up playing golf after Ouimet's popularizing victory, George won the Oklahoma State Amateur, qualified for the British Open, and maintained a reputation as an accomplished amateur, which led to a lasting friendship with Bing Crosby in the late 1930s, when George became one of the Clambake's earliest competitors. His pairing in a 1942 pro-amateur resulted in an even closer friendship with Ben Hogan. Their relationship deepened as Hogan realized his greatness after the war, reeling off nine major championships in six years to emerge as the dominant player of his era.

Lean and good-looking, educated, socially gifted, and a phenomenal success in business, George Coleman represented for Ben Hogan something close to the model American man. The two men were not only contemporaries, they could have been twins separated at birth; born within two weeks of each other in 1912, in neighboring Southern states, at opposing ends of the class spectrum. A kid who had worked his way up from nothing, Hogan, as an adult, saw in Coleman the business tycoon he hoped to become when his golf career ended. Coleman in turn appreciated the lonely struggle Hogan had endured to reach the summit of his sport, reshaping himself as a sophisticated man of the world; he embodied Coleman's ruling-class vision of the self-made, self-reliant American.

Although he had agreed to play in the 1956 Clambake as Bing Crosby's partner, returning to the tournament for the first time in five years, Hogan would spend the week of the Crosby Pro-Am as the houseguest of George Coleman. After making an early, brief appearance at George's place that Tuesday evening for drinks, Ben and his wife, Valerie, moved on to Bing's house at about seven thirty for dinner.

At about the same time the Hogans left the Coleman party, Eddie Lowery and his partner and houseguest that week, Byron Nelson, arrived with their wives. If Ben Hogan and George Coleman had begun life as social opposites, they shared a stoic and reserved code of personal conduct. They were gentlemen in the classic Anglo-Saxon sense, and among the many things a gentleman did not do in polite company was talk about himself, brag about his accomplishments, or by any conspicuous display indicate how much money he was making. In a modern business world dominated by egomaniacal headline-grabbing CEOs, the strong silent type who'd conquered worlds but never bored you with the details might seem an antiquated male stereotype, but in mid-century America he was an admired ideal, seldom better personified than by these two singular men.

Eddie Lowery, another self-made multimillionaire who had risen from circumstances every bit as dire as Hogan's, most certainly did not fit that profile.

Eddie

When his main chance, in the virtuous form of Francis Ouimet, first appeared to Eddie Lowery—a ten-year-old dirt-poor pugnacious Irish runt, who'd lost his father the year before in an industrial accident—he grabbed hold and rode him as if his life depended on it. Eddie's instincts were faultless, and his contributions as a psychologist and cheerleader to Francis's success cannot be underestimated. When his impossible long shot came home to win the 1913 U.S. Open Championship, and the gracious amateur Ouimet refused the crowd's spontaneous generosity, his animated little caddie ended up with a hatful of cash: a fortune of 125 bucks. Eddie hung on to every one of them. From his newly elevated station, as he observed how this grown-up world around him operated, and turned the same precociously discerning eye on himself, Eddie decided he'd been blessed with only two marketable gifts—gab and hustle—and to say that he went on to make the best of both of them is a colossal understatement.

Although successful in the advertising business in Boston, by the mid-1930s Eddie had few ties left to bind him to his hometown—his first wife had died not long after their only son was born—and feeling confined by the city's rigid social structure, he hungered for new horizons. Eddie decided that California's gold-rush frontier mentality offered a wide-open playing field, so he traveled west, re-married, and bought into a car dealership in San Jose. His timing was impeccable. Benefiting from the abundance of cheap oil, Presi-dent Eisenhower's creation of the U.S. highway system, and the post-war ascendance of the automobile as the symbol of upwardly mobile American affluence, by the mid-1950s Eddie had turned the three showrooms of Van Etta Motors into the most successful Lincoln Mercury dealership in the country.

Eddie's association with the sport of golf had continued through-out his life, and apart from the business world it remained his con-suming passion. He had matured into a player of no small talent, won both the Massachusetts Junior and Amateur during the 1920s, and remained a competitive amateur at the national level for de-cades. Eddie was among the first American businessmen to exploit the now commonplace bond between the corporate boardroom and the privileged playing fields of private golf. Established in San Fran-cisco's business community, he joined the golf clubs in the area that catered to its grandees, San Francisco Golf Club and Cypress Point. He forged strong friendships with famous contemporaries who shared his love of the game, like Bing Crosby and Ed Sullivan, and with the next generation's greatest players, Ben Hogan and Byron Nelson. At a time when the sport provided little financial security to even its brightest stars, Eddie was quick to dispense favors, business advice, or financial support to cement those relationships. In time, with the crucial support of the game's elder statesman, Francis Ouimet, he networked his way onto the influential USGA Executive Committee in 1953 as Northern California's regional representative.

Eddie had made it to center stage in life and his sport, but didn't get there without stepping on a few toes. Although he made friends easily, and devoted himself to them, he could also be a controversial figure. Slightly less than five foot nine and 150 pounds, animated by a pepper-and-vinegar vitality, Eddie had the personality of an alpha wolf in the body of a terrier and never relinquished the underdog's perspective that had been a defining part of his birthright. Cold experience had taught him that life was a Darwinian battlefield, survival was at stake on a daily basis, and the poorhouse awaited the losers. His credo was work hard, play harder, take what's yours, and never back down from a fight. So there were grumbles. Whispers about hardnosed tactics, in business, in backroom card games, even on the golf course. No one who ever met him described Eddie's personality as anything less than electrifying, but there were a few civilized souls who didn't appreciate the extra voltage. "He's a hustler," was the complaint from some gentrified quarters; "a car salesman, yes, but almost a *used* car salesman. He pushes deals a step over the line when he doesn't need to—why, it's almost as if he can't help himself."

Maybe he couldn't. Eddie didn't possess the temperament to rest on his laurels. He was a scrapper, who thrived on excitement of any kind, lived for it. His second wife, Louise, died of cancer in 1951, and while grieving he devoted himself like never before to the game and the action around it. During golf tournaments at his clubs you could always find him at the center of the Calcutta, a form of parimutuel betting where players were "bought" at a pretournament auction and sums in the tens—and even hundreds—of thousands were won and lost below the radar of the IRS. The regular presence of unknown pros brought in to compete as amateurs under a variety of ruses—known as "ringers"—was indicative of how seriously big gamblers took these events. A public fixing scandal about the Calcutta at Deepdale Golf Club, outside New York, broke late in 1955, and as the Attorney General's Office moved in to investigate, the traditional "Calcutta" disappeared around the country. Bing Crosby canceled the Calcutta for the upcoming Clambake in 1956. Eddie Lowery, winner of the '55 Crosby Pro-Am, had bet on his own team and cleaned up at that last Calcutta. Eddie used the cash to finance an all-expenses-paid overseas trip with Byron Nelson, during which Byron played for only the second time in the British Open and then won his final professional title at the French Open.

Eddie for years hosted an evening poker game at Thunderbird Country Club in Palm Springs, where he kept a third home. After hours, he often moved the game to his house, kept the liquor flowing, and there were complaints that an occasional pigeon got plucked cleaner than polite company should have allowed. A lot of cash changed hands in those cutthroat smokers, sometimes handed over the next morning in brown paper bags after angry trips to the bank, and if you hadn't made good Monday's losses you could forget about playing in Tuesday's game. Eddie also built a bunker and green in his backyard, and would gamble for hours, even with pros, on closest to the hole for a quarter a ball. Byron Nelson couldn't remember Eddie ever losing one of those bets, not even to him.

Then there were the private matches Eddie arranged on the golf course. Before establishing himself on the West Coast, Eddie had always made a practice of supporting gifted amateur players. Unless they came from privileged backgrounds, every American amateur champion from Francis Ouimet and Bob Jones forward struggled to maintain his skills at the highest level while trying to make a living. Many found a way to write off golf expenses as a business cost related to their profession. Some lesser-known amateurs occasionally entered paying events under assumed names, allowed to compete with a wink and a nod, in order to make ends meet. That kind of rule bending went on regularly, and it accelerated after the war when golf became a part of doing business, but as long as it didn't directly affect the outcome of national championships, no one blew the whistle.

Eddie Lowery had always gone out of his way to encourage young amateur talent within the letter of the USGA's stringent guidelines. He described it as giving back to the game that had given so much to him, and after losing his only son during the war, it also gave him a way of filling that void as a surrogate father. As a member of the

USGA's Executive Committee Eddie knew he was expected to uphold its standards and would operate under greater scrutiny than almost anyone else on the amateur side. Which makes the inherent contradictions of some of his subsequent actions all the more intriguing.

Eddie decided once he established himself in California that the aboveboard way to support the game's best amateurs was to offer them jobs as car salesmen. They were expected to sell Lincolns and Mercurys in the morning and play golf in the afternoon, often with important clients—company golf, as the practice came to be known—with time off as needed to compete in important tournaments. If they brought home a trophy, Eddie saw only benefits to his business interests; reputations sold cars, and everyday joes loved to rub shoulders with jocks from the sports pages. Eddie also helped his players gain memberships to local clubs and often paired up with them in weekend matches against well-heeled, high-caliber opponents. Eddie put up the stakes and absorbed any losses, but if they won those bets, as they usually did, he'd split the winnings with his junior partner. That extra cash came in handy for a young salesman at the start of his career. Everyone went home happy, even the losers, who dined out on the tough scrap they'd given Lowery and his thoroughbred protégés.

On that Tuesday night during Clambake week in 1956, when he arrived at the Colemans' party, Eddie was feeling particularly bullish about two young salesmen/golfers working on his showroom floor. The possibility that either might become the first amateur in a generation to follow down Jones's path and win the Masters or an Open again glittered before him like golf's Holy Grail. This wasn't wishful thinking; Eddie was a superb evaluator of talent. He had been there at the start for Ouimet's breakthrough as the first American amateur champion, and could close the circle on his journey by mentoring the man who planted the amateur standard back in its rightful place at the summit of the game. This was the prize at the end of

the rainbow for Eddie Lowery, a ticket to the Hall of Fame and im-
mortality in his sport.

After an obligatory appearance at Crosby's party, Eddie had a
couple of drinks under his belt—Byron Nelson, who never touched
a drop, did the driving that night—and to anyone at Coleman's party
who would listen he continued talking up his two young amateur
stars. Through his relationship with Bing, Eddie had arranged entry
in the Clambake for both of them. Their names were Harvie Ward
and a young man who had just recently returned home from a two-
year hitch in the army named Ken Venturi.

The Bet

George Coleman didn't own his own mansion in Monterey, but he'd been a member at Cypress Point since 1932, and ever since his father had first brought him out to the new resort at Pebble Beach as a teenager he'd spent part of every winter on the Peninsula. He rented the same house from an old friend in the oil business, a New England–style "cottage" in the hills above Pebble Beach. The Colemans were looked after by their Italian butler and man Friday, Franco Rosiello, who ran the household staff and organized their frequent entertaining with continental efficiency.

Franco served Eddie Lowery his third cocktail of the evening as the party sat down to dinner. During the salad course Eddie resumed singing the praises of his two amateur salesmen stars, Venturi and Ward, predicting certain victory for one or the other of them in the Pro-Am that week. His broadcasting now attracted the attention of his host; George Coleman and Eddie had a long and complicated history.

They were fellow members at Cypress Point, Augusta, and Seminole and, as experienced single-digit amateurs, enjoyed a spirited rivalry whenever they stepped on the course. Years before, George had given Eddie's candidacy at Cypress a boost with the membership committee at a moment when it looked far from assured. Both were fiercely competitive and, with their partners, contended in every Crosby Pro-Am they entered. Both bet heavily in the Clambake's annual Calcutta pool and had been known to lay down healthy wagers between themselves. Within the last month they had played a big money four-ball match at Brookhollow Golf Club in Dallas, partnered with their respective best friends, Byron Nelson and Ben Hogan, relationships of which they were equally proud.

But George and Eddie were in every other way opposite numbers. While George summered in Tuscany and wintered in West Palm, Eddie was more at home at the track. George was old money and old school; Eddie never made it past tenth grade, and the ink on his fortune was, by comparison, still coming off on his hands. Two indelible characters—dry Oklahoma panhandle versus brassy backstage Broadway—they could've walked off the pages of Edna Ferber and Damon Runyon. In each other's presence their personalities generated friction as naturally as heat and water produce steam, which they usually defused by giving each other the needle, Eddie jabbing like a hyperactive welterweight, George winging well-timed sarcastic one-liners like roundhouse rights.

George usually tolerated Eddie's unpolished brass with his characteristic low-key forbearance, but for some reason on this night and on this subject, Eddie's relentless boosterism about his two young golfers got under George's skin. Maybe he didn't like the way Eddie walked right up to the line on rules supporting amateur golfers. Maybe the recent bet he'd lost to Eddie at Brookhollow was still gnawing at him. When George's blood was up, he went ominously quiet, and so he sat back, said nothing, and listened to Eddie's patter. Byron Nelson, sitting between them, aware that George's thermostat was rising, watched them like a man at a tennis match, sensing something was about to blow.

"And I'll tell you this right now, Kenny and Harvie are the two best amateurs in the world today," said Eddie, by now to no one in particular. "One of 'em, either of 'em—maybe *both* of 'em—are gonna win a Masters or the Open before they're done. I like their chances this year; they're both peaking at the same time, and the sky's the limit."

"So let me get this straight: you think your two kids are going to win the Masters," said George finally.

"Or the Open, hell, yes. They'll shock the world. And if they play the way they're capable of, I swear to Christ there isn't anybody in the world who could beat these two boys as a team."

"Anybody in the world."

"Anybody in the world. Against them in a best-ball match the way they're playing right now? I don't care who it is."

"You're saying your two amateur car salesmen can beat any two players in the world, straight up."

"You heard me, George, that's exactly what I'm saying, and I'll back it up, you name your price."

"You'll put your money where your mouth is."

"I'll do that, and you know I'm good for it—"

"I certainly know where your mouth is."

"You hear me, any two players in the world," said Eddie.

Byron saw George glance his way, and his discomfort grew a little greater.

"Including pros?" asked George.

"Yes, including pros, including any goddamn players in the world. Any twosome breathing. Whoever you like."

"Well, I've got a couple of fellas in mind."

"Fine, bring 'em on, my boys can beat anybody."

"What do you want to bet on that?" asked George.

We reach the first point in this narrative where some principal accounts begin to significantly vary. There's no dispute that Eddie now proposed a substantial wager, perhaps as a bluff, or perhaps as bluster to back George down. But both were wealthy men, far from shy about putting their hands in their pockets, who'd squared off over poker tables and three-foot putts on dozens of occasions, and this time nobody blinked. The initial amount Eddie suggested ranges in accounts from five to as high as twenty thousand dollars. Whatever the number—and according to some reports it would continue to escalate the next day—George didn't bat an eye.

"Agreed," said George.

With that, George got up and left the table.

"Where are you going?" asked Eddie.

"I'm going to make a phone call," said George.

"So who are your two players?" Eddie yelled after him.

"I'll tell you in a minute."

George picked up the phone in his office, called Bing Crosby's house, and asked to speak to Ben Hogan; a minute later, Ben came on the line.

"Where are you playing your practice round tomorrow?" asked George.

"At Pebble, eleven o'clock," said Ben.

"With who?"

"Why?" said Hogan, an edge of suspicion creeping into his voice.

"I've got a game for you. The kids want to play you and Byron."

"What kids?"

"Ken and Harvie," said George.

Silence.

"Eddie's arranging it," said George. "A four-ball. Against you and Byron."

"What did Byron say?"

"Byron says he'll play if you'll do it," said George.

"He did, huh?"

"That's right."

"And Eddie's arranging it."

"That's right. And he says they can kick your ass."

There was a moment of silence.

"How big is the bet?" asked Ben.

"That's between me and Eddie," said George.

"I'll bet it is," said Hogan, with a small chuckle.

"So how about it?"

"I don't want any big crowd," said Ben, as George heard him light a cigarette. "Against a couple of amateurs."

"I'll take care of that," said George. "We'll keep the crowd out of it." George waited.

"Okay, I'm in," said Hogan.

"Cypress Point all right with you?"

"Sure," said Ben. "But I'll keep that tee time at Pebble. In fact, why don't you call in the morning to confirm it."

"I'll do that," said George, with a smile.

George hung up the phone, went back in the dining room, and gestured for Byron. Byron, sensing what was coming, excused himself, rose from the table, and joined him in the hallway. In the middle of another conversation, Eddie noticed him go.

"Okay," said George, moving Byron out of Eddie's sight. "Ben says he'll play 'em if you will."

Byron smiled. "You don't say."

"That's right. So how about it?"

Byron glanced back at Eddie. "You know I love playing those kids anytime. That's fine with me."

"It's all set then."

"We'll probably have a little Nassau," said Byron. "The four of us. But that other bet's between you and Eddie."

"Yes, it is," said George.

Byron followed him back to the table. Franco saw George take his seat again and started serving the steaks. George waited a minute for a lull in Eddie's conversation.

"The match is on," said George.

"That's great, George," said Eddie. "Who are your players?"

"Nelson and Hogan," George said, and took a bite of his steak.

Conversation around the table came to a dead stop. Eddie swallowed hard and looked over at Byron, who confirmed it with a smile and a slight shrug. Byron's wife Louise stared at him, too. Byron smiled and patted her hand under the table.

"Well, they'll beat them, too!" blurted Eddie.

"We'll see about that. Ben's already got a tee time," said George. "Pebble Beach, at eleven, all right with you?"

"That's just fine," said Eddie. "My boys will be there."

"One thing I'd like your help on here, folks," said George, glancing around the table. "We don't want word of this leaking out and attracting any big crowds. So please, everybody keep it under your hat."

Everyone agreed.

The rest of the dinner passed without further incident. As his guests were getting ready to leave, George took Eddie and Byron aside.

"I'm going to call Cypress first thing in the morning and arrange a time," said George quietly. "We'll go out around ten."

"But you told everybody it was Pebble at eleven," said Eddie.

"That's right," said George. "And by the time word of this gets around tomorrow that's where everybody's going to show up to watch."

All three men laughed.

"Why didn't I think of that?" said Eddie.

"Given time," said Byron, "I'm sure you would have."

"Maybe you and I'll play tomorrow, too," said George to Eddie. "Have ourselves a little side bet."

"You know I love taking your money, George," said Eddie, shaking his hand.

"Just make sure your fellas show up," said George.

"Don't you worry about that," said Eddie.

"You'll have to find Harvie first," said George.

"That's no problem," said Eddie. "He's staying right over at Bing's."

"Like I said," said George.

When Eddie and his houseguests arrived back at his home up on the hill above Cypress Point around ten thirty, the Nelsons went straight to bed. Eddie called Ken Venturi at the old hotel where he was staying in Carmel, the Pine Inn.

"You and Harvie were planning to play a practice round together tomorrow, weren't you?" asked Eddie.

Ken confirmed that they were, with their Pro-Am partners.

"Kenny, let me ask you: if you could play a best-ball match tomorrow against any two men in this field, or in the world, who would it be?"

Ken didn't hesitate; it was a subject they'd talked about many times. "Byron and Ben. Why?"

When Eddie told him the match was on, Ken was so excited he had to get up and walk around the room. In the last few years, as his career advanced, he had played with both of the game's greatest living professionals, but never together, and never against either of them head-to-head in match play competition. This was a dream come true.

"You think they'd mind a little side bet?" asked Ken, with a grin.

"No, Kenny, I don't think they'd mind at all," said Eddie.

Eddie hung up and called over to Bing's house to speak to Harvie and let him know about the match. No one could find him at the party. In fact, no one had seen Harvie all night long.

Ken

Eddie Lowery and Ken Venturi were the first of their group to arrive at the Cypress Point clubhouse on Wednesday morning, January 11, shortly before nine o'clock, in Eddie's luxurious Lincoln Continental Mark II. Introduced to compete with the top-of-the-line Cadillac DeVille, less than three thousand of the new luxury models had been built in the last two years, most of them sold to millionaires and celebrities like the Shah of Iran and Elvis Presley. The pride of American productivity, Detroit owned the American road, and Eddie had reserved for himself one of the first cars that rolled off the production line.

They changed their shoes in the small, unadorned men's locker room—names were handwritten and inserted into slots in its few lockers for members to use whenever they were in town—and stepped outside to roll a few putts on the practice green. Wearing a tie and cardigan, his usual golf togs, Eddie then moved to the small driving range across Seventeen Mile Drive, to the right of the first fairway. The day had dawned cool and mostly clear, the sun already promising to break through a light cover of sea mist, a happy circumstance whenever that occurred in January. Eddie had called the

Cypress Point pro shop just after rising at daybreak that morning, to confirm that George Coleman had already arranged their ten o'clock tee time. But George hadn't told the club's head professional, Henry Puget, who else they were playing with that morning, and Eddie didn't mention it either, on the phone or when they arrived.

The Crosby Clambake didn't officially begin until Friday, with the first two rounds splitting the field between Cypress Point and Monterey Peninsula Country Club, and ended with the third and final round on Sunday afternoon, by which time only half the amateur field would have survived the cut, at Pebble Beach. Wednesday was the Clambake's first scheduled day of practice rounds, a chance for the amateurs to relax and work out the midwinter kinks, for the pros to focus on a few specific shots or early season swing thoughts. And almost all of them greeted the day with a hangover from Tuesday night's festivities.

Twenty-five-year-old Ken Venturi felt no ill effects from his evening before, other than that he'd been so excited by the prospect of playing against Nelson and Hogan he had hardly been able to sleep. The foremost thought racing around his mind that night: the realization of what a milestone this represented, a measure of how far he'd come since his caddying days at Cypress Point. Devoting himself to his game all through high school, even to the exclusion of baseball, where he'd shown considerable talent, Venturi had garnered a reputation as one of the Bay Area's up-and-coming amateurs. Ken's home course became the city's outstanding municipal track in Harding Park, where after retirement his father later took a job as the starter and ran the pro shop.

At sixteen, in 1948, Ken had participated in the inaugural U.S. Junior Amateur Championship in Michigan, losing in the finals, and went on to capture an impressive string of local and California state junior titles. After months of regular coverage about him appeared in the *San Francisco Chronicle*'s sports pages, he was being introduced to local baseball deities like Joe DiMaggio and Lefty O'Doul. Two years later, in 1950, playing head-to-head against an adult field at Harding Park, Ken became the youngest winner in the history of the amateur match play San Francisco City Championship.

Throughout his developing public success, Ken continued to struggle with his private stammering problem. Decades before society was conditioned to react sensitively to speech disabilities, Ken felt compelled to conceal it from people as best he could, or risk ridicule and scorn. As a result, seldom willing to chance saying more than a few words at tournaments or in response to reporters, he developed a reputation as an arrogant, cocky young kid with rough edges. Instead of offering a more nuanced response to a question like "Who's going to win this week?" Ken would simply say "Me." There was no question he now possessed a teenager's bulletproof self-assurance, much of it justified by compiling so much early success, the rest perhaps to help compensate for the years of shame and abuse he'd endured because of his stutter. Ken's confidence was strong, but somewhat brittle; although he would later learn to forgive and forget a slight, during this time in his life he tended to do neither. In that way he possessed the classic chip-on-the-shoulder perspective that had fueled so many working class caddie-turned-player careers in the early history of the American game. That tendency, and his entire subsequent professional career, was about to be turbocharged by a powerful new presence in his life.

Shortly after his win at the San Francisco City Championship, Venturi was introduced to another local legend, Eddie Lowery. Eddie had been following Venturi's amateur career with interest, and when he invited Ken to play a round with him at San Francisco Golf Club, Ken eagerly accepted. During his years as a caddie there, Ken had always promised his fellow mules in the yard—in return suffering their perpetual scorn—that he'd come back to play the exclusive course with a member one day. As he walked onto the first tee following Eddie Lowery, his former running mates in the yard came out to give Ken Venturi a standing ovation.

"What's all the noise about, Ken?" asked Eddie.

Venturi couldn't answer. He was easily the most famous caddie in American history, and when he saw Ken trying to hide the tears in his eyes, Eddie knew exactly what the fuss was about and threw him a wink. Both men split the fairway with their drives. Their friendship was off to a solid start.

Ken Venturi had been blessed with a strong family and a caring, dedicated father, but in Eddie Lowery he found a mentor who was willing and able to guide him to the next level in his sport and in life. Like many self-made men, Eddie Lowery knew how the operating systems of the world worked, particularly the arena of championship amateur golf, and he was eager to pass that knowledge along. It's also safe to say that in Ken Venturi, Eddie Lowery had found a surrogate son, nearly the same age as the boy he'd lost to the war. The two were cut from the same cloth: tough-minded, combative, and self-reliant. In both men their tough exterior concealed a more sentimental and emotional side they showed only to their families, and every once in a while on the golf course. On a more practical level, Eddie had also found a gritty, dependable playing partner for those high stakes weekend matches he liked to arrange, and until Ken was able to cover his own bets, Eddie agreed to bankroll him.

Lacking the money to pay for private college, and years before major universities poured big money into golf programs, Ken had earned a partial scholarship from nearby San Jose State in 1949, the defending national collegiate champion. As he worked his way through school, Venturi's future plans never for one moment involved becoming a professional golfer; the grind of eking out a living on the fledgling PGA Tour, or putting in backbreaking hours as a resident club pro—which he knew killed most men's games—held zero appeal for him. Hard as it is to believe by today's standards, this was the prevailing conventional wisdom of the day. Ken had also watched his proud father struggle in blue collar jobs and wanted to establish himself as a professional in the business world, so he began studying dentistry at San Jose State, with the intent of building a practice that he hoped would underwrite a long and distinguished amateur playing career. The growing influence of Eddie Lowery in his life can be keenly felt here as well; this was the exact path Eddie had watched his friend Francis Ouimet take after winning the U.S. Open thirty years earlier, and then followed himself.

While Venturi continued to flourish as a player at San Jose State—winning the California State Amateur title at Pebble Beach in 1951—his interest in dentistry, and academics for that matter, began to evaporate. The fast-paced business circles to which Eddie Lowery was introducing him offered a lot more pizzazz than a life spent staring into people's mouths. In 1952, at Eddie's behest, Ken received a personal call from Bing Crosby, inviting him to play as a last-minute replacement in the Clambake for the first time. Six months later, after a disappointing first round, final hole loss in that year's U.S. Amateur in Seattle, as Ken walked off the eighteenth green, Eddie stepped out of the crowd with a guest he'd brought to watch Ken play.

"Ken," said Eddie. "I'd like you to meet Byron Nelson."

Ken was speechless, not for fear of stuttering, but by the unexpected appearance of his lifelong hero; he had been so focused on his game he hadn't even seen Byron in his gallery. Eddie explained that his old friend Mr. Nelson had been playing an exhibition in the area and accepted his invitation to watch Ken play his entire round that day.

Ken didn't mention that they'd met briefly once before, during the 1946 San Francisco Open at the Olympic Club, Byron's final year on tour. The fifteen-year-old Venturi had followed Byron all around the course that day, captivated by his style, modest self-possession, and effortless ease of play, on his way to winning the tournament over Ben Hogan by nine strokes. An amateur photographer, Ken had brought along his camera and decided to sneak under the ropes to snap some shots of Byron as he prepared to hit his approach to the fifth green. Byron pulled out of his backswing when he heard the click of the shutter, turned to Ken, and said firmly: "Son, take that camera of yours and get back under the ropes with the rest of the gallery." Ken did as he was told, hurried home on his bike after the round was over, and ran in to tell his mom excitedly: "Byron Nelson spoke to me today!" When he elaborated about the circumstances, she tried to explain that this exchange didn't exactly qualify as a conversation, but Ken wouldn't let go of the idea that they had made a real connection.

Now that they had actually connected, Ken struggled to gather himself in Byron's courtly presence in Seattle. Byron helped take the sting out of his defeat by asking Ken if he'd be interested in playing a round of golf together. Venturi leapt at the offer.

"When are you going back to San Francisco?" asked Byron.

"Right away," said Ken.

"Me too. Let's play tomorrow then. San Francisco Golf Club. You, me, and Eddie."

After Ken accepted their offer, Byron and Eddie left immediately for the airport. Only after they were gone did Venturi remember that'd he *driven* to Seattle. He tossed his clubs into his beat-up 1942 Buick Roadster and drove frantically all through the night—changing a three A.M. flat tire by flashlight in the middle of nowhere—in order to reach the San Francisco Golf Club for their lunch hour tee time.

Determined to put on a good show for Nelson, Venturi played one of the best rounds of his life, a career low 66 on the demanding San Francisco course, even besting Byron by a couple of strokes. Byron said little to him during their game, other than the standard, small talk, "good shot" etiquette remarks. But when they sat down for soft drinks afterward, and Ken expected to finally be showered with praise about his remarkable talents, Byron said nothing. He wore his beatific smile and was the perfect gentleman, as always, but offered not a single compliment. Finally, Venturi could no longer resist fishing for one.

"So, Mr. Nelson, what did you think of my play?" he asked, with a cocky grin.

"Kenny, Eddie asked me to take a look at your game to see if I could help out a little bit."

"Uh-huh."

"I'll be in town for a few days. If you're not busy tomorrow, why don't you come out here about nine o'clock, because there's about six or seven things we've got to work on right away."

Venturi felt the blood rise in his throat.

"That is, if you want to be a good player," said Byron, smiling benignly.

Although stunned, Ken swallowed his wounded pride. "I'll be there."

Ken Venturi had never taken a professional lesson in his life, but for the next three days—working four to six hours a day on the San Francisco Club range—Byron made up for it. Byron had observed that Ken was a superb short game player and putter, but he had hit a lot of bad shots during both days he'd watched him and Byron correctly assessed that his full swing would never carry him to the championship level of their sport. Ken hit the ball primarily with his hands and hadn't developed the timing and rhythm he needed to incorporate the strike with the power of a full-body turn. Once they were on the range, Byron set out to convince him that his swing was guaranteed to break down under pressure and desert him when he needed it most.

Reeling and discouraged from having so much thrown at him at once—he realized halfway through their first day that Byron was demolishing his game down to the studs and starting from scratch—Venturi managed to see the evident value of what was being offered to him and tenaciously applied himself. Byron spared no aspect of his swing: grip, stance, weight shift, balance, transition, swing path. A talented mimic, Venturi learned by copying the changes Byron demonstrated for him. Toward the end of their last session, they talked about Ken's upcoming schedule; he was about to defend his title in the California State Amateur.

"You have got to stay with what we're doing," said Byron, with the stern tone of a martial arts master. "You can mimic it now, but you haven't learned this new swing yet deep down and you'll be tempted to go back to what you know when the pressure comes. If you do that, even for a few holes, you'll have learned nothing."

"I won't go back," said Ken.

"Good," said Byron. "You may not win anything for a while, but that doesn't matter. What matters is what happens down the road."

Ken didn't successfully defend his title at the California State Amateur that year or win anywhere else for a while, as Byron had predicted, but he stayed committed to the changes, and gradually all of the lessons Venturi had learned found their way into a reconstructed and dependable swing. The following spring, Eddie Lowery arranged a series of exhibitions for Byron and Ken to play together up and down the West Coast, during which young Venturi's education entered its postgraduate phase.

With Ken's new swing under control, Byron now concentrated on teaching his charge the larger strategic issues of course management and the mental approach to the game: how to break down a golf course and identify the best route to approach a green, when to be aggressive in a match, when to lay back, play for par, and take what a hole gives you. As they dissected their round each evening, Venturi detailed all of Byron's lessons in a notebook he would carry with him everywhere, and refer to often, from that day forward.

Byron also imparted to him timeless lessons about the spirit of the game. In each exhibition they played against the host club's head professional and reigning amateur champion in a best-ball match. At every stop Byron made a point of inquiring who held the local course scoring record, which usually belonged to one or the other of their opponents that day. Byron told Ken that wherever he went, no matter how well he was playing, he should never break that record, as a show of respect to his host; that was the way gracious visitors were supposed to behave. Ken never forgot it.

Their hard work paid off in national recognition when Venturi was invited that fall to join the 1953 Walker Cup team, the biannual competition between America and Great Britain and Ireland's best amateurs. Playing at the Kittansett Club, a seaside links on the coast south of Boston where the Brits were expected to excel, the American team beat them decisively. Ken Venturi and his partner, Sam Urzetta, won the key foursomes match against Britain's best twosome—which had never lost in international competition—and then Ken won his singles match going away, 9 & 8. That Walker Cup team was so good, there was even talk of them challenging their professional American counterparts on the Ryder Cup team. Ben Hogan, among others on that Ryder Cup team, quickly put a halt to that idea; as far as he was concerned, men who made a living and built their reputations playing golf for a paycheck had nothing to gain by playing amateurs, and everything to lose. The proposed match never came to pass.

Venturi's personal and professional life came together that year as well. When he graduated from San Jose State in 1953, Ken accepted an offer that had been long in coming from Eddie Lowery, to work for him as a salesman in the used-car lot at Van Etta Motors. Eddie threw in a complimentary membership at nearby California Golf Club, where Ken would play his customer golf in the afternoon. He also became engaged that fall to his college sweetheart, Conni MacLean.

Later in 1953 Ken was joined at Van Etta Motors by a new member of the sales staff. They had first met a year earlier as partners at the inaugural America's Cup, a team competition against Mexico and Canada, and followed that up as teammates on the victorious 1953 Walker Cup squad.

Harvie Ward had arrived in San Francisco.

The First Tee

At nine fifteen on Wednesday morning Byron Nelson drove into the Cypress Point parking lot in the showroom Lincoln Continental loaner that Eddie Lowery gave him to use whenever he came to the Crosby. His arrival drew hushed words and curious looks from the players waiting to begin their practice round on the first tee; although a decade removed from the prime of his playing career and, after a decade of ranching, noticeably thicker than the lean, Lincolnesque figure he had been at retirement, Byron retained the aura of superstar status reserved for the true immortals of the game.

Joey Solis, the Cypress Point caddie master, saw Byron arrive from his post behind the pro shop and hustled out to meet him. Byron opened the trunk. His clubs and shoes were in back.

"Nice to see you again, Mr. Nelson," said Joey. "Playing today?"

"That's right, Joey," said Byron. He had an uncanny gift—actually a talent that he worked hard on—for remembering names. Joey Solis made that easy; he had been a fixture at Cypress Point for twenty-five years, starting as a teenage caddie.

"Who with?"

"Ten o'clock," said Byron with a smile, offering nothing more.

Henry Puget came out of his pro shop to welcome Byron personally and show him to a locker.

"Playing with Kenny and Eddie today?" asked Henry, concealing the suspicions that the events of the morning were starting to arouse.

"That's right, Henry," said Byron.

"Who's your fourth today?"

"Not exactly sure who Eddie has in mind."

"Eddie mentioned six of you might be going out."

"Did he?"

"Mr. Coleman called this morning to make the time, so I think he's playing with you."

"Good. George is a fine player." Byron finished tying his shoes, gave Henry his best Buddha smile, and walked outside.

"Kenny and Eddie are already here," said Henry, following him out. "I'll send your bag over to the range."

"Thank you, Henry."

Byron strolled down the lawn that sloped gently to the north toward the Seventeen Mile Drive and the range. Henry Puget was conferring briefly with Joey Solis about which caddie to put with Mr. Nelson—Mr. Lowery's regular man, Jimmy Tyree, would take care of Eddie and Venturi—when Joey spotted a sleek black Cadillac Fleetwood turning off the Seventeen Mile Drive onto the winding, quarter-mile-long Cypress Point driveway.

"There's Mr. Coleman," said Joey.

They watched Coleman pull into the lot and park next to Byron's Lincoln. Someone was in the passenger seat.

"Who's that with him?" asked Henry.

Coleman got out first. The passenger door opened, and over the top of the car they saw the distinctive white cap emerge. They didn't need to see anything else.

"It's Hogan," said Henry.

Ben Hogan wore impeccably tailored light gray worsted slacks, with a center crease sharp enough to open an envelope. A charcoal button-front cashmere sweater covered his custom-fitted English white cotton knit three-button polo. His trademark short-billed linen cap on his large square head, he stood tall at five foot nine, never tipping the scales during his playing days at more than a middleweight's trim 145 pounds. He flicked away a cigarette butt and looked up at the flag flying above the elegant white colonial clubhouse. Checking the wind. Sniffing the air.

"Put Turk on Hogan's bag," said Henry Puget, immediately walking out to greet them. He knew all Hogan wanted in a caddie was an assurance that he knew the rules, and Turk had carried for him before. Other than that, he was expected to keep up and keep quiet. "How many more groups before they go off?"

"I think two."

"Take one of the buggies and drive them out to ten, start 'em on the back. Same with the next two groups after them. Let's give 'em some room."

"They're going out as five?"

"Six. There's one more."

"Think it's Mr. Crosby?"

"I don't know. Guess we'll find out."

Joey Solis carefully removed from the trunk the black stitched-leather tour bag bearing Hogan's name and hustled back toward the caddie shack, as Henry Puget welcomed Coleman and Hogan. A refuge from the demands of universal fame, Cypress Point had become one of Hogan's favorite places in the world, and he greeted Henry as a friend, his usual reticence less on display with a fellow veteran professional, but his eyes darted around the grounds and clubhouse. Henry wasn't sure, but he thought the famously shy Hogan seemed concerned that there might be a crowd waiting for them, and seemed relieved to realize there wasn't one.

"I tell you it'll work," said George, reading Ben's body language. "They'll all be at Pebble."

Ben glanced at him skeptically.

George smiled at Henry. "We're having a little friendly match today."

"Byron's down at the range," said Henry. "You want to hit a few?"

They indicated that they did and went into the locker room to change their shoes, while Henry sent their bags across the street. He always instructed his caddies to take extra care of Hogan's clubs, which most golfers regarded with an awe reserved for the relics of a saint; those less religious by nature had been known to pilfer one of the Hawk's prized sticks. In the locker room Coleman watched Hogan go through his practiced pre-round rituals; he tied his black kiltie tasseled brogans as meticulously as a man defusing a bomb. Crafted by a master London boot maker, the sole of each shoe included an extra cleat just behind the ball of the foot, an innovation Hogan had asked for to help stay connected to the ground throughout his aggressive swing. By the time the two men emerged, word of Hogan and Nelson's presence had ripped through the clubhouse. Everyone on the grounds, player or employee, materialized to get a glimpse of Hogan as he and George Coleman walked down toward the range.

Byron Nelson had retained his celebrity ten years past his retirement through equal parts lasting respect for his achievements and enormous personal likeability. Although he'd announced his own retirement from the regular tour six months earlier, Hogan's reputation as the game's dominant player remained current based on the mystique and awe aroused by his phenomenal success and an unapproachable persona that inspired a touch of fear. If Byron always seemed especially human, warm, and accessible to everyone he knew and most he didn't, Ben at first glance appeared almost superhuman, wrought from some unearthly material beyond common understanding. Byron welcomed any conversation and never seemed to meet a stranger, while Ben's mere presence commanded silence and he listened more than he spoke, even with friends. For golfers and employees on the grounds, the chance to see both these legends on the range at the same time was bigger than Cinerama, and a small crowd began to gather across the street around the first tee.

Henry Puget went back to the card table that served as his desk in the pro shop and made a few calls around the Peninsula, one of them to colleague Art Bell, the head professional over at Pebble Beach, who he knew was scheduled to play as Venturi's partner that week in the Crosby Pro-Am. The fifty-four-year-old Puget had been the first and only head professional Cypress Point had known since 1931. Henry and his older brother Cam had started their careers as caddies at Pebble Beach; Cam had gone on to become the head professional at Pebble, and later at Monterey Country Club. Both men were accomplished players, and teachers of great repute, although they had an ongoing family disagreement about teaching philosophy; Henry believed the left side was dominant in the golf swing, while Cam favored the right. Henry also developed a reputation as a master club maker, which along with lessons constituted a pro's primary source of income in those early days.

Henry Puget possessed the ideal temperament for one of the great low-stress jobs in golf; to watch him at work in his simple, wood-lined pro shop, you'd have thought his heart beat only forty times a minute. With the club's small and exclusive membership— only a few full-time residents of the Peninsula—a week could pass during the off-season at Cypress Point with no more than three or four groups going out on any given day. The Clambake represented by far the club's most active and aggravating week of the year, and Henry Puget always had his staff and crew and golf course meticulously prepared.

But nothing could have prepared them for today. Henry Puget knew that Hogan and Nelson never played a practice round together, and as far as he knew hadn't ever played as teammates. And it was common knowledge that the perfectionist Hogan did not like to play with or against amateurs, which was the main reason he'd been back to compete in the Clambake only one time since he'd last won it in

1949. Nothing bothered the taciturn Hogan more than excessive praise, and amateurs tended to gush helplessly in his presence on a golf course. (When a corporate playing partner wouldn't stop admiring Hogan's ability to stop his seven iron on a dime, and kept pestering him for a tip about it, Hogan finally asked the man how far he hit a seven iron. "One hundred and twenty yards," came the answer. Hogan replied: *"Why the hell would you want it to stop?"* Not another word passed between them during the round.) Henry Puget also knew that Hogan had only played one public, competitive round—during a celebrity pro-am at the LA Open only the week before—since losing the U.S. Open in a play-off the previous summer. Hogan playing *anywhere* was news. With this group, it was headlines.

Henry asked Art Bell if he was coming over to play with his partner, Ken Venturi, against Hogan and Nelson that morning. Bell said no, he was playing Pebble that day, and for that matter he had Hogan penciled in at Pebble as well for an eleven o'clock start. Henry Puget told him that Hogan was about to tee off at Cypress with Nelson and Venturi, thanked him, and hung up the phone.

Ben exchanged handshakes and a few pleasantries with Eddie and Byron, then assumed his customary place at the far right-hand side of the range, which the others had as a courtesy left vacant for him; this was his office, where Hogan could keep his back to any other golfers while he practiced. After he finished rolling it around on the putting green, Ken Venturi had felt too self-conscious to warm up on the range alongside Byron and Ben, so instead fell back on an old trick he'd used during his youthful days as a Cypress Point caddie: he grabbed a small bucket of balls from the caddie shack and snuck around to the back of the clubhouse, the deserted side facing toward the ocean, where he teed up and whacked one drive after another all the way down to the water.

Once he broke a sweat and found his rhythm, Ken walked over toward the range and watched Hogan as he eased into his established routine with a half dozen crisp wedges. The sight of Hogan at work was never less than mesmerizing, but Ken had to remind himself that today was not the day to stand back and watch Ben Hogan craft perfect shots in wonder; he was the opponent, not a hero, and the objective was to beat him. The same went for his longtime friend and mentor Byron, who despite his gentle Christian soul was one of the fiercest competitors alive, and whose game, Ken knew firsthand, had hardly lost a step. He also knew both men well enough by now to know they wouldn't be giving him any quarter, particularly as two pros playing a match against a couple of amateurs. After two years in the army, his soaring ambitions forced to the sidelines, he was also dying to show that he could stand alongside Harvie and back up Eddie's boast that they were the best young players in the world. Success today could be the springboard he needed to vault him to the top of the game.

Ken edged over to Eddie and glanced at his watch. 9:45.

"Where's Harvie?" Ken asked quietly, feeling a twinge of anxiety.

"He'll be here," said Eddie.

Eddie sounded a little less certain of that than Ken would have liked, both of them throwing glances back at every car that passed on the Seventeen Mile Drive or entered the parking lot.

"You spoke to him; you didn't just leave a message."

"Yes, I spoke to him, for Christ's sake," said Eddie. "Seven o'clock sharp. Woke his ass right out of bed."

"You sure he'd *been* to bed?"

Eddie scowled and yanked the head cover back on his driver. "He said he'd be here, he'll be here."

Hogan hit one last soaring drive that faded off the left edge of the range, and watched until it landed. As if responding to a silent signal, all five men headed back across the road toward the first tee together, while their caddies picked up the bags and trudged after them. George glanced at his watch as he passed Eddie.

"Where's Harvie?" he asked dryly.

"He'll be here," said Eddie.

The five men gathered on the tee and prepared to begin their round, marking balls, putting tees in their pockets. Hogan lit a cigarette. George and Eddie walked off a short distance and conducted a quiet and somewhat animated conversation; Ken and Byron had the impression they were arguing about, or perhaps renegotiating is a better word, their wager. From the tone of Eddie's voice, it sounded as if the number might be headed north of its original destination. A few more Cypress members appeared to join the discussion—including Paul Shields, Ben Hogan's Wall Street broker and another early investor in his company, who hadn't been at last night's dinner; word of the match was getting around—and it looked to Ken like Eddie had started to augment the Coleman bet with some side action.

At five minutes to ten, a sporty new red Mercury Montclair came roaring along the highway, turned into the parking lot, stirring up dust on the gravel drive, and screeched to a halt right below the clubhouse.

Ken and Byron exchanged a smile, and both shook their heads.

Harvie Ward bounded out of the car, shouldered his own bag from the trunk, and ambled straight toward the assembled group on the first tee. Impeccably dressed as usual in tapered black trousers and a plush burgundy cashmere sweater, he wore dark aviator shades and had his custom-made black leather golf shoes on already, although he hadn't yet bothered to tie them. His handsome shock of wavy brown hair didn't look to have a single strand out of place.

"Hey, boys, is this a private game or can anybody play?" asked Harvie, with a grin.

He shook hands all around, even eliciting a smile from Hogan when he said something like "Guess they didn't tell you you'd be playing a couple of *amateurs*." Hogan said he'd been assured, at least, that Harvie and Ken would be the only amateurs they'd see that day. Harvie knew why: although hardly the fastest of players himself, Hogan hated waiting for amateurs—"they're slower than a week in jail," as Harvie used to say—and that was the main reason he hadn't been back to the Clambake for so long.

"You playing much, Ben?" asked Harvie. "Bing's awful worried he's gonna have to carry you around all week."

"I'll manage," said Ben, with a smile.

Seeing that Eddie and George were still engrossed in a private dialogue about their wager, Harvie proposed the four men generate a little side bet of their own, which immediately piqued Hogan and Nelson's interest.

"How much?" asked Byron.

Swinging his driver back and forth to loosen up, Harvie and Ken exchanged a wink and a nod.

"Hundred dollar Nassau," said Harvie.

Ken felt an involuntary twinge in his wallet: a hundred for the front nine, a hundred for the back, a hundred for the match. That was a little more downside than he liked to be exposed to if they lost; three hundred bucks was nearly a whole week's salary. On the other hand, thought Ken, if he and Harvie played to their usual team standard, the upside looked even better.

"Done," said Hogan.

Eddie and George wrapped up their negotiation and walked back down to the tee to shake hands again and wish everybody luck. The subject of their bet came up briefly, as Eddie learned about the players' Nassau.

"What kinda action you two got going today, Eddie?" asked Harvie. "You guys gonna bet your houses?"

"You worry about your bet, Harvie," said Eddie. "We'll worry about ours."

"Eddie and I were just saying maybe we won't play a full round today," said George. "Don't want to hold you youngsters up."

"Yeah, maybe we'll just hit a few shots while we watch you scratch it around," said Eddie. "Fire away, boys."

Hogan turned to Harvie and Ken. "You fellas have the tee."

"After you, Harv," said Ken.

"With pleasure."

Harvie teed up his ball, turned, and smiled at Hogan and Nelson. He gave them a frank and confident smile that said, not in so many words or in a rude or disrespectful way, that he almost felt sorry for them.

"Play well," he said.

Now that the life of the party was here, the party was ready to begin.

The Opening Holes

From the tee box on the clubhouse side of the Seventeen Mile Drive, the first fairway at Cypress Point runs 418 yards down a broad, sweeping expanse of lawn to the edge of the dunes, where an elevated, undulating green sits perched, bracketed left, right, and behind—where the dunes rise ominously toward Spyglass Hill—by the first of course designer Dr. Alister MacKenzie's naturalistic bunkers. Considered a stern but negotiable opening hole, in keeping with MacKenzie's philosophy of the golf course as a dramatic three-act progression, it quietly introduces all the visual themes to come: forest, dunes, and sea. Looking out from the tee box, the player's eye can easily be distracted from the task at hand by the stunning vistas of Fan Shell Beach, Seal Rock, and Spyglass Hill to the north. A tall stand of cypress trees dominates the right center of the fairway 210 yards out. The bold line is to carry them with the drive, which greatly shortens the second shot and improves the angle to the green. The safer approach—and for the golfer just easing into his round the more traditional—is to aim for the broad landing area down the left side, away from the cypresses; but it sets up a much longer second and brings the front left bunker into play.

Known as one of the straightest hitters in the world, Harvie had the job as first man up on their team to land a ball safely in play. He did just that, sending his opening drive booming down the left-hand side of the fairway.

Venturi stepped to the tee. Still loose from his private session driving balls behind the clubhouse, and with Harvie's ball in perfect position, Ken ripped his opening drive, a high-power fade over the cypresses and out of sight into the dead center of the fairway beyond. He'd cut forty yards off his second shot.

"Good shot, Kenny," said Byron, and Eddie echoed him.

Hogan said nothing, his eyes fixed on the fairway. Byron followed Ken to the tee and, taking Harvie's line down the left-hand side, drove it roughly the same distance. Hogan teed up his ball and precisely followed his pre-shot routine. Ken and Harvie glanced at each other. Would the Hawk try to follow Ken over the trees? An early signal he was ready to slug it out with them? Or would he play the percentage shot down the left side, his usual approach? Hogan always computed the odds on every shot, weighing risk and reward, with nothing left to chance. Which way would he go today?

Down the left. Long, beyond both Harvie and Byron, with just a little fade at the end.

Ben pulled his tee without even watching the flight of his ball— he knew where it was going—turned to Ken and Harvie, winked, and started walking down the path toward the road. The other five men followed him, their caddies trailing, and a small gallery of about fifteen men who had gathered around the tee went after them.

Back at the clubhouse, after hurriedly rearranging the foursomes on either side of the match, Joey Solis picked up the phone and began calling friends around the Peninsula to tell them about what was going on at Cypress. The caddie master at any course serves as its unofficial information officer/gossip columnist; he's the eyes and ears of the club's staff, the head professional's confidant who's closest to the action on the ground and what's really going on with the membership. Keeping the often unruly caddie ranks in line requires the discipline of a drill sergeant; keeping a membership of worldly, demanding, successful people content about their golf course requires the contrasting skills of a diplomat; the best caddie masters possess both qualities and so tread a delicate line. Joey Solis always aimed to please, and he had a kind of mascot's devotion to his members, but he privately got a kick from his regular proximity to important people and events, and few events in his long memory at Cypress could compare to what he'd just witnessed. As he saw it, it was not only his right but his obligation to help spread the word. With Joey's help, news of the match would travel quickly around the Peninsula.

Harvie played first from the fairway, to the left and just in front of the cypress stand, a hundred and seventy yards to the flagstick, tucked on the back left shelf of the deep, contoured green. Usually damp with ocean mist, the springy turf at Cypress didn't offer much roll, particularly in the morning. Harvie's ball landed on the front of the green, kicked forward, but didn't have enough juice on it to complete the climb, and it rolled back onto the lower level. Byron followed, landing his ball on the back right of the green, about hole high and twenty-five feet away. From about 165 yards, Hogan played a textbook six iron to the middle of the green, leaving an uphill putt for birdie of twenty feet.

Left with the best chance to cash in his long drive, Venturi faced a shot of about 140 yards, straight at the flag, and he hit a nine iron that started right for it. The ball landed, bit hard, and rolled to a stop about twelve feet to the right of the hole, a solid chance for birdie.

The governing strategy in a best-ball match dictates that the player with the longer putt lags to guarantee the par, leaving his partner a free run at birdie. That style just wasn't Harvie, who never met a birdie chance he didn't like; his forty-five-footer ran too long and to the right, and in the spirit of generosity common to early round match play etiquette, Byron and Ben conceded his par. Sticking to the more orthodox method, and equally in character, Byron lagged his putt a few inches short of the cup; he had secured his team's four. With their partners both in for par, Hogan and Venturi were free to make their run at birdie.

Hogan stood over his ball for a long time, staring at it hard, a habit that had increased of late with alarming frequency. Few people knew the reason for this change, but many had noticed it and wondered why. When he finally let it go, the putt came up a foot short; Hogan walked to it and swatted it away, mildly annoyed. Ken stepped quickly to his ball—he played best at a brisk pace, trusting his instincts—and putted firmly. The ball didn't take the hard break to the left he'd anticipated, edged the rim, and rolled two feet past the cup.

Eddie groaned and slapped his thigh in disappointment, and wrote down their scores; both he and George kept separate cards. Ken silently picked up and the group walked up the hill behind the green to the second tee.

All square after one.

Alister MacKenzie had been the first golf architect to codify and publish his guiding philosophy of course design, and one of his fundamental principles was to open with a couple of long holes that encouraged separation between groups to avoid logjams on the course early in the round. The second hole at Cypress Point is a brawny 532-yard par five that turns east toward the Del Monte pine forest and confronts the player with an intimidating carry from the elevated tee box over a deep, natural valley that slashes diagonally through the dunes from southeast to northwest. The fairway runs in that same direction above the valley, at the same elevation as the tee box, so only a thin sliver of green is visible as you stand over your ball. At about two hundred yards out, another of MacKenzie's deep bunkers breaks up the line of the slope leading back to the fairway; left of that bunker is the target line for the bold player, and success helps ease the problems offered by the second shot. The cautious route is to the right of the bunker, encouraged by a more inviting visible spread of fairway, but the timid face a greater challenge once they reach their ball.

There were no timid players in this foursome. Maintaining the same order, they all cleared the valley to the left of the bunker, with Venturi's ball again the longest of the group. As they trekked down into the valley and began the climb back up to the fairway, Harvie walked out front, in time to a tune he quietly hummed to himself: Count Basie's "Every Day I Have the Blues." Although he never suffered from anything approaching the blues, what Harvie did have on this day was a monstrous, black dog hangover after only two hours of sleep. He was no stranger to playing golf with his senses crisply fried, particularly at the Clambake, but if he'd known about this match the night before, instead of finding out about it from Eddie Lowery at seven that morning, he might have altered his plans and bunked in at a decent hour. Emphasis on might.

But even had he known about it, Harvie wouldn't have arrived at Cypress Point that morning any closer to their tee time than he did. He was admittedly one of the worst practice range golfers in history; whenever he tried to hit balls before a round, all he succeeded in doing was gouging huge chunks out of the earth and fouling up his natural timing. Harvie's idea of a proper warm-up was to listen to an LP by Count Basie and his orchestra for twenty minutes, feel that syrupy, syncopated rhythm seep into his muscles, and then carry that out onto the course. But after Eddie's call dynamited him out of a dead sleep, he hadn't even had time to pop a record on the stereo over coffee at Bing's house that morning, so he kept humming as he walked along, trying to find his rhythm as he moved.

Eddie fell into step alongside Ken as they walked at the head of the pack.

"For Christ's sake, what the hell's wrong with Harvie?" whispered Eddie.

"Nothing," said Kenny.

"He's still wearing dark glasses, for Christ's sake."

"He's fine," said Kenny.

Kenny knew perfectly well that Harvie was suffering from a severe overdose of fun—he was no stranger to the condition himself—but that had never held his partner in crime back on the golf course in the past, and he didn't expect it to today. A few holes of walking in the crisp morning air with the sun on his face and Harvie would be restored to his usual well-oiled efficiency. If that didn't do the trick, and the queasiness persisted, Ken figured Harvie could always repair into the woods and expel the toxins out of his system by a more direct method; severely hungover players retching the wretched remains of last night's excess among the Monterey pines between shots was hardly unprecedented in the early, ribald days of the Clambake. In 1947 Sam Snead's amateur partner, a Los Angeles lawyer named Roger Kelly, an exceptional player and even more notorious carouser, had staggered into the woods twice before they finished the first hole, and Snead nearly walked off the course in disgust. But Kelly rebounded within a few holes, played an astonishing round, and the two men went on to win the Pro-Am; with a winning check in hand, Sam never complained about Kelly's drinking again.

But Ken didn't have a five-figure bet down on today's game either, as their boss clearly did, and a big part of their job was making Eddie happy. Ken also knew that Eddie had recently been notified he was coming under the unsettling scrutiny of the IRS for possible tax evasion, which made him a good deal more sensitive about monetary issues than he had been in the past. He decided he would have to bear down early in the match until Harvie leveled his load.

MacKenzie's second challenge, on the second hole, consists of two deep, yawning bunkers on either side of where the fairway sharply narrows about 150 yards out from the green. The player who pulled off the heroic carry on his tee shot would be left with a good chance to fly those bunkers and set up a relatively easy approach to attack the flag for birdie; anyone who laid back now had to play short of them and would be left with a third shot of 170 yards.

The flagstick was set up in the front left corner, protected by a sprawling, sculpted bunker to the left. None of the four men could reach the green in two, and only Ken now tried, but all carried the two fairway bunkers with their second shots. Harvie's shaky nerves showed up in his third shot, a poor effort with his wedge that stopped two feet short of the green. Hogan's wedge landed pin high and right, about fifteen feet. Byron and Ken, playing near each other, both feathered their third shot within ten feet of the hole.

"Good shot, Kenny," said Byron, as they walked up together.

"You too," said Ken.

Harvie's chip scooted just past the hole, and the pros conceded his par. Now Hogan stood over his second birdie putt of the round and froze again, this time for nearly a minute. No one else moved as he stood there, stock-still. Finally he pulled the trigger; this time the ball ran past the hole on the high side. His par was conceded, and he knocked the ball away without comment.

Byron's ball was inside Hogan's on a similar line, and he benefited from watching the first one roll, calculating it would break less toward the ocean than the eye suggested. Byron had always been a natural putter and often criticized himself for not working on it as hard as he might have to improve. Eddie rode him about it constantly when they played together and was forever writing him letters about various tips and drills, even mailing him newfangled putters to try. Today, for once, Eddie was pulling for him to miss. Byron glanced over at Eddie as he stood over the ball and smiled at him.

Then he drained the putt for the day's first birdie. Eddie rolled his eyes.

Now Eddie's pressurized gaze shifted to Ken, who stepped quickly to his ball, on the other side of the cup, took one look, and banged it into the back of the hole for a matching birdie.

All square through two.

That broke the ice. Ken and Byron shared a little laugh and mutual compliments as they walked off the green, where Eddie patted Ken enthusiastically on the back. Harvie thanked his partner for bailing him out. Hogan said nothing—"You're away" was a full conversation for him under any circumstances—and walked behind them to the next tee with George Coleman. He was limping slightly; his badly damaged legs hadn't warmed up yet in the cool morning air.

From the third tee box MacKenzie makes his first notable use of camouflage on the course. It's the day's first three par, slightly down-hill and not long at 156 yards, and not overtly difficult unless your concentration should wander, which MacKenzie does his damnedest to encourage. A towering sand dune rises behind the green to the left, and two cross bunkers in front of the green—which appear much closer to it from the tee than they are—create problems in perceiving the actual depth of the green. MacKenzie also added a strip of closely mown fairway extending twenty yards toward the tee from the front of the green, making it difficult to determine where the putting surface actually begins. A large bunker guarding the back left of the green merges with the towering dune behind it to trick the eye as well—its artfully ragged handcrafted edges make it look as if they're both of a piece—particularly when the hole is set in that back left corner as it was on this day. MacKenzie also deliberately aimed the tee box to the right of the green and left standing two tall pines on either side of the forward tee box that are not actually in play but cause the entire approach to the hole to feel pinched and constricted. All of the above effects conspire to make the green appear much more severely sloped from back to front than it actually is; it's not until you stand on the green that you realize the slope is quite severe, but largely from right to left. The net effect: no small challenge for what's rated as the second easiest hole on the course.

MacKenzie's genius is that the casual player might never become consciously aware of all these hidden effects conspiring to throw him off stride, but they affect him just the same. The better player who does notice them begins to believe the shot is more difficult than it is, and suffers the consequences. Only the great player, taking in and discounting these subtle attempts at mental and emotional sabotage, aims straight for the flag and fires away.

Knowing that the back left hole position was designed to lure you toward the bunkers, Harvie played safely to the right side of the green, about pin high, leaving a difficult downhill putt but a certain par. Ken, who could work the ball in a little easier, tried to start it right and draw it in toward the flag but overcooked it slightly, leaving the ball short and left, on the edge of the front left bunker.

Feeling a surge of confidence from his birdie at the second, Byron stepped up and fired straight at the flagstick. The ball pitched in just to the right of it, checked up, and rolled left down the slope, coming to a stop three feet below the hole. A perfect tee shot. Eddie stared at the ground for a moment and slightly shook his head.

Hogan murmured a compliment and landed his tee shot in the middle of the green. A short walk later, after Harvie's aggressive birdie attempt flirted with but failed in finding the hole, Ken's chip came up short, Hogan putted close for another conceded par, and Byron drilled his putt into the center for his second straight birdie.

The pros had the first lead of the morning, one up.

This time no one laughed as they walked to the next tee.

Byron

After his caddie career came to an end, Byron Nelson left high school halfway through the tenth grade in 1928 to enter the workaday world and pursue his dream of playing amateur golf. Admittedly no fan of the classroom, he scratched out a living as a low-level railroad clerk and at various odd jobs around Fort Worth, winning a few local tournaments as an amateur, until he qualified to play in the U.S. Amateur in 1931 at the age of nineteen. After losing early in the tournament, Byron couldn't afford to hang around in Chicago to watch thirty-nine-year-old Francis Ouimet win his second Amateur title, seventeen years after his first, a dry spell that ended, not coincidentally, the first year after Bob Jones retired.

The Great Depression had continued to layer darkness across the country, and jobs everywhere were increasingly hard to come by. Byron was still living with his parents on their cotton farm outside Fort Worth, and when he lost his railroad job, unwilling to burden them for a loan, he was forced to sell the few silver trophies and cups he'd won over the last three years to underwrite his golf expenses. If he hadn't lost that job, Byron might have been content to live out his life working for the railroad and playing amateur golf, but the Depression rewrote almost every man's story in those years. At the age of twenty, he'd never even been on a date; he just couldn't afford it. The Nelsons' rural existence had barely been touched by the twentieth century. Byron never owned a pair of shoes until his fifth birthday. The family farm, even in 1931, didn't yet include a phone.

On his way to play in the Texarkana Open in 1932, struggling to find another worthwhile job, Byron took a long look at the way his life was headed and decided to change direction. Amateur golf might have been the ticket for college boys and lawyers like Mr. Jones, but it wasn't putting any food on Byron's table; at that point nothing was. Once he arrived, he asked a tournament official at the Texarkana Country Club what he needed to do to turn professional in order to compete for the $500 in prize money.

"Pay five dollars and say you're playing for the money," he was told.

No tests were required, no tournaments, no trial by fire; that's how few men wanted, or could in any reasonable way expect to prosper from, the job. So on November 22, 1932, with that simple declaration Byron Nelson turned pro. He ran into his old friend Ben Hogan that evening before the Texarkana qualifying rounds, bunking in at the same rough rooming house for three bucks a night. Ben had already joined the professional game, declaring himself into their ranks two years earlier, the year of Bobby Jones's grand slam when he captured the Open and Amateur titles of both Britain and America. Hogan's timing had been unfortunate. After Jones abruptly announced his retirement from competition a few weeks later, the sport of golf lost its only superstar at the apex of his popularity and suffered a body blow from which it had yet to recover.

As the national economy slid into the jaws of the Depression, the professional game had nearly collapsed. Attendance evaporated, prize money steeply declined, and hundreds of private courses that had sprouted up around the country in the go-go twenties went into foreclosure, eliminating more club professional jobs. The winter tour, such as it was, had been cobbled together as a way for resident club pros from the East Coast to chase a few bucks when their home courses shut down for the winter, from December to April. A paltry amount of money was on the table, none of it guaranteed, and hardly a soul showed up to watch them play, but the whole experience offered a companionable soldiers-in-arms camaraderie that these itinerant, solitary practitioners came to appreciate as much as the pocket change.

Giving voice to these reservations, Hogan warned his old friend Byron that night that prospects now were even harsher for the touring pro; Ben had already called it quits once and was back living at his mother's house in Fort Worth, working odd jobs: mopping floors and parking cars; working as a stickman at a speakeasy craps table and dealing cards in private poker games—both of which required his packing a pistol for self-protection—or hustling pocket money from wealthy oil men in private matches on the weekends. By Hogan's reckoning a touring professional needed to win at least $3000 during the season just to break even on expenses, a nut that would only get tougher to crack every year. Showing more fortitude than aptitude, Hogan had lost his shirt the last time he'd gone out on the tour, and he'd only ventured back out for another try that winter because he'd been staked $150 by a Fort Worth businessman and patron he'd befriended at his home course, department store owner Marvin Leonard. That second grubstake was nearly gone now, too; at one point, earlier in the year, Hogan had been down to his last fifteen cents and was picking fruit in the orchards near courses in California to keep from going hungry. Every once in a while, when he knew he was out of the money in a tournament, which was more often the case than not, he'd hook a drive out of bounds into an adjoining grove just so he could secretly fill his bag with oranges.

Even if you make it through qualifying, Ben explained grimly, prize money at tour events was only handed out to the top ten or twelve finishers. At the Texarkana Open, a private event organized by the country club, money would go only to the top six. Byron knew that Ben was engaged to be married to a young woman he'd met in Fort Worth and as a result was under increasing pressure to earn a living. Byron wasn't sure if Ben was out on the tour because the game was in his blood or if he truly had no other choices. Hogan had never been anything close to a lighthearted soul, but he seemed haunted by the specter of bottomless failure that night, a look his old friend Byron had seen in a lot of men's eyes of late.

The next day both men made the cut and qualified for the tournament. When the Texarkana Open came to a end, Byron had finished third in his professional debut and won $75, which they paid out in cash; it was the most money he'd ever held in his hand in his life. But Ben Hogan finished well out of the running and had already slipped quietly out of town by the time Byron made it back to the boarding-house to share his unexpected good fortune.

On the strength of his showing at Texarkana, a group of Fort Worth friends staked Byron $500 for a trip to California and what was then emerging as the opening leg of the winter tour, a group of four tournaments and a couple of pro-ams in and around Los Angeles. Byron was astonished by the mild West Coast weather and lush green golf courses, so unlike anything he'd ever experienced in hardscrabble Texas, but Hogan's warning about tough times echoed throughout his stay; he won a grand total of $34.50 for his entire month's work and had to hitch a ride back home to Fort Worth, dead broke. This playing for money notion would have to wait until he established himself as a working pro. The next year, after another jobless season living and working on his parents' farm, Byron applied for and was awarded the job as head professional at Texarkana Country Club, where he'd won his first tournament paycheck the year before.

Moving away from home for the first time at twenty-one—125 miles was a much longer distance then—Byron bought his first car, a sporty roadster, for $500 on a dealer's hardship deal: three years' credit, no interest, and no money down. Soon after he landed in Texarkana, he fell in love with the first girl he ever took out on a date, a pretty, self-possessed nineteen-year-old hairdresser named Louise Shofner, who'd just come home from Houston. Byron took one look at the petite brunette in his Bible study class, tasted one bite of the lemon-frosted angel food cake she'd baked for the occasion, and went to work chasing off her only other suitor—a cashier who worked in a local bank—after which they were almost immediately, though unofficially, engaged.

Byron settled into a quiet work routine at Texarkana Country Club, giving his first tentative lessons and working every spare moment on his own game; the desire to make something of himself in order to impress Louise now fueled the engine of his ambition. When it came time to shut down the club for the winter in 1934, Louise convinced her father, who owned the local grocery store, to loan Byron the money so he could make another run at the West Coast tour. Recognizing that failure to hold up his end of this financial arrangement might seriously jeopardize his matrimonial aspirations, Byron played more effectively his second time in California and won a little over $100 in prize money, but by the time he traveled back to Texas, he had only broken even on expenses and still owed $660 to Mr. Shofner. Only two tournaments remained in the abbreviated Texas swing of the professional season for him to dig out of the hole he was in with the man he hoped would be his future father-in-law.

At the Texas Open in San Antonio, playing like a man with everything to lose, Byron led a pro tournament for the first time after the first round, firing a 66, and he eventually finished second, cashing a check for $450. The next week in Galveston he finished second again and won $325. Before he had a chance to spend a penny of it, Byron jumped in his car and sped back to Texarkana, walked into Mr. Shofner's grocery store, and paid him back his $660 in cash. He then marched down the street to Arnold's Jewelry store, bought a hefty $100 engagement ring with the last of his winnings, and he and Louise were married in the living room of her parents' home three months later.

The next winter, Byron took Louise along with him to California for the winter tour's West Coast swing. They made an endearing young couple, only three generations removed from the original pioneers, drawn west by the same dream of a better life, taking a flyer on the wings of Byron's innate optimism and born belief in the simple power of faith. To keep his bride warm in their unheated roadster, Byron heated a handful of bricks in the stove of their motel room each night, then wrapped them in newspaper and set them on the passenger floorboards under her feet. Once they reached California, he scratched out just enough cash to cover expenses until they reached the San Francisco Open, a match play event that Byron played his way into through a qualifier, only to find that he was paired in the first round against the fearsome Lawson Little.

Guileless and openhearted, fearful but willing to stand up to a challenge, tall, straight, and true as a stalk of wheat, Byron at this time in his life possessed the uncluttered purity of a frontier folk tale hero. Any child acquainted with the genre knows that such a young man eventually comes up against the adversary who provides the stern test that determines his character. Lawson Little filled the bill like an actor straight from Central Casting.

Little was the two-time defending U.S. and British Amateur champion, a feat never accomplished before or since. Easily the most celebrated amateur since Bobby Jones and his all-but-crowned heir apparent, Little had just collected the Sullivan Award as the country's outstanding amateur athlete, the first golfer to do so since the man from Atlanta. He was, in short, *the* golfer of the moment, at the height of his powers. Lawson Little was also everything Byron Nelson was not: a sophisticated Stanford man who had lived on three continents, the son of the commanding colonel of the army base at the San Francisco Presidio, where the tournament was being played at the Presidio Golf Club, Lawson's home course.

An unyielding, deliberate, cerebral juggernaut, who not surprisingly, given his military background, viewed every round of golf as a combat experience, Little was riding an unprecedented streak of thirty-two straight victories in international championship match play events. He hadn't lost an important match in two years, and he hated to lose with a passion that left him nearly friendless among his peers, but his unrivaled excellence inspired an equal fervor from followers of the game who were still hoping against hope for another Jones. The tournament's organizers had granted the twenty-five-year-old golden boy a favorite's pass straight into match play, sparing him the indignity of qualifying, and a huge crowd of local fans turned out for Lawson Little's first round, expecting him to rout this unknown hayseed professional qualifier from somewhere down south.

His stomach turning over from nerves, just before they teed off, Byron received a key piece of advice from one of the older pros that Little—a shortish, burly, barrel-chested man whose nickname was "Cannonball" and who took exceptional pride in his prodigious length off the tee—absolutely despised being out-driven. After Little smashed his opening drive to tumultuous applause, a pumped-up Byron walloped one that passed Little's ball on the fly by twenty yards. Little looked stunned, then furious, then flummoxed when this upstart nobody birdied the hole to take the early lead. Byron kept his head down, refused to be intimidated, and continued to outdistance Little off the tee, while the renowned amateur strained to catch up, lost his rhythm, then his vaunted concentration, and never recovered. Byron walloped the champion 5 & 4, an earthshaking upset that stunned Little's hometown crowd and earned the unknown Texan his first national headlines. Byron played on into the quarterfinals of the event, pocketing a mere $150 for his efforts, but the attention he got from spanking the great Lawson Little turned out to be worth a whole lot more.

His showing in San Francisco earned Byron an invitation to the 1935 Masters Tournament, only the second to be played at Bobby Jones's splendid new creation, Augusta National. Byron spied the great Jones from a distance during his practice rounds but felt too shy to introduce himself. He also fell in love with the golf course, which suited his game perfectly, finished tied for ninth and won $137, and privately predicted he could win Mr. Jones's fancy tournament in three years. Byron had started to realize he belonged. During that week in Georgia, Byron also accepted an invitation to become the assistant pro at Ridgewood Country Club in New Jersey. He had never traveled east of the Mississippi River, and he knew Louise would be reluctant to leave Texas, but to ascend the professional ranks in those days a head pro job at an established eastern club was a necessity.

Ridgewood Country Club was one of the oldest private New York metropolitan area establishments, dating to 1890. It moved from its original location to nearby Paramus, New Jersey, in 1929, with a course crafted out of old celery fields by Arthur W. Tillinghast, known for his challenging designs as "Terrible Tilly," the celebrated creator of American classics like Winged Foot and Baltusrol. Still a raw young country kid, Byron had as much trouble understanding the nuances of the locals' New York–New Jersey accent as they did his Texas twang. He was six foot two, rail thin but strong, tan and good-looking, soft-spoken, painfully polite, eager to please, and although not extensively educated, he was smart enough about people to know what he needed to find out to get where he wanted to go. He learned a whole lot more from Ridgewood's sophisticated membership, among them some wardrobe tips from "Terrible" Tillinghast himself, than he was able to teach them on the practice range.

They played the Ryder Cup at Ridgewood in 1935, so Byron also had a front row seat to watch America's best pros—led by a fading, forty-two-year-old Walter Hagen in his last appearance as their playing captain and Gene Sarazen near the end of his prime—crush the British team 9 to 3. Byron had not seen the mighty Hagen play since the semifinals of the PGA Championship in Dallas eight years earlier, when he briefly loaned him his baseball cap on the eighteenth fairway. Byron didn't remind Hagen of their brief encounter when they met at Ridgewood, and if Hagen remembered him he didn't mention it, not even when they played their first round together— and Hagen showed up forty-five minutes late—in a tournament the following year.

That year Byron began keeping a meticulously detailed record of all his tournament appearances, winnings, and expenses—down to the penny—in what he called his Little Black Book. He missed the cut at his first U.S. Open in 1935 by one stroke but shortly afterward recorded his first professional victory at the New Jersey State Open, a $400 check that matched his entire year's salary at Ridgewood. Byron played in thirty-one tournaments in 1935 and between his winnings and salary took home a total of $5146.40. After expenses, the Nelsons showed the first profit of their married lives: $1200. They were still living in a $9-a-week New Jersey boardinghouse, with Louise knitting his argyle socks for him, but they were on their way.

Byron got up the gumption to introduce himself to Bob Jones at the Masters in 1936, and noticed Jones following him during a practice round, tantamount to a blessing from the pope. In spite of which, Byron dropped back to twelfth that year and won only $50. But he recognized that two years of steady practice at Ridgewood were paying off; he now started to play consistently in competition, with his concentration—what he called "head work" in his notebook—seldom wavering, the key he had identified to playing professional golf for a living. A few weeks later he won his first important tournament, the Metropolitan Open in New York, beating a field that included all the pros he'd watched at the Ryder Cup only the year before. Money continued to be tight; Byron drove two hours back and forth to the tournament in Westchester every day to avoid springing for a room, and he could afford only a hot dog and Coke for lunch. He gave his first extensive interview to a grizzled, one-eyed New York sports reporter after his victory, answering every question with his most polite yessir or nosir. Byron was so thrown off by the piratical patch over the man's missing eye he couldn't think of anything else to say. The reporter concluded: "This young man can really play, but he sure doesn't know how to talk."

There would be no more wins in 1936, but Byron finished in the money in twenty-four out of the twenty-seven tournaments he entered, including two more second-place finishes during a swing through the Pacific Northwest that boosted his earning for the year to nearly $8000. By 1937 the outline of what we now think of as the modern PGA Tour was starting to take shape; after the four opening tournaments in California, the pros would pack up their cars or caravans and travel east for stops in Arizona, Texas, and then Florida, then the North & South at Pinehurst, ending up, for the lucky ones who earned an invitation, at the Masters in Augusta.

This was only the fourth Masters Tournament. Although years away from being ranked in importance with the Open, the Masters had started to generate some national press attention in 1935, when Gene Sarazen's lightning-bolt double eagle at the fifteenth secured the second Masters and the Squire's reputation as the grittiest pro since Walter Hagen. That win would be the seventh and most memorable of Sarazen's major victories; it would also be his last, which coupled with Hagen's departure by 1937 left the professional ranks desperately in need of a new star. No amateurs had appeared since Lawson Little, who had turned pro the previous year, who could sustain the same interest either. Seven years removed from retirement and only thirty-five years old, Bob Jones still played in all four rounds of the Masters in only a ceremonial capacity, but his presence was enough to attract one of the finest fields of the season. From their ranks, a new star was about to emerge.

After finishing third at the North & South, Byron had accepted his first offer to work as a head pro, at a club in Reading, Pennsylvania—for a sixfold rise in salary—so he arrived in Augusta for the Masters, as he put it, "as high as a kite." That feeling translated to an opening 66, a record first-round tournament low that would stand for thirty-nine years. For what it came to mean to him, Byron always referred to it as the best round he ever played. He held on to his lead through the second day, then faltered and fell three strokes behind fellow Texan (and soon to be two-time U.S. Open winner) Ralph Guldahl by the time there were nine holes to play in the final round. After catching him with birdies at the tenth and twelfth, Byron stood in the fairway of the short par five thirteenth, watched Guldahl make bogey on the green ahead of him, and faced a life-changing moment: lay up short of Rae's Creek and play for par or go over the water for broke.

"The Lord hates a coward" is the phrase that rose up from the soles of his Christian shoes.

He smashed a three wood to twenty feet, just off the back of the green, and from there chipped in for an eagle three. Confidence soaring, Byron closed with a flawless 32 on the back nine and won the Masters over Ralph Guldahl by those two strokes he'd picked up on thirteen. They didn't hand out a green jacket to the winner in those days, but a gold medal from Bob Jones and a fat check from Clifford Roberts—one year ahead of the victory Byron had boldly predicted for himself during his first visit two years earlier—was more than enough to certify the feeling that this sweet-souled, tee-totaling country boy could match nerves with any hard-drinking, flinty-eyed professional in the land.

Jones's faithful old friend and chronicler O. B. Keeler, now fifty-five and still covering the sport for the *Atlanta Journal,* was on hand to witness his victory and interviewed Byron in the locker room afterward. The unfailingly literate Keeler mentioned that Byron's back nine charge had put him in mind of Lord Byron's poem about Napoleon's defeat at the Battle of Waterloo. His headline the next day read: "LORD BYRON WINS MASTERS."

He had won the 1937 Masters, national respect in the game, and an eternal nickname on the same day. The antithesis of an aristocrat in every way but spirit, Byron accepted his faux title graciously, pointing out that the name had come from his grandmother's admiration for the poet when she named her son John Byron Nelson. John Byron Nelson, Jr., had dropped the John and the Junior at an early age to avoid being confused with his father, but once he found out a little more about the original "Lord Byron" he thought less of his flamboyant namesake. "Not a very admirable man it turned out," he later wrote, "who drank himself to death at an early age."

That would not be the path for Byron Nelson.

Into the Woods

Byron held the honors on the fourth tee. Always a dead straight driver of the ball, he played his shot down the left-hand side, carrying all of the daunting sixty-yard-long bunker that MacKenzie had planted there to discourage players from testing the most direct route home. Hogan hit his standard, commercial towering fade that drifted into the right half of the fairway, leaving a poorer view of the green over a gaping fairway bunker and creating a more difficult approach. Harvie and Ken blasted away, landing safely between them.

The par four fourth hole travels 410 yards up a slight but constant grade, carrying into the edge of the Del Monte Forest and the shelter of the Monterey pines that surround the green on three sides, as do another threatening band of MacKenzie's bunkers. The green is deep and subtly slanted back to front, making it difficult from the fairway to gauge the distance to the back center pin position, where it was today.

Ken watched Byron strike a pure four iron to the center of the green. The straight, upright, one-piece takeaway and powerful, pistonlike leg action that pulled the club down and through the ball hadn't changed over the years, and was as familiar to Ken as his own swing, which had, after all, been meticulously modeled after Byron's by the man himself. Seeing the original in action was always a sound reminder for Ken to stay within himself and play to his strengths, but this was better-ball match play, where slow and steady meant nothing if the other team made birdie. He knew Byron was a streaky player who prospered and fed off success; Ken had seen him run off five birdies in a row before, in an unconscious groove like the one he was apparently in now. The prospect of going more than one hole down to the seasoned pros this early on was daunting, to say the least.

Nothing of the sort seemed to be troubling Harvie, still humming and chatting away with Eddie and his caddie between shots, but he left his second shot short of Byron's ball on the green, a long way from birdie. Hogan bent silently to his task, his pre-shot routine as set in stone as the Catholic mass. His five iron ended up hole high, at the back right of the green, twenty feet from the cup, leaving a solid chance for birdie.

Ken hit a five iron, high and soft—as with Byron, long irons were the strength of his game—that landed and settled ten feet below the hole. Eddie offered another little pep talk to him on their way to the green. Harvie, who overheard it and caught Ken's eye along the way, took off his sunglasses and rolled his eyes in sympathy behind Eddie's back.

Doing his part, Harvie got safely down for his par four, and Byron shortly followed him. Ben and Ken glanced at each other briefly on the green as they lined up their birdie putts. This wasn't an attempt at a psych job on Ben's part, not yet anyway—the two men had a friendly relationship, as warm as any the remote Hogan had fostered with one of the young guns in the game—but a look of appreciation: *Isn't this a fine way to spend a morning?* Ken read the look correctly and smiled in return.

Yes, it is.

Hogan stood over the ball for a shorter length of time, but he still didn't have his mechanics worked out. The ball lipped out.

Ken moved quickly to his ball. He was an instinctual putter, who felt the line as much as saw it, and when both were working, the ball usually dropped, as it did now for a birdie three, his second of the day.

Back to all square.

Harvie hummed a little louder as they hiked up to the fifth tee, and Eddie yakked away at Coleman as he jotted down their scores. Ben kept his own counsel as usual; even Byron seemed a little reserved. Ken glanced over at Harvie and saw a twinkle come back in his eye; the competition was starting to spark his interest. Good news, thought Ken; Harvie had a huge engine under the hood, and it might be getting ready to rev up.

Alister MacKenzie felt informed enough to define the orthodoxies of course design, and bold enough to break them. Which he did with his next two holes at Cypress Point, both of them par fives; three par fives among the first six. The fifth is only 468 yards long, but the second half of it plays almost straight up a hill. The tee box slots back into the pines and offers a miserly view of the fairway, compressed now by woods on either side. The drive is also challenged by a gigantic bunker on the left, which, if carried, awards the player a long but negotiable second shot to a steeply elevated green. Drive safely to the right, and your second shot will either have to carry two of the most dangerous-looking fairway bunkers in the world—after which you then face a completely blind uphill pitch for your third over another pair of bunkers dug into the slope—or, if you play short of them, leave you a long and difficult approach to a slick, back-to-front slanted green you can't completely see on top of the hill.

Taking the tee again, after seeing what he spotted in Harvie's eye, Ken didn't bother to play their first shot safely and hefted a powerful draw over the right edge of the left bunker. Harvie showed Ken that the sparkle he'd seen in his eye was as advertised and walloped his first big drive of the day down the same line, twenty yards farther. Although deeply conservative by nature, Byron had it going now, and he didn't play safe either, taking the same aggressive line. Always re-luctant to flirt with the hook that had nearly ended his early career, of the four only Hogan didn't follow, lofting his drive out long but fading sharply right.

Playing first from two hundred yards out, Hogan drilled a fairway wood toward the green, but the trajectory was a little flat; the ball kicked into the hill and died there, thirty yards short. Byron, Ken, and Harvie now all went flat out for the green in two; Byron reached the apron and Ken the left side of the putting surface. Harvie hit his second perfect shot of the day in a row, a rocketing four wood that parachuted softly down about ten feet past the flag, which was cut six paces off the front edge.

Hogan's pitch up the slope rolled twelve feet past the pin, a dis-appointment, but Byron chipped to six inches, a gimme birdie four. Hogan picked up and took five. Facing the longer putt, Ken lagged to about the same distance for a birdie to match Byron again. Harvie was left with his putt for eagle to win the hole. He crouched low at the ball, nearly doubled over, in his hands that same old rusty hickory-shafted putter he'd used since he was twelve years old. He'd learned to putt on old-fashioned oiled sand greens back home in Tarboro, which were by their nature perpetually rolled flat as a parking lot, and that experience had given Harvie an uncanny knack for reading the line and keeping the ball on it. That was why he always putted so aggressively and sel-dom worried about going long; once he'd seen the break going past the hole, he almost never missed a come-backer.

Harvie tapped it. The ball rolled straight down for the hole, slid ever so slightly to the right and stayed out, hanging on the lip. Birdie, not eagle.

The teams were all even after five holes.

As they walked off the green, Eddie asked Ben if he wanted a four for his score—which would mean taking the twelve-footer he had left for a gimme after Byron had made his birdie.

"Five," said Hogan tersely.

Byron and Ken were both three under par after five, and Harvie was now off the schnied at one under. Only Hogan had yet to record a birdie; he knew it, and his frustration showed. *Amateurs.* George and Eddie might be keeping the scorecards, but all four players knew exactly where they stood, and would all day. Hogan lit another cigarette and kept his head down as they headed to the next tee. But he was no longer limping; his heavily bandaged legs had started to loosen up.

The sixth tee sits on the highest ground of Cypress Point. Still in the woods, you gaze down from there back toward the dunes and the sea below, where the course now returns; 503 yards, the second of the back-to-back par fives, and given the immense scale of the sand hills and ocean in the background, the green looks tiny and farther away than it actually is, another of MacKenzie's deft sleight-of-hand illusions. The fairway snakes out 220 yards from the tee and then tacks sharply left; a vast bunker guards the right-hand side and demands a two-hundred-yard carry, which if successful will result in the ball kicking left down the hill into position for a positive go at the green. But if you drive left to avoid that bunker, a swale will pull the ball farther left behind a downhill stand of pines that obstructs any attempt to reach in two, and make even par an uncertain proposition; all four men knew from experience this was one dogleg that did not reward a tee shot that cut the corner.

Ken launched a perfect drive, drawing over the middle of the bunker, sidespin pulling the ball left onto the downslope, generating maximum roll and ending up nearly three hundred yards away near the bottom of the hill. Harvie and Byron hit straighter shots that both flew the left edge of the bunker and landed in the middle of the fairway, trailing Ken. The pressure shifted to Hogan, but you'd never know it to look at him; every move, every gesture was executed with the same deliberate, ritualized tempo.

But then a surprise: Hogan played the draw, flirting with the dreaded hook, the perfect line, and if Venturi got 95 percent of his,

Hogan caught 99 percent. It bounded well past Ken's ball, a 320-yard drive, all the way down around the dogleg to where the fairway pinched in beside a massive fairway bunker on the left. Without expression, Hogan watched the ball land, roll, and stop, acknowledging all the compliments that followed with barely a nod.

Uh-oh, thought Ken. *Ben's awake.*

George Coleman walked alongside Hogan down the hill, complimenting the shot again.

"Perfect drive, Ben," said George.

"Hit it too far," said Hogan. "Nearly reached the bunker."

"But it didn't."

"It could have," Hogan said, refusing to take any credit, and lit another cigarette.

Harvie's ball had kicked twenty yards left off the swale in the fairway, bringing the pine trees into play, so he was forced to lay up sixty yards short and right. From 240 yards out, Byron played for the small, T-shaped green, the pin in its back left corner, and came up twenty yards short. Cigarette cupped in his hand, Hogan stopped to watch Venturi hit his ball. Ken felt the Hawk's eyes on him as he pulled his four wood and struck a beauty, a high arching shot that reached the front of the green and skittered to the right fringe.

Hogan pulled his own four wood, a heavy black varnished beauty, and stood to the ball, his feet together, measuring the shot with his eyes. He widened his stance and waggled once, twice, never lifting the club above the level of the ball—a miniature swing, thought Ken—then let it go. The swing itself happened in a flash of efficient effort and power after all that deliberate preparation. His arms never moved above shoulder height; he wanted the same feel of a boxer rearing back to throw a hard right hand, and he descended on the ball with devastating force, his blacksmith hands releasing into it only at the instant of impact. The ball leapt off the club face with a crack, rifled straight for the green, where it pitched into the middle, rolled, and settled to the back, exactly hole high, fifteen feet away.

Hogan didn't look at anyone after he hit, holding the finish, his eyes on the green; then, satisfied, without a backward glance he handed the club off for his caddie to grab. He still had the cigarette in his mouth. Exhaled. Started walking.

"Good shot," said Ken, and meant it.

This time Hogan accepted the compliment.

Harvie's short pitch to the green for his third was inside Ken's ball, but not by much, an indifferent effort. Byron's short pitch up rolled to within three feet of the cup, a perfect play, almost assuring another birdie so Ben could play for eagle. Ken felt the pressure pinging inside him for the first time that day as he stood over his long putt from the fringe, but his touch was sure and he lagged to inside a foot.

"Take it away," said Byron.

With his partner in for birdie, Harvie picked up; no point wasting a long one if they didn't need it.

Without even bothering to check with Hogan about whether he should finish, Byron stepped up and putted first, and sank his three-footer for birdie to half the hole with Ken.

Hogan examined the line from both sides of the hole, then stood over the ball again for an agonizingly long time. Did he have the putter going yet? He had the line, when he finally let it go, but this time the ball came up one turn short from dropping. But he showed no irritation this time, just curiosity as he examined the grass around the hole. Was it heavy with unexpected moisture? A slight imperceptible rise circling the cup? Whatever the reason, by his actions he appeared to lay the blame on some external condition; this time he found no evident fault with his stroke or the weight he'd given it. And that, thought Ken, was not good news for him and Harvie.

All square through six.

Byron and Ken were both four under, playing lights out, Harvie was still gathering himself, and all of a sudden the Hawk was on his game.

Harvie

Harvie Ward, the 1949 NCAA Intercollegiate Champion, graduated into a world that wanted nothing more than to throw a meaty arm around his shoulder, pour him a double Scotch rocks, introduce him to the girl next door, teach him the secret handshake, and hand over the key to the executive washroom. You didn't need a crystal ball to see that worldly success waited just down the road for Harvie; he wore the "can't miss" sign in neon lights a mile high and exuded the rare, intangible confidence of a man supremely comfortable in his own skin. That future appeared all mapped out; Harvie just had to fill in the details on the requisition, sign on the dotted line, and start living the life of Reilly. As he surveyed the landscape ahead of him, amateur golf, naturally, occupied the high ground. Not that he wasn't willing to work, but whatever career he decided to pursue with his all-purpose degree in "economics" would in truth be there, so the understanding with any prospective employer would go, to support his annual pursuit of the game's coveted international trophies.

Harvie had already played in his first Masters in 1948, fresh off his North & South victory while still a Chapel Hill senior, and he made his first trip down Magnolia Lane in a borrowed pink Cadillac convertible, trailing a string of tin cans and a hand-painted sign that read "Masters or Bust." That kind of free-spirited self-expression would have earned most rookies a perennial non-invitation from the conservative Masters stewards, but it's a testament to Harvie's formidable charm that not even Augusta's feared chairman Clifford Roberts took offense. Harvie debuted in the U.S. Amateur the same year, losing in the second round, but in '49 he demonstrated he was ready to contend, making it to the quarterfinals before losing to eventual champion Charlie Coe. Harvie picked up two more winners' trophies that same season at the Carolinas Amateur and the Tournament of Golf Champions, and made it back to the finals of the North & South, giving back his title to the man he'd taken it from the year before, Frank Stranahan. He also stepped into his business career that year, taking a job selling life insurance as he commuted back and forth from Pinehurst to nearby Greensboro, North Carolina. Not fooling anybody that he was truly more interested in actuarial tables than golf, he left for greener pastures in Atlanta in January of 1952 and a position with one of the city's oldest brokerage firms, Courts & Company, as a junior stockbroker.

Not long after he settled in Atlanta, Harvie accepted an invitation to lunch at the downtown Atlantic Athletic Club with Bob Jones, who had admired his early showings at the Masters, and their first meeting turned into a regular date. Golf world insiders watched with interest; for twenty years, ever since Jones had retired and sent the game tumbling back into another Dark Age, they had been hoping against hope for another godlike amateur player to rise above the professional ranks, charge to victory in a major championship, and restore the greater glory of the gentlemen's game.

The establishment grandees bore no grudge against professionals per se, and it seems at best a remote, even quaint notion today, but a man who played the game of golf and won championships for love instead of money reaffirmed all their cherished upper crust ideals about class and sportsmanship. This was their older generation's Victorian era code of chivalry and fair play in action, a shared remnant of British-American high culture, the same impulse that had given rise at the start of the century to the revival of the modern Olympic Games. A gentleman amateur sporting champion unconsciously represented the most eloquent and refined expression of the classical idea of "empire" on either side of the Atlantic; men who chose to play sports because they could afford to, not because they had to. When the immortal Jones had recently begun to suffer from and show the effects of syringomyelia, the as-yet-undiagnosed spinal disease that would cripple and eventually kill him, the nostalgic memory of his golden championship reign had infused the search to find a successor to his throne with even greater urgency.

A string of possible successors had happened along in Jones's wake. The first had been Johnny Goodman, an Omaha farm boy who in his national debut shockingly eliminated Bob Jones in the first round of the '29 U.S. Amateur at Pebble Beach. Goodman went on to win the U.S. Open in 1933, the last man to win America's national championship as an amateur, but after one additional win at the U.S. Amateur four years later, he reached his high-water mark and was never a factor again. The next had been Lawson Little, the man who inadvertently kick-started Byron Nelson's career in 1935, who had won those four amateur majors in an astonishing two years. But Little had turned professional the very next season, unable to resist the prospect of a windfall, and had gone on to win his own U.S. Open in 1940, in a play-off against Gene Sarazen. That would be his fifth and last major championship—his brilliant amateur career failed to translate as most assumed it would; he won only seven times on tour as a pro—and by the early 1950s Lawson Little was battling alcoholism, a shadow of the player he'd once been, nearly a forgotten man.

Frank "Muscles" Stranahan emerged as the next contender for Jones's throne, after the Second World War. Harvie's nemesis from

Pinehurst had captured the British Amateur twice by 1950 and been a factor at least once in every other important championship, but he had yet to break through in any of the American majors, which by the early 1950s, by most experts' reckoning, now included the Masters. Many thought such a victory could still happen for him, but Frank was now twenty-nine, already a year older than Jones had been when he called it quits. "Muscles" was considerably more popular with the professional tour's rough-and-tumble pros, who were forever cooking up creative side bets to tap into Frank's cavernous pockets, than he was with the USGA's blue-coated custodians of the amateur game. Stranahan had also incurred the antipathy of Augusta National in 1948 by thumbing his nose at Masters traditions and playing more than one ball during a practice round, an offense he then compounded by angrily confronting the on-course official who dared to bring it up to him. When he completed his round, a larger group of officials were waiting to inform Frank that his invitation to play in the tournament was withdrawn and he was to leave the premises at once.

Stranahan had earned the most dubious distinction of his enigmatic career: the first golfer whose playing privileges in the Masters had ever been suspended. A tempest of he said/they said controversy erupted, with Frank and his father campaigning in the press for reinstatement, to no avail. He bought a ticket at the gate to get back onto the grounds, hoping to secure an audience with Jones to plead his case. The two men did finally meet face-to-face on the eve of the tournament, but Stranahan's ardent self-defense fell on deaf ears—denying him his place in that year's tournament was the whole point of the exercise, which he didn't quite seem to grasp—and so he slumped away in disgrace. Trusting he'd learned his lesson, Jones invited Stranahan back in 1949, but similar frictions over his willful behavior persisted well into the next decade; he was compelled to write a series of letters of painstaking, personal apology to Jones as late as 1956 to again retain his playing privileges in the tournament.

Given all these self-generated dramas, any chance that Frank Stranahan could challenge Jones's decade-long dominance of the game was fading fast, and his personality was so aggressive and problematic there were many insiders rooting against him making that leap.

So Bob Jones's taking a keen personal interest in Harvie Ward and setting him up with playing privileges on his Atlanta home course at Peachtree Golf Club were interpreted by many as signals that he might be the game's next Chosen One. It's impossible to say if anyone, including Jones, ever said as much to Harvie in so many words, but the inference was unmistakable. Not that it made any difference to him either way, because the plain truth about Harvie was, as matter-of-factly and removed from egotism as you can imagine, he already felt that way about himself. He had played in all the major domestic championships an amateur could earn his way into, surveyed the field, and taken stock of his competition, and if there was an opponent on the current scene whom Harvie thought he couldn't beat when he was on top of his game, that man hadn't yet revealed himself. As he later described his attitude at that time, "There wasn't enough mustard in the world to cover me."

Harvie's skills on a golf course flowed through him so naturally, and he won with such effortless ease and lack of nervous strain, that the game just didn't take that much out of him. As a boy growing up in the South, he had modeled his swing after the fluid move of Sam Snead, and it expressed perfectly Harvie's cool inner thermostat. Bob Jones suffered so grievously from the stresses generated by the highest levels of championship play, he could lose twenty pounds in four days during a major championship. He walked away from the game at the height of his success, an old twenty-eight, to spare himself any further torment. High-level tournament competition created no trace of the same sort of agony in Harvie Ward; his personal confidence was so bulletproof that the struggles inherent to the game didn't appear to have the ability to wound him at any deep level.

The statesmanlike last word in golf writing, Herbert Warren Wind, called Harvie "archaically relaxed on the golf course." Even more useful, he also possessed some eerily precocious form of sage-like wisdom that allowed him to greet both failure and victory as imposters.

Not that Harvie thought his talent couldn't benefit from additional refinement; he always maintained a clear-eyed view of his own strengths and weaknesses, and during this period of his life he worked harder to improve his game than he ever had or would. Couple a perfectly simple swing that never broke down under pressure, his dashing swordsman's go-for-broke playing style, with a breezy on-course personality that made him an overwhelming fan favorite, chatting and joking with his galleries between every shot, and it's no wonder both experts and casual observers alike had sized up Harvie Ward as custom-made for once-in-a-generation greatness.

On top of which, everybody he met was just plain crazy about the lighthearted, happy-go-lucky son of a gun, and Harvie seemed to genuinely like everyone in return. He wore his feelings on well-upholstered sleeves; a dedicated clotheshorse, Harvie had incurred the wrath of his frat house roommate at UNC one night when the building next door caught fire and Harvie first made sure his stash of cashmere sweaters were carried to safety before waking the other boy up to warn him. (The fire never seriously threatened their frat house, and Harvie was, as usual, quickly forgiven.) The weaknesses of the flesh Harvie was heir to were all too human and right up front for everyone to see—they came part and parcel with his considerable charm—and he certainly never made any secrets of them. Within them dwelt the seeds of potential downfall—he liked his cocktails, and he loved women, especially women who loved Harvie, a group that constituted a substantial percentage of any random sampling—but in early 1950s America those traditional male prerogatives hadn't exactly risen to the twenty-first-century level of confessional talk show pariah.

Harvie's Atlanta career culminated in back-to-back wins at the

Dogwood Invitational, a prestigious amateur championship played the week after the Masters at Druid Hills Country Club, another local course with a strong Jones connection. Between those victories, in the summer of 1952, at the urging of Mr. Jones, Harvie traveled to England to play in the British Amateur, a trip not many American players were willing or financially able to make in non–Walker Cup years. Harvie's march up the national ranks had stalled out at the U.S. Amateur during the previous two years, where he'd been unable to get past the quarterfinals, and he was eager to try his hand at the British style of play.

The Amateur was played at Prestwick in Scotland that year, the quirky old course that had been Old Tom Morris's first professional home and the birthplace of the British Open. Having grown up on a bump-and-run course in North Carolina, Harvie quickly discovered he felt supremely comfortable playing the ball low to the ground in the links manner. Harvie qualified for match play near the top of the field and then ran the table that week, ending up in the finals pitted against none other than his old American rival, two-time British Amateur champion Frank Stranahan.

Harvie's rusty old putter didn't have the same magic in it when they began their thirty-six-hole final; he went two down to Frank after fourteen holes. But it heated up at exactly the same moment Stranahan's driver lost its sense of direction. Harvie played the next sixteen holes at four under par and finished off Frank on the thirty-first hole, the winner 6 & 5. Taking the British Amateur title the way he did, against a formidable two-time former champion, and with his free-swinging, man-of-the-people swagger, Harvie Ward stole the hearts of the discerning Scottish galleries. Their customary reserve melted; they hadn't encountered such a warm and winning American amateur since you-know-who. Hopeful comparisons to "our Bobby" in the press on that side of the Atlantic became commonplace.

After returning to Atlanta with his first major title, Harvie dutifully posed with his British Amateur trophy for a photo session with

Bob Jones, and two weeks later made the papers again when he married for the first time. He had proposed by phone from Paris, somewhat abruptly given his enthusiastic bachelor's proclivities, while playing in the French Amateur. Another marker of his rising fame, a photo of their big society wedding made the front cover of *Golf Digest*. Harvie's bride, Suzanne Smith, an industrious, down-to-earth young woman who worked at a large Atlanta bank, began encouraging the dedicated fun lover in the direction of diligence and respectability. This new success, as far as she could see, cried out for her husband to capitalize on opportunities to advance his off-course business career. His developing relationship with Bob Jones also influenced Harvie's growing conviction that the life of a golf professional would never be in his future.

More than any of the celebrated amateurs since Jones, Harvie truly did play golf for the joy of competing, and he knew himself well enough to know that grinding out an uncertain livelihood from it would soon reduce the sport to drudgery and kill his love for the game. Nothing about a touring professional's life appealed to him. Living hand to mouth, on the road week after week shacking up in cheap motels, hawking sweaters in some cramped pro shop to support his habit, giving lessons to weekend hackers and bored housewives for chicken-feed pocket change? No, thank you.

It's difficult to imagine in an era when the sport's top players soar high above the earth like titans in their private jets, but in the mid-1950s an amateur with the education and natural advantages with which Harvie had been blessed would have been crazy to turn pro and refuse the easy, guaranteed living that beckoned from the business world. The Fortune 500 crowd all wanted him to keep playing as much competitive golf as his heart desired; most of them had someone like Harvie working for them already; smooth, companionable men who could close a few deals and defend the company's honor on the golf course. Once he'd established himself as an amateur champion, tycoons were practically standing in line to hand out jobs that would allow Harvie to indulge his governing passion; aside from his easygoing amiability, it was the largest part of what they liked about him. At this point in life Harvie had already hit a triple and was standing on third base; turning pro would have been like trying to steal second.

Shortly after his return from winning the British Amateur, if any further confirmation of his rising stock were necessary, he received a letter from Augusta's Clifford Roberts extending an extraordinary additional privilege that had seldom, if ever, been offered to anyone: a lifelong exemption to play in the Masters. Roberts went on to mention that he and Mr. Jones would be pleased to see him win a few more of their Low Amateur trophies, but would prefer that he "make up his mind to acquire the Winner's Plaque as well." All that remained to complete the picture was for Harvie Ward to live up to what everyone else saw in him and win an American championship. He appeared to have every intention of doing exactly that. Later that season Harvie was awarded a spot on the country's America's Cup team, the inaugural of a new biannual amateur competition between the U.S., Canada, and Mexico. Harvie found himself paired in his first alternate-shot match with a young teammate from San Francisco whom he hadn't met before named Ken Venturi. Their aggressive playing styles fit together like a lock and key; Harvie's first words to Ken were "Boy, if I get you on the green, don't you be lagging any putts out there today, you understand? I can make anything coming back."

Ken ended up testing Harvie's resolve on the first green, when he blew his twenty-footer for birdie five feet past the hole. As good as his word, Harvie sank the come-backer for par with barely a glance at the ball. The team of Ward and Venturi won both of their thirty-six-hole matches that week by ridiculous margins, 13 & 12 and 10 & 9, and an impregnable partnership was born. Just as important, a lifelong friendship was born off the course; they were soon as close as brothers, and because their wives got along as well they became inseparable couples. As an indication of the duo's rising fame in the

Bay Area, when their wives, who had both just taken up the game, went out to Harding Park to play a round together and the starter announced "On the first tee, Venturi and Ward," within moments the two women were surrounded by a crowd of over a hundred people. Suzanne whiffed her tee shot, and they hurried down the fairway to get away from them.

During his trip to England in 1952 Harvie had also met Eddie Lowery, who made the trip with a number of other USGA officials. Harvie and Eddie seemed to grasp each other's essence with the ease and speed of complementary molecules. Early in 1953 Eddie invited Harvie to move out to San Francisco and join his sales staff at Van Etta Motors. After Harvie got his first extended look at the California weather and lifestyle, complete with the understanding that on the strength of his British Amateur win and Eddie Lowery's good word every door in San Francisco would open for him, he said yes and made the move, dragging his skeptical young Southern belle Suzanne, who'd never been west of Alabama, along with him.

The move might seem puzzling, given how well his life was going in the South, but Harvie had privately come to the conclusion that although he was frequently compared to Bob Jones, and had long been the beneficiary of the man's support and friendship, trying to follow all the way in the trail of those giant footsteps while living in Atlanta would become a burden next to impossible to bear. Jones cast a towering shadow over the traditions and values of golf in the South; Harvie's admiration for him would never wane, but he felt a strong need to break out in his own direction. California, as it has for millions of Americans eager for a new way of life, provided the territory.

San Francisco suited Harvie perfectly. He realized at once that he preferred the concrete, tactile business of selling cars to the ephemeral numerology of securities and bonds. And it was a lot less work kicking tires and tossing the keys to some starry-eyed desk jockey who came in eager to buy his Lincoln from a famous athlete than it was sweating the daily tickers on the stock exchange. Harvie was not only gifted at sales, he loved working in a field that depended largely on his formidable personal charm, and he was soon banking $35,000 a year from Van Etta, a princely sum that translates to over 250,000 contemporary dollars. To earn that kind of living on the PGA Tour, he would have had to win more than half the tournaments he entered, and grind it out on the road all year round just to have the opportunity. Selling cars meant a guaranteed paycheck, and the big-money private weekend matches with Eddie or Ken as his partner that started rolling his way only served as candles on the birthday cake. With Eddie running interference for him, Harvie was soon invited to join prestigious San Francisco Golf Club, and within a few months he broke the course record with a 63.

That year Eddie also arranged for Harvie to play in his first of many Crosby Clambakes, and he was a perfect fit into its boozy bonhomie, making fast friends and raising hell with CEOs and movie stars. Bing Crosby himself took a powerful shine to Harvie, recognizing in the younger man some of the same insouciant charm that he possessed in such abundance. The young Wards became favorite houseguests of Crosby's, and within a year Harvie and the recently widowed Bing would travel overseas together to play in the British and French Amateurs, pursuing extracurricular interests with gusto between rounds. (One story Harvie loved to recount years later: Late one night while serenading the apartment window of a pair of Parisian mademoiselles from the backseat of a rented Cadillac convertible, the two men's amorous plans died an inglorious death when they became the target of a disgruntled neighbor's emptied chamber pot. As quick with a quip in life as he was in the Road movies, Bing had this immediate response: "Everybody's a critic.") As a disappointing conclusion to his most dominant season to date, Harvie made it back to the finals of the 1953 British Amateur before losing to Joe Carr, and a few weeks later reached the quarter finals of the U.S. National Amateur for the second time, where he was beaten by another eventual champion, a rising young star from San Diego named Gene Littler.

On the heels of those setbacks, just as he'd done earlier with Ken Venturi, Eddie Lowery arranged some practice range sessions with Byron Nelson for Harvie. Unlike Ken when he'd first studied with Byron, Harvie had no obvious flaws in his game; if anything, the only complaint they had was that he hit the ball too straight, and lacked the final degrees of finesse to work it left or right when a demanding shot required it. Byron spotted a flaw in Harvie's grip and taught him how to work the ball; Harvie was such a natural he incorporated it all in a couple of brief sessions. Eddie then arranged an exhibition tour of Northern California for the two of them, like the one Byron had previously played with Ken Venturi, and they tore through their competition undefeated.

Harvie's education and his game were just about complete. With his one-of-the-boys affability, he had become friendly with all the top name players in the game, amateur and pro. In the spring of 1953, when he won his first Low Amateur trophy at the Masters, he'd even broken the ice with the notoriously hard-to-know Ben Hogan, who won Jones's prized tournament that year for the second time. The taciturn Hogan always preferred the locker room company of self-confident extroverts like Jimmy Demaret and Tommy Bolt— they embodied the easygoing virtues he lacked but also longed for— and Harvie was cut from that same cloth. The two got along so well that when Harvie recommended a Scottish caddie he'd befriended, the man ended up on Hogan's bag when he won the British Open that year at Carnoustie, his third major of that season, the most dominant performance since Jones's grand slam. That was the kind of personal favor that Ben Hogan never forgot.

After making the quarterfinals of the U.S. Amateur, Harvie Ward and Ken Venturi were both selected to the 1953 Walker Cup team, the amateur version of the Ryder Cup, captained that year by one of Bob Jones's first Atlanta protégés, another former winner of the

British Amateur, Charlie Yates. Harvie served as the team's number one player and handily won both his matches, keying a 9 to 3 trouncing of the Brits. Shortly afterward the successful playing partnership of Venturi and Ward would be placed on hiatus, when Ken received notification from the draft board that he'd been tapped for two years of service in the army. But when he finished his eight weeks of basic training at Fort Ord in Monterey, and before he reported for active duty, Ken received a week's leave from the camp's commander—a fan, as it happened—which allowed for one last golfing highlight: his first trip to Augusta, Georgia.

On the strength of making that year's Walker Cup team, in 1954 Venturi earned his first invitation to the Masters, and Eddie Lowery arranged to have him paired with Harvie in his first round. Supremely comfortable in each other's company, both men played well. The next day, with the help of an influential Augusta member, Eddie helped arrange a second-round pairing for Ken with defending Masters champion Ben Hogan, whom Venturi had forever worshipped but never met. Harvie knew Hogan well enough to give Ken some valuable advice about establishing an accord on the course with the prickly, intimidating Hawk: the first time he needles you, needle him right back, or he won't respect you. You had to earn the great man's respect, because Hogan never handed it to anyone. And if he didn't respect you, you might as well be playing on the moon.

Their round began smoothly, with Hogan courteously advising Ken on the first green that the younger man should putt out before he did on each hole so that Hogan's massive gallery wouldn't stampede toward the next tee with Ken's ball still on the green.

"Thank you, Mr. Hogan."

"Call me Ben," he said.

When Ken hit a three iron to within six feet on the par three fourth, and Hogan stuck his three iron in the front bunker, he asked to have a look at Ken's club, then derisively dismissed it as second-hand goods. Instead of bearing the insult in silence, and sensing he was being tested, Ken found the nerve to challenge Hogan and give the needle right back.

"That's great," he said. "I'm in the army making seventy-two bucks a month. These are the only clubs I have. You want me to call you Mr. Hogan again?"

Hogan stared at him for a moment, perhaps a little in shock, then with a twinkle in his eye said: "No. Call me Ben. But I want your address when we get in."

The next week Hogan mailed Venturi a brand-new set of Ben Hogan signature irons, free of charge.

Venturi made the cut at his first Masters, finished tied for sixteenth as the third low amateur behind Harvie Ward—a meaningful honor in Jones's tournament that Harvie had now won twice in a row—and earned an invite back for the following year that he knew he wouldn't be able to accept. A few days later Venturi reported for active duty back at Fort Ord, was shortly thereafter shipped off to an American base in Austria, and bid good-bye to golf for the next sixteen months.

Before Venturi's departure, playing as a regular team for over two years in organized competition or Eddie Lowery's private matches, Harvie and Ken had never lost a single match. With Ken in uniform, Harvie, playing his own ball, now embarked on the most impressive stretch of golf in his career. He had already won the '54 Crosby Pro-Am earlier that year. After his fine showing at the Masters, he captured the Canadian Amateur Championship, paired in the finals against the redoubtable West Virginian Bill Campbell, a former Walker Cup teammate and good friend; Eddie Lowery traveled along to watch, and picked up expenses, conducting some car business while Harvie trampled the opposition.

After another undefeated performance for the America's Cup, Harvie repeated the feat on his second Walker Cup team in 1955, playing brilliantly against the British. He finished eighth at the '55 Masters, low amateur for a record third year in a row. A few weeks later at the 1955 U.S. Open at Olympic Country Club in San Francisco, Harvie shared the second-round lead before finishing tied for sixth place, low amateur again, his best showing in America's biggest championship. He arrived at the Country Club of Virginia in Richmond for the 1955 U.S. Amateur that September as the odds-on favorite.

That year marked the silver anniversary of Bob Jones's grand slam, and the USGA kicked off the week's festivities of their longest running tournament with a dinner honoring the Great Man. By now barely able to walk even with the aid of canes and leg braces, Jones rose from his seat to give eloquent thanks for the silver goblet they presented him. Harvie and Suzanne Ward were seated at Jones's table, more evidence of his favorite-son status; as low amateur that year at both the Masters and U.S. Open, Harvie had come closer than anyone in a quarter of a century to duplicating Jones's enduring championship run. To cap his season by winning the U.S. Amateur would seal the deal on his own greatness.

But two days later, out on the course in his first-round match, Harvie nearly fumbled it away; one down at the eighteenth to an unheralded youngster, Harvie manufactured a birdie to force extra holes, and then bombed in a thirty-five-footer for birdie on the nineteenth hole to advance. He was never seriously challenged again during his next five matches—he missed only *two* fairways all week—and marched into the finals against one of his former Walker Cup teammates, a Philadelphia insurance executive ten years his senior named Bill Hyndman.

Nearing forty, out of shape from years behind a desk, worn down by a week of intense competition, and walking gingerly on badly blistered feet, Bill Hyndman never knew what hit him. He played well; only one over through nine, but he already trailed by five. Harvie roared out of the gate in that morning round to shoot 66, and established an eight-hole lead by the lunch break. Hyndman won only a single hole from Harvie all day, their twentieth, sinking an improbable seventy-five-foot putt for birdie. The scheduled thirty-six-hole final match required only twenty-eight to settle the issue; Harvie waxed Hyndman 9 & 8, one of the most spectacular final-round performances in National Amateur history. Harvie Ward had written the perfect ending to his fairy tale year.

After the president of the USGA handed him the Havemeyer Trophy and introduced him as "the world's greatest amateur," Harvie thanked his father for giving him a love for the game at such an early age; Palmer Maples, the head pro at his little home course back in Tarboro, for first teaching him the fundamentals; then Bob Jones, Eddie Lowery, and particularly Byron Nelson for helping him realize his potential. Visibly full of emotion, he elaborated about his dedication to amateur golf and what it meant to him, relating a promise he had made to his parents when they helped him out financially at the start of his business career.

"I will never turn pro," he said. "I like to play golf for fun. I intend to continue to earn a living by other means than golf."

This was an issue much on the minds of everyone from Bob Jones, to the USGA, to all the officials and players dedicated to the amateur championship. As opportunities steadily increased through the decade for players to make a better living on the professional tour, the last two men to win the U.S. Amateur title—Gene Littler and Arnold Palmer—had immediately announced they were turning pro. The underlying fear of money creeping into the collegiate and amateur ranks, corrupting its young players and undermining its august traditions, threw a chill into fervent supporters of the game. The USGA had that year even begun to canvass pretournament contenders, and if they stated an intention to turn professional right after winning the National Amateur, they were politely asked to withdraw. This advancing trend warned of a day when the best up-and-coming players might bypass amateur events altogether, eroding sixty years of tradition and culture that centered around the storied amateur championship and the pioneering players who'd made them so memorable: Francis Ouimet, Walter Travis, Jerry Travers, Chick Evans,

Bob Jones. Despite recent advances, the professional game still had a lower-class aura about it, and the taint of prize money, which left it only a few steps up from the boxing ring. On the night of his triumph in Richmond, the best and brightest current bearer of the amateur standard tried his best to set the audience's fears to rest the only way he knew how. Harvie loved the amateur lifestyle; he liked making money at the office, sleeping in his own bed in his own house every night, and playing golf for the love of the sport, and he promised the audience at the end of his speech that he would return the following year in 1956 to defend his amateur championship.

But after all the congratulations and backslapping after the dinner, as he relaxed with his wife, friends, and his new hardware over cocktails in the bar, Harvie was approached by a reporter who, after lobbing a few softballs, asked him some pointed questions about the legitimacy of his employment by Eddie Lowery at Van Etta Motors and, by implication, the authenticity of his amateur status.

"I work for a living," said Harvie emphatically. "I sell cars. If I don't work I have no income, and nobody pays me to play golf."

The reporter retreated. The usually unflappable Harvie remained agitated for hours because he knew he'd done nothing wrong. Every successful amateur had to walk a fine line on issues of generating income from the sport or accepting financial support to play in championships; the USGA's guidelines were painstaking and assiduously spelled out. Harvie trusted his boss to guide him through this dangerous thicket. Eddie Lowery was a legend in the game, a mainstay of the USGA's Executive Committee, and he had assured Harvie point-blank that with whatever help he'd afforded him they'd always played inside those rules.

But the question hung in the air.

The Dunes

They climbed the path to the elevated seventh tee box above the sixth green. A great wall of sand rises sharply there, a primeval parapet dividing the forest landscape from the shore beyond. The tee shot on the par three seventh angles steeply up the slope to the right, to a two-tiered green cut into the ascending hillside, 155 yards away but playing much longer. Cavernous bunkers protect the lower right-hand side, ready to severely punish a fade, push, or under-clubbed effort. The flagstick is cut seven paces from the back right edge, the most difficult position on the green, with a large waste area waiting just beyond the back border of the green. The tee box atop the dune wall exposes the player again to the prevailing ocean wind, adding uncertainty to its effect on the upcoming shot. But there are no tricks of the eye or camouflage to the challenge MacKenzie confronts you with here: a tough, uncompromising line to the hole.

The amateurs still held the tee. It was nearly eleven thirty now, and the last of the morning fog had just about burned off, leaving milky blue sky fleeced by a few scudding high clouds. Looking down toward the ocean, Ken could see whitecaps forming off Fan Shell Beach; the wind was picking up, blowing toward them with a salty tang of the sea. He briefly noticed what appeared to be a flurry of activity, cars swarming down near the Seventeen Mile Drive where it rounded south toward the clubhouse, but focused on his task he thought nothing of it. Ken went down a club accordingly, pulling a six iron. He led off with a high fade, the favored approach to that back flag, which reached the middle of the green. Harvie tried to follow the same line and take it deeper, but his ball refused to fade as much, and it rolled just off the green into light rough near the back left. Ken thought Harvie wobbled slightly during his swing, and wondered if the wind had affected him. Harvie had suffered all his life from a malformation of the mastoid bones in his ears, resulting in a series of painful childhood infections. Whenever the wind blew, particularly a cold breeze like the one just picking up off the ocean, it adversely affected his balance. He could usually counteract it by stuffing wads of cotton in his ears, and he carried them in his bag, but he hadn't yet needed to today.

Byron played a steady, commercial five iron to the middle of the green, a few feet from Ken's ball. Hogan stepped to the tee. Nothing ever varied in his routine over the ball, but Ken detected a sharpening in his gestures and eye, a heavier sense of physical presence, and he knew exactly what that meant.

Hogan shaped his six iron high, soaring above the dunes, then turning as precisely as a target-seeking missile toward the back of the green. Impact. Slight roll to the right, where it settled less than a foot from the hole.

Cold stiff.

Murmured "good shots" were the only words spoken until they reached the green. Hogan was the last man up the hill, concealing the effort that the climb demanded, his eyes fixed on the ball near the flag as he crested the front of the green, confirming what he knew he'd done at first impact.

"That's good, Ben," said Ken.

Hogan swept the ball away. Byron picked up for the par that would have certainly been his without a word. Harvie went first, chipping from off the green, rolling past the hole and then knocking it away. Ken had a thirty-footer left for birdie, a five-foot uphill breaker to halve the hole. It passed the hole and rolled three feet beyond.

The pros had regained their advantage, one up.

There followed another short climb to the eighth tee, up the dune to the right, where the box slashed into the escarpment, the only tamed grass on the hillside. Dead silence, but all four men felt it now, triggered by Hogan's burst of brilliant play, the gravity that settles over a round when they feel themselves reach beyond the ordinary and tune up toward the apex of their game. The setting, the opponents, the partner, the day. Competitive juices lit up and flowing. Distractions falling away. Senses heightened and alive. The defining reason why they played the game.

And what a golf hole awaited them: the first partially blind tee shot, turned west now, dead into the wind, facing a broad, uncertain carry across a vast, falling, broken shoulder of sand. A broad stretch of fairway is visible below and to the left, but the green sits sharply right, perpendicular and dead uphill from what you can see, not so far away as the crow flies, only 321 yards; but the bold shot demands you fade it out blind over that sandy waste toward where you know from past experience the fairway chokes down to a narrow sliver of grass and disaster awaits on either side. Play it safe toward the visible slice of fairway and chances are the ball will kick farther left and away from the green, greatly complicating the approach.

Hogan led off now, aiming straight for that bold and educated route, a sure-handed fade, his bread and butter, ignoring all MacKenzie's warning signs and ripping it high and hard out of sight. Byron, knowing precisely his role in this moment now that Ben had come alive—and without hard evidence that his daring drive had found a safe landing—followed with a gentler fade over the edge of the dunes, still a two-hundred-yard carry, in sight and in play.

The most emotional player in the foursome, Venturi rode the surging competitive high kicked up by Hogan's brilliance and stepped to the tee committed to match him blow for blow. They'd grown close during the last two years, as close as Hogan let any other player get, but he'd never let up on any man in competition; you could give no surer sign of disrespect. Ken took the same aggressive line with a three wood and killed it, his best of the day: *I love you like an older brother, Ben, but take that.* He watched it sail out of sight, confident he'd stuck the landing, then turned and smiled at Hogan.

Hogan winked at him.

Harvie followed with a more aggressive version of Byron's supportive play, and the four of them tramped down through the dunes across the top of the parapet, their step quickened and lively, out to the fairway that barreled and narrowed up the sandy canyon to the green. They rounded the corner of the dunes and reached the grass. In front of them, one of the caddies who'd scurried ahead gave them the safe sign.

Both Hogan's and Venturi's balls were in the fairway, less than ninety yards from the green.

Byron and Harvie played their seconds from well back in the fairway, 130 yards, playing a third again as long to a flagstick pinned in the front center flap of the T-shaped green, five paces from the apron. Byron's nine iron spun back just off the front edge, eighteen feet away. Harvie stuck his shot hole high, fifteen feet to the left, a slippery downhill leave for birdie.

Hogan and Venturi walked up the vale along the edge of the dunes, Hogan's stride measured and slow, pacing himself up the steady grade. His caddie waited for him at his ball, a hand resting on the sand wedge, but he waited until Hogan asked for the club before he pulled it. Hogan measured his distance, flicked the wedge at it, and, judging by his reaction, knew instantly he'd hit it too hard. The ball struck, danced once, and planted twelve feet above the hole, perfectly on line but hanging on the lip of the next ledge above.

Venturi pulled his sand wedge as he walked ahead, hardly hesitated over the ball, already feeling the shot, and his abbreviated half swing sent the ball spinning in high toward the stick. It dropped and stuck less than a foot below the hole, only a fraction off line, a certain birdie.

Byron secured his par from the front edge. Harvie went ahead and made a run at birdie, just misjudging the line and running five feet past. He marked his ball and picked up. Hogan looked at his line for a long time from the front of the green before moving to his ball. He looked as though he had it measured, and kissed it with a tap, but the grain or the gravity of the sea pulled it three inches right before it got there. This time Hogan glared at the ball with genuine anger. Venturi knocked it back to him as he moved past it and set his down.

Less than a foot. No hesitation. Firm. Up and in for birdie. Ken Venturi was five under through eight holes and the kids had erased the veterans' lead for the second time. All square.

"Glad to know ya," said Harvie, nudging Ken with an elbow as he walked by to pick up his coin marker. Venturi nudged him back, unable to keep a straight face.

The view from the ninth tee box was described by Alistair MacKenzie as one of the wonders of the world. High atop the crest of the dunes, all of Cypress Point spreads out below in either direction, back into the woods and out toward the sea. Once again, Ken Venturi noticed an unusual amount of activity on the road near the shore, cars clogging the normally tranquil scenic drive. The ninth is a perfect twin, almost a mirror, to the preceding eighth, another short par four, 295 yards, with an elevated tee and a slight right-to-left bias. All the choices are visible in front of you, but here, perched on what feels like the top of the world, the sheer beauty of the surrounding views is MacKenzie's greatest weapon of distraction. The fairway runs straight back toward the sandy hill, widens with a distinct bulge to the left after a waste area, then rises toward the top of the dune parapet, where the undulating, three-level green is terraced in at a sharp right angle just below the summit. Vast sand wastes lie below the green to the left and rise sharply behind it like a snow-clad

Alpine peak. The flagstick sits on the uppermost shelf on the left side of the green, a small and precarious target.

With the wind behind them, Ken knew he could reach the green in one, and pumped up from his birdie at the last, he went for it with a blast that turned over and rode the wind all the way to the front edge, but took an unfortunate hop upon landing and trickled into the broad, deep bunker on the left. Harvie stepped up and grinned at Ken, not the look of a man about to play it safe even with his partner in jail, and slammed an even more powerful drive that kicked once on the slope leading up to the green and rolled forward onto the putting surface.

Hogan and Nelson, who had hardly glanced at each other all day, now met each other's eyes, and Byron nodded; he understood Ben was going for the green. He took it out over the waste area on the left, then faded the ball back perfectly over the fan-shaped bunker below the green and set it down on the lower level a few feet from Harvie. Byron followed with a drive to MacKenzie's proscribed, strategic landing area, about forty yards short to the right side of the green, the ideal angle for attacking the back-shelf flag.

Byron's short wedge to the green crawled onto the upper terrace and clung there, twenty feet from the hole. Ken could only carve his ball out of the steeply angled bunker onto the green's middle level. Now it was a putting contest between Hogan and Ward.

The green rises precipitously from front to back over a distance of thirty yards, making the putt from the lower level notoriously difficult to assess. Hogan was away, and he didn't wait for his caddie to climb up and attend the flag—you could still hit the flagstick while it was in the hole without penalty at the time—his eye running up and down the line from his ball to the stick and back. Then he spanked it, turned only his head, and watched the ball ascend with his raptor's stare, climbing both terraces, judged perfectly, settling less than three feet from the hole.

Harvie went him one better. Bent over, clutching his old hickory-shafted blade, with a wristy stroke he launched the ball on an even more aggressive line, taking it up and over both roller-coaster rises, heading straight for the hole, where it caught a corner of the lip and curved around to stop less than six inches away. From sixty feet.

Byron and Ken picked up their balls and trailed Hogan to the upper level, where he had the three-footer left to tie Harvie with a birdie three. Hogan never expected anyone to concede a putt, or anything else for that matter.

He stood over the ball, stock-still, then with a firm stroke rammed it into the back of the hole.

All square through nine. Both sides six under par.

As they began the short walk to the tenth tee, Hogan hung back from the others a moment. He met Byron's eye as he passed, concerned, and spoke the first full sentence he'd uttered to his partner since they left the first tee.

"We've got our hands full with these guys," said Ben.

"You can bet on that," said Byron.

Ben

The black secret of the Hogan family that's only recently come into the light of day was this: when Ben was nine years old, his father, Chester, suffering from what was believed to be depression at the collapse of his blacksmith business, shot himself in the family's Fort Worth home. Accounts suggest that this immediately followed a bitter argument with his wife about moving the family back to the small rural town of Dublin, where they had previously lived and prospered, before the arrival of the automobile rendered irrelevant the blacksmith's stock in trade. The most heartbreaking detail: it appears that little Ben ran into the room after his father, whom he adored, perhaps to comfort him after the fight, just in time to witness Chester hold the revolver to his chest and pull the trigger.

Chester Hogan lingered for twelve hours, before dying at a local hospital, and remained conscious long enough to express anguished remorse at his actions before he passed. Newspaper accounts in the days that followed mention that Chester Hogan had been treated during the preceding year at a Fort Worth sanatorium for an unspecified mental illness. Bipolar disorder or manic depression, the most likely diagnosis given the symptoms Chester Hogan exhibited, remained at that time a mysterious and shameful affliction, and in this case the surviving victims of its merciless assault would suffer the consequences for the remainder of their long lives. According to all the future biographies that were written about his famous son during his playing career and lifetime, Chester Hogan, only thirty-seven years old, died of a "sudden and unspecified illness."

Young Bennie had rushed into that room after his father a sweet-natured, innocent, and loving little boy, and in that instant his childhood came to a shocking end. That Ben Hogan survived at all is a testament to his mother's iron will, the granite support of his rugged older brother Royal, and the forging of his own formidable character as it was forced to stand up against the wake of such disaster. Both sides of the family came from hard-nosed, pioneering stock, no strangers to calamity, and Clara Hogan rallied them around her like Mother Courage. They all went to work; survival was at stake, and after selling newspapers at the Fort Worth train station for a year or two, Bennie fell into the caddying job at Glen Garden Country Club, a three-mile walk outside of town.

Ben Hogan never spoke of his family's hardships. He hardly spoke at all. Byron Nelson, who met him in the caddie yard at twelve and knew him all his life, never heard a word about the Hogan family's private torment. Ben quickly developed a tough, leathered exterior, a consequence of the beatings he endured from, and then learned to efficiently dispense to, other newsboys and older caddies. One of Byron's first vivid memories of Ben was him putting on gloves and boxing an older caddie who had challenged him to fight. He fought the much larger boy to a draw, absorbing the punishment necessary to get inside and hit back without complaint. Hogan at twelve already appeared entirely without pity for himself, or any other evident sentiment. Drummed into him by Clara and hard-bitten necessity was the belief that work afforded the only possible road to survival, let alone salvation. And not long after he joined the caddie yard at Glen Garden, as unlikely as the prospect appeared on the facts of the matter, he decided golf would serve as the vehicle of his deliverance.

Ben quit high school after the tenth grade, just as Byron did, and, a good deal sooner than his friend, reached the conclusion that amateur golf was a luxury men from their class could ill afford. Hogan began his professional career running the pro shop at a rudimentary nine-hole semipublic course near Fort Worth that almost no one wanted to play, scrounging lost golf balls from the weeds for his own games. At the age of twelve he'd already met in school the girl he would marry, Valerie Fox, who lived down the block, the daughter of a movie house projectionist. But theirs would be a prolonged courtship, in contrast to Byron's, with Ben uncertain about committing to marriage until he found his financial footing. His first two stabs at playing on the primitive pro circuit came up painfully empty, netting less than a few hundred dollars, exhausting his patrons' generosity, and leaving him deeper in debt. He continued to work long hours away from the golf course—for a local petroleum company and whatever other odd jobs he could scrounge—to pay the bills.

During these years of deprivation, Hogan developed the brutal practice regimen he followed for the rest of his career, hitting hundreds of balls with every club in each session, working his way up through the bag from wedge to driver. No golfer since Harry Vardon had ever worked so long or hard to find himself as a player or as a man. What emerged was the apocryphal legend that Ben Hogan practiced until his hands bled, but in reality this solitary, quixotic pursuit began his journey down the road to mastery. "If you can't outplay 'em, outwork 'em" became his motto. Pounding balls day after day, season after season, he found not only uncommon skill but profound emotional solace in his lonely, uncompromising routine. Gaining control of every aspect of his swing, by painstaking stages he slowly fought to gain control of a devastating hook that routinely surfaced under pressure in tournaments and sabotaged his attempts to play the game for money.

Hogan never had a formal relationship with a teacher and only credited one other older pro—the stylish, established Henry Picard—with ever giving him a piece of advice that he directly incorporated, a slight weakening of his grip that helped contain his dreaded hook. But Hogan watched every player he went up against carefully, picking and choosing the elements from each he thought he could use. In this way, over the years he came to understand and synthesize his deeply personal mechanics like no man ever had before; his swing evolved from a self-conscious effort to unconscious method and eventually grew into something approaching a philosophy of life. Ben and Byron shared this tireless work ethic early on and spent lean months as running mates on the road chasing their shared dream of middle-class respectability. Byron, the more naturally talented of the two, got there first.

Ben and Valerie finally married in 1935, the year Byron beat Lawson Little, debuted at the Masters, and took his first important step up the professional ladder by moving east to Ridgewood Country Club. The Nelsons played hosts to the Hogans during the 1936 U.S. Open at nearby Baltusrol; both men qualified, and neither made the cut, but Nelson broke through with his first professional victory weeks afterward, and when he won the Masters the following spring, his struggles were all but over. Other Texas compatriots, like a colorful part-time crooner named Jimmy Demaret, Ralph Guldahl—about to win back-to-back U.S. Opens—and Lloyd Mangrum, began to make their mark in the national game that year, leaving Hogan in their dust, and painfully aware of his also-ran status. By the fall of 1937, the Hogans had scraped together enough cash for Ben to make his third attempt at the professional circuit. His sole means of emotional support, Valerie, would travel with him this time, and Hogan privately determined that if it didn't work, it would be his last try.

By the time they reached the Oakland Open being played in Northern California in the winter of 1938, the young couple was down to their last $50 and Ben Hogan was on the verge of giving up. In order to avoid paying the hotel parking fee, he left their car in a vacant lot across the street. When Ben went down the next morning to leave for the first day of play, he discovered the front and back end had been jacked up on blocks and all four tires stolen. His spirits sank to a new low.

"That's all," he said out loud. "That's enough."

Hogan went back to their room and told Valerie he didn't have one bit of hope left in him; it was time to call it quits and find another line of work. As she had often had to do during the early years of their marriage, his wife stood him up and talked some fight back into him. Ben had to call Byron, staying in the same hotel, to ask for a ride to the course that day—in his brand-new Studebaker—another body blow to his pride.

But scraping bottom forced Hogan to dig down into some un-tapped reserve of sustained fury that enabled him that day to silence his core issues of self-doubt and insecurity, and he rode it to a sixth-place finish, good for the biggest check he'd ever cashed in his life, $285. A trickle of confidence flowed in him for the first time in memory. The following week in Sacramento, more encouragement: Hogan moved up to third place for $350. The missing piece—the as-surance to trust his years of hard work, banish his demons of doubt, and just play the game—had suddenly clicked into place. An offer to work as an assistant pro at the Century Club, a prominent Jewish country club outside New York City, soon materialized. He played in his first Masters on his way back to the East Coast to begin that job, made the cut, and by the end of the year had wrestled home $4800 from the professional tour.

Through part of 1938 and most of 1939, the Hogans and Nelsons traveled together around the country on the professional circuit. The wives bonded, and the two couples drew a protective curtain of pri-vacy around themselves from the rough-hewn, carousing hard cases who made up most of the PGA Tour. The joyful Byron never drank or smoked and didn't even dance, living simply and happily by his Christian principles, and at that time Ben seldom touched a drop. Both men were devoted solely to their wives and their work, in Ben's case not necessarily in that order, although aside from Byron, Valerie Hogan was Ben's only other real friend. That left little time or appetite for hanging out with the boys in the locker room after their competitive rounds; penny-ante poker, chasing skirts, and boozy camaraderie, the main attractions for many of the scrappy rascals who lived the early tour life, weren't on the menu. From his years dealing poker in the back room of Depression-era speakeasies, Hogan could make cards dance like a riverboat dandy, but there wasn't a gambling bone in his body.

Instead of nursing swollen heads, both Ben and Byron would be back on the practice tee not long after sunup, clear-eyed and refreshed, working on some angle that had come up during the previous day's play. As a result both men were considered slightly out of round by their peers, although Byron was universally liked—there simply wasn't anything *not* to like about him—while Ben Hogan remained harder to warm to. Nothing about the man invited anyone a step closer than arm's length; he was wary, shy, judgmental, and uncompromising about himself and others. No one knows exactly who hung the name on him, but his fellow competitors on tour began calling him the Hawk that year, for his steel-eyed raptor's gaze out on the course, where nothing got past him and he existed in a silent, self-absorbed state of concentrated ferocity. Although he had at last started to earn a decent living, and few men were now his peer at hitting pure golf shots, Ben was also still winless on tour, and as Byron's superior tournament play lifted him into the game's highest echelon that year, their friendship began to suffer.

As they made their way back east from California in 1939, Byron won the Phoenix Open that spring, with Ben trailing by twelve strokes, a more than distant second. That widening gap between them continued to expand. Byron followed that up a month later with a victory at the North & South in Pinehurst, worth $1000 and at that time still considered a major victory on tour. Byron afterward was offered and accepted the job as head professional at Inverness in Toledo, Ohio, one of the country's most storied clubs, twice host to the U.S. Open. And then, as the season headed into summer, Byron made it into a play-off at the U.S. Open at the Philadelphia Country Club, with a former Masters champion, Craig Wood. In the play-off Byron trailed by a stroke going to the eighteenth hole but benefited from some strange good fortune; Wood badly hooked a three wood for his second shot to the par five green and struck a man in the gallery, knocking him unconscious. The players stood by while they carted the victim off to the clubhouse. Wood, visibly shaken up by the incident, still managed to carve a wedge to six feet, which appeared to secure his victory. Byron's third shot left him just outside Wood.

Standing over the ball, Byron suddenly flashed back to the last hole in his first play-off with Ben Hogan for the Caddie Championship back at Glen Garden all those years ago, when he'd told himself he was putting for the U.S. Open. Here it was, at last, the real thing. Comforted by the memory, Byron drilled the birdie. His rattled nerves now reaching the putter in his hand, Craig Wood missed his clinching putt, and they finished in yet another tie. USGA rules dictated they return the next day for a second eighteen-hole play-off. Early in that round Byron airmailed a one iron into the hole for eagle from two hundred yards out—still considered the greatest single shot in U.S. Open history—and rode it to a three-stroke victory. He polished off his remarkable year by reaching the match play finals of the PGA Championship, which he lost in a play-off, and then won the Western Open in Chicago, another tournament considered a major during that era.

As the 1939 season ended, Byron Nelson was now crowned by the national press as the finest golfer in America: three major victories, tops on the money list—$11,235.90, accounted to the penny in his Little Black Book, about $165,000 in contemporary money—winner of the year's Vardon Trophy for lowest scoring average. The sport had a new emerging superstar. Ben Hogan, convinced he had every bit as much game as his old friend, had yet to win his first PGA tournament.

The Hogans and Nelsons set out together again in early 1940 for another eighteen-thousand-mile roundup odyssey on the tour, with Ben feeling ready and more determined than ever to end that winless streak. After finishing second to Jimmy Demaret in San Francisco, third at the Crosby Clambake, and second in Phoenix, Hogan grabbed what appeared to be an insurmountable lead in the last round of the Texas Open. But playing in the final group, Byron Nelson closed hard with a birdie at the last for a 67 that tied Ben and forced an eighteen-hole play-off the next day between the two childhood friends. Leaving the locker room, they drove together to a San Antonio radio station for a live interview to talk about facing off against each other for their home state championship.

Byron made customarily polite and respectful reference to how difficult it was to go up against Ben under any circumstances, but when Hogan was tossed the same softball question, he responded with what he later tried to defend as an ill-considered stab at humor.

"Byron's got a good game, but it'd be a lot better if he practiced. He's too lazy to practice."

The comment froze the air between them. If it had been intended as a joke, Ben now made no effort to explicate or elaborate as such. He may have been as stricken at what came out of his mouth as Byron was plainly hurt by it, but there was a painful grain of truth in what he'd said that neither man had the impulse or social wherewithal to patch up then or afterward. The truth was that Byron had in the last year given up on the relentless practice range sessions they used to share; since his breakthrough at the previous year's U.S. Open the demands of success on his time made that same level of commitment impossible.

More to the point, Byron at last had his game grooved exactly where he wanted it—one couldn't argue with the results—and no longer felt he needed to devote the same endless, obsessive hours to its pursuit. Absolute devotion to the perfection of his craft was central to Hogan's identity, and would forever remain so; the slightest glimpse of perfection, no matter how fleeting, was its own reward. But Byron had already found everything he wanted and needed from his golf swing, learned to trust it, and moved on. The game was only there now to serve a new and bigger dream that he'd just identified: Byron wanted to buy a cattle ranch, get off the road, and settle down like his parents, and he and Louise were already devoting every penny he recorded in his Little Black Book toward that goal. Byron never lost his love of golf, but he didn't even like the lifestyle the professional game demanded of them, living out of suitcases half the year for subsistence pay, or in cramped rented apartments, and when they returned to Texas after the season was over, they were still staying with either his or Louise's parents. He craved a home they could call their own, stability and simplicity, and a return to his rural roots. By 1940 playing professional golf was becoming no more for him than a means to that end.

Byron didn't share this ambition with Hogan, but at some perhaps unconscious level Ben felt abandoned by his oldest friend. What corrosive part envy had started to play in prying apart their early bond is harder to calibrate, but not to understand. As the two men advanced on tour, and found expression for their tremendous talents, they were destined to collide competitively at the game's highest levels. Fellow feeling has often been a casualty of such battles between champions in the lonely crucible of their sport. But this went beyond just two young bucks who'd grown up together coming into their own and butting heads for supremacy. Ben Hogan had survived his various ordeals by virtue of unending labor and manful pride, an approach Byron, in the elusive embrace of worldly success, had to Hogan's way of thinking now apparently forsaken. So out the thought slipped, and in Ben's one unguarded utterance at the radio station, the damage was done.

Theirs had forever been a friendship based on shared experience, communal but never confiding—Ben had never shared his secret heart with anyone but his wife; not many men of their generation had any idea how or the impulse to do so—and to the end of their days Byron maintained that Ben Hogan had always remained an absolute mystery to him. Why did he never reach beyond himself? What prevented him from trusting even the people who knew and liked him the most? Byron gave vague voice to some of those misgivings in an interview of his own a few years later at which Hogan took offense, deepening the rift. Whatever the exact accounting of whose feelings were bruised when and by whom, from this awkward moment in San Antonio forward these two decent, hardworking friends would drift slowly, almost imperceptibly apart. There's no way of knowing whether they discussed the moment on the long ride home from the radio station that night, but the odds seem stacked against it. Byron later said he forgave Ben's comment—that was his nature—and Ben would block it from memory as if he'd never said it. But neither would forget.

The next day brought a result that crowbarred the gap between their fortunes another painful inch wider: Byron won their play-off to capture the Texas Open by a single stroke. Neither man appeared to take any pleasure in the ordeal. Hogan could barely force himself to speak about it, heading quickly for his car and the next stop on tour. Instead of talking about his victory, the ever-gracious Byron spent more time explaining to reporters afterward that Ben Hogan would break through and win his first tournament any day now. Just not this one.

After seven top ten finishes in the season's first ten events, Ben Hogan's breakthrough would come, as Byron had predicted, within a month, at the North & South Championship in Pinehurst, after the U.S. Open the country's second-longest-running professional championship. One of the fruits of Byron's arrival at the top was a generous endorsement contract with MacGregor Sporting Goods, one of the leading equipment manufacturers, with whom Ben had also signed a considerably less lucrative deal. Byron arrived in Pinehurst with a pair of new prototype drivers the company had just sent him to try out. Byron had already decided on his favorite of the two, and on the range he offered Ben the other one to swing.

In that driver, its shaft so stiff hardly another man who swung it could ever hit it anywhere but sideways, Ben knew instantly he had found his Excalibur. With the heavy, black lacquered persimmon weapon in his hand during the first round of the North & South, Hogan tied the course record on Pinehurst's legendary Number Two with a flawless 66. (Byron refused Ben's offer to pay for the driver, insisting he keep it as a gift.) Hogan split every fairway that day, went on to break the tournament record by two, and win the North & South by three strokes over Sam Snead, with Byron finishing third. Pinehurst's presiding godfather, the venerable Donald Ross, was on hand to present a beaming Ben Hogan with his first PGA Tour trophy and congratulate him for his unprecedented assault on the master's prized real estate.

Once he'd secured his first victory, the dam broke: Hogan won the next two tournaments in quick succession, at Greensboro and Asheville. Offers for profitable exhibitions and product endorsements began to stream his way, evidence that in the wake of the Depression golf was finally moving back toward center stage of the national sports scene. Ben won twice more before the year was out, and made his best showing at the Masters and the Open, both top ten finishes.

Ben Hogan became the PGA Tour's leading money winner in 1940, ahead of fellow Texans Jimmy Demaret and Byron. He took home the Vardon Trophy as well, for the year's lowest scoring average. He also landed a better paying job as head professional at the Country Club of Hershey, Pennsylvania, another crucial step forward on the road to financial security. This was his first gravy train gig, with no formal duties required other than some client golf and a few ceremonial appearances promoting Hershey's candies. From the confines of that new office, after he'd been eliminated in the quarterfinals, Ben watched Byron beat Sam Snead at Hershey to win his third major in the 1940 PGA Championship. Despite his progress, Ben wasn't satisfied; more than ever he wanted a major championship of his own to close the gap with Byron Nelson. He would have to wait eight more years, and then, hardly a moment after Ben had it all in his grasp, he would nearly lose everything.

The Back Nine

T hey made the short walk up from the ninth green to the tenth tee in silence. Perched high atop the parapet, the tee box towered over the tenth fairway that stretched out below them, making one last uphill run toward the Del Monte Forest. The uniform canopy of the tall, slender Monterey pines lend an arboreal, rain-forest look to the leading line on the horizon. It is the last of the par fives on the course and at 475 yards the shortest of the four and the easiest to reach in two, making it a frequent turning point for match play. The view from atop that wall, which ranges again from the sea to the woods, is every bit as spectacular as the one from the ninth tee, but by now neither the pros nor the amateurs were the least bit interested in scenery.

Eddie and George Coleman had given up any idea of playing their own match, or even carrying on conversations; they wanted nothing to distract them from this trance-like exhibition. Both men told their caddies to head back in with their bags, but the caddies asked if it would be all right to stick around and watch. A few dozen others had joined their gallery during the last few holes, most of them players who'd been out on the golf course and had heard what was going on.

A group of nearly fifty people now trailed behind the players in respectful silence. From the tee Eddie saw that more were gathering down below along the tenth fairway. He quietly ordered his caddie to head back to the clubhouse and spread the word: if his amateurs could come out on top against the two greatest pros in the world, he didn't want anybody on the Peninsula to miss it.

Other than Harvie, who always had friendly words for people who came out to watch him—if Harvie didn't have anyone to talk to, he'd happily talk to himself—none of the players ever even noticed their gallery was there. Coming off the birdie at nine, even Harvie felt the screws start to tighten, knowing the tenth hole represented their best chance for an eagle on the course. Match play was his game— it was *the* amateur game—and because an occasional wretched hole meant little or nothing to the eventual outcome, it suited his sometimes wayward concentration perfectly, just as it used to Walter Hagen's. Match play refocuses the game from a battle against par to a form of hand-to-hand combat, imposing your will on an opponent, with the ball as your stand-in, and Harvie favored his odds in that arrangement with any man walking. With the wind at his back, Harvie now blasted a deep drive down the perfect left center line, more than long enough to reach the green in two. A statement shot; his will to win expressed. Ken followed him down the middle, short and safe.

Hogan, intent and still, hit a precision drive that trailed Harvie's by a few yards. Byron's drifted slightly to the right, bringing a large bunker on that side of the fairway into the line of his second shot.

They made their way down the great sand hill to the fairway, where the people waiting adhered into a larger gallery that now formed around them on both sides. Hogan trailed the others as they descended, forced to negotiate the steep downgrade with more care, and Ken and Byron slowed their pace to let him catch up. Ken always automatically walked to Hogan's right, knowing Ben was hard of hearing in his left ear, on the off chance a conversation might break out. None did here. He saw that Hogan already had his eyes fixed on his ball in the fairway ahead, thinking about the next shot.

Their second shots presented a crucial decision about laying up or going for the green. Byron's line up the right side brought a squall of bunkers into play as he approached the green, so he laid up short and left with an iron, leaving a hundred yards and the perfect angle to the back right pin.

Ken, trailing Harvie, hit a similar textbook layup, freeing his partner to let it rip. Playing first, Hogan surprised them all by gearing down and hitting short with his four wood. At first Ken thought it was a mishit; his ball landed just inside Byron's, a good eighty-five yards short of the flagstick. But Ben's inscrutable mask didn't betray any signs of disappointment. That's where he wanted his ball.

Harvie let loose with a powerful, penetrating three wood that flew on a perfect line and kicked onto the front of the small green, leaving him a forty-foot putt for eagle. Advantage amateurs.

Five bunkers surround the tenth green, leaving only the narrow channel Harvie had negotiated in front to reach it. Ken played his wedge approach in first, about twelve feet to the left of the flag and an excellent chance for birdie. Byron followed with a high approach that landed just inside him.

Hogan pulled his wedge, a club with a leading edge so sharp and deadly he called it his "equalizer," like an old gunslinger's trusty Colt .45. His hands came in low, and he held them short of a full release on the follow-through, a soft, held finish, pure finesse.

The ball landed six inches short of the flag, hopped once, and rolled delicately into the hole without even touching the flagstick for an eagle three. The shot of the day. Byron jumped a foot in the air and let out a whoop, and the gallery erupted.

For the first time all morning, Hogan smiled broadly, a sight as welcome and unexpected as the sun bursting through the clouds. He flashed another wink at Venturi, then went to work tapping down the divot his caddie retrieved for him.

George Coleman tried to catch Eddie Lowery's eye, but he was having none of it, already marching past Hogan, yakking at Harvie as they headed toward the green.

"Come on, kid, don't let an old man get you down," he said, pitching the same brand of self-improvement he'd given Francis Ouimet over forty years earlier. "You can still sink this to tie 'em."

Everyone settled around the green while Harvie crouched over his ball, told his caddie to pull the flag. He'd had that old putter reshafted recently for the third time, still trusted it like a hunting dog.

The ball slid just off line and stopped a foot past.

"That's good," said Hogan.

Taking an exaggerated stance, Harvie tapped it in left-handed, for a laugh, and got one. Byron and Ken each picked up his ball, and took par fives on the hole, forsaking chances for meaningless birdies. Both men were slightly superstitious; they didn't want to waste a red number now, because the way this was going they knew they'd need every stroke they could wrest from the holes ahead.

George and Eddie tallied the scores, comparing cards by the side of the green. The amateurs were seven under through ten holes, and down one to the pros. Hogan, Nelson, and Venturi were all five under par, Ward three under.

The eleventh hole turns right around and heads back to sea, the longest par four on the course at 436 yards, lined with pines on the left, slightly downhill but dead into the ocean breeze. Two long, angular bunkers split the center of the fairway, out of reach from the tee but in sight and psychologically intrusive.

All four men took their foot off the brake with their driver, four perfect shots that you could have thrown a blanket over on the left center of the fairway. From close to two hundred yards out they played their seconds toward the center of the green, guarded by deep sand on either side. Ken's ball caught a bad bounce and rolled into the sprawling bunker on the left. Byron hit a low, piercing two-iron that landed, rolled, and died just short of the green. Ben and Harvie both hit almost identical four woods—they were just about the two best fairway woods players alive—and both balls ended twenty feet from the flag, bracketing the hole on either side.

Byron chipped up to within four feet. Ken's bunker shot flew long over the flag, twelve feet past, and he nodded to his partner that he'd have to salvage the hole. Harvie took the news in stride, stepped up, and for once lagged to within inches for an easy par. Hogan followed with a lag that left him more than a few feet short, but Byron calmly stroked in his four-footer for the tie. The teams had parred a hole for the first time since the opening.

The pros held on to their slim lead, one up through eleven.

They walked around the southern shoulder of the dune wall where it ends just beyond the eleventh green. As if you are walking through a huge, natural gate, a whole new terrain presents itself once you round that corner: a treeless valley of rolling green amid sea level dunes running straight down toward the blue water, the flag of the distant twelfth green framed against it, visible in the distance.

The twelfth was Ben Hogan's favorite hole at Cypress Point, and he thought it was one of the best par fours in the world. He said it "fit his eye," which usually meant it suited his favored fading tee shot: 402 yards, the fairway slanting left to right, a large waste area separating the fairway from a long, narrow green complex. The toughest hole on the back nine.

Ben followed Byron's strategically sound tee shot with an immense booming fade that flew a small depression running through the middle of the fairway and kicked another fifteen yards down and to the right, where the line to the green opened up; perfection.

Harvie matched Byron's effort, and then Ken cranked up and tried to equal Hogan again, coming close, landing just behind him. As they walked to the fairway, the crowd buzzed around them, growing in twos and threes as word continued to spread through the course about the match. Many players up and quit in the middle of their own practice rounds to hurry over and join the growing gallery.

The bunkers protecting the slightly elevated green are all short of it, and with the open blue water and sky behind, MacKenzie again consciously distorts and foreshortens the perception of distance to his green. Byron asked his caddie where the flag was—in the middle but difficult to perceive from the fairway—and from 160 yards hit a six iron to the front edge. Harvie's ball was ten yards closer and a little farther left, down in the central depression. He faded a ball in over the bunker on the left and ended up running nearly to the back of the putting surface.

Then Venturi and Hogan traded punches again, dueling nine irons from 120 yards out that both danced and stopped less than six feet from the hole. Hogan had gotten out of the practice of firing directly at flagsticks early in his career, when he hit so many balls that then bounded farther away that he realized his accuracy was costing him strokes. Now he usually aimed for the flattest spot nearest the flag. But not today.

Not a word was spoken as they walked to the green, each man absorbed and focused, and their gallery followed with equal gravity. Byron and Harvie lagged their birdie putts close for par, clearing the green for Ken and Ben. This time Ken went first and holed his sixth birdie of the day.

Hogan stroked the ball and turned his upper body, braced in his stance, a miniature version of his full follow-through, and watched it roll with that raptor's stare until the ball dropped into the dark again to halve the hole. Since starting his spectacular run, Ben had now broken par on five of the previous seven holes, and he showed no signs of letting up.

The pros still held their lead after twelve, one up.

They hiked up to the thirteenth tee box, perched above and to the right of the twelfth green. From there the thirteenth fairway runs on a slightly diagonal line from left to right, challenging the players to carry as much of a dunes and high-grass wasteland along the right as they dare; the more one is willing to gamble, the better the resulting line to the thirteenth green, tucked into an elevated bowl just below the peak of the last tall dune before you reach the sea, 353 yards away.

As they got to the tee box, Eddie and George saw an unbroken black line crowning the dune above the distant thirteenth green. A gallery of people twice the size of that already following them had gathered there; this was the reason for all the cars and commotion they had spotted along the Seventeen Mile Drive from up on the ninth tee box. Caddie master Joey Solis had banged the jungle drums, and crowds from all over the surrounding courses on the Peninsula who'd come to watch the day's practice rounds had flocked to Cypress Point.

If he even noticed anyone standing there, Hogan gave no indication of it; there was work to do. The thirteenth was an additional hole that favored Hogan's fade, and he smashed another low runner into the wind. Byron followed with one more dead straight efficient drive. Ken pulled his slightly to the left into the first cut of rough, but Harvie covered for him with his longest blow of the day.

It was past noon now, the sun almost directly overhead, the air sparkling with the filtered, crystalline light particular to the Peninsula. As they stepped onto the fairway, Harvie broke into a brief, pitch-perfect impression of Bing Crosby singing the opening bars of his familiar golf tune, "Straight Down the Middle." Harvie had honed his impression to perfection during his travels with Crosby; even Bing conceded it was one of the best he'd ever heard. (He could also do a spot-on Eddie Lowery, mimicking his pepper-pot New England patter with deadpan perfection, although Eddie remained less amused by it than Bing.) The other men all broke up, which briefly relieved their steadily growing tension; even the gallery laughed.

Harvie always explained his enduring lack of interest in academics and boring repetitive work by saying he had a ten-second attention span. Born today, he might well have been diagnosed early on with ADD and pumped full of prescription drugs, but whatever the underlying reason for his agitated nervous system, golf turned out to be the ideal activity for him. Lining up a shot and executing any shot seldom took him longer than ten seconds—about twelve minutes in total per round—and the *quality* of his concentration in those minutes was never less than exceptional. That left the rest of his four hours on the course for a pleasant stroll communing with nature, feeling the sun on his face, and cracking up his friends and galleries, which was Harvie's idea of the perfect day.

The flagstick had been set five paces from the back on what many consider the most difficult green on the course, long and undulating, a difficult ridge snaking almost straight down the middle from back to front and a steep falloff into sandy waste to the right.

Neither Ken nor Byron could threaten the flag with their seconds, but first Ben and then Harvie challenged the tough back position, each landing inside twelve feet, in birdie range. The crowd gathered behind the green applauded both shots, as they merged with the walking gallery and surrounded the green.

Byron and Ken played for their pars and secured them. Hogan lined up his flat-bottomed, center-shafted putter behind the ball. He had a diabolical break to read, sharply downhill and then right toward the cup; he waited until the line appeared to him and then rolled it.

The ball trickled in for birdie, Hogan's sixth in the last eight holes. The crowd let out a roar: as much as they loved their local favorites, Ken and Harvie, and admired the great Byron, Ben Hogan was still the game's reigning superstar, and this was the Hawk at his finest, in what was supposed to be a casual practice round. It was as if they'd wandered into their neighborhood bar and found Duke Ellington playing the piano while Sinatra sang a few tunes.

As he put his ball back down in front of his marker, Harvie looked over at Ken, smiled, and shook his head—*Can you believe this old guy?*—and ten seconds later he'd matched Hogan for his fifth birdie of the day, and fourth in the last five holes. No one present had ever seen anything like this; an amateur, standing up to Hogan at his finest, trading shots with the champ like Rocky Marciano.

The amateurs were ten under through thirteen holes, and still one down to the pros with five holes to play. Hogan's eagle at the tenth remained the difference.

As Ken trudged up the dune to the fourteenth tee, he had to ask himself: How much longer could Ben Hogan keep this up?

Byron and Ben

Ben Hogan's relentless drive to succeed continued gathering momentum; in 1941, playing in thirty-nine tournaments, he finished lower than fifth place exactly once. He took home $18,358 for his efforts; over a quarter of a million in current value, but about a quarter of the average first-place check for one PGA tournament today. He finished first on the money list for the second time, won three tour events, captured the scoring title for the second year in a row, and moved up to a third-place finish at the U.S. Open, his best showing in a major championship to date. Byron won four tournaments, winning $12,205 to fatten his savings for the ranch, but he trailed Ben on the money list for the second year straight. Although they didn't face each other directly in play-offs or even contend in many of the same events that year, Byron was clearly the man Ben was gunning for now; it didn't mean a damn thing to earn more money if he couldn't beat him head-to-head. The two men from Fort Worth no longer traveled out on the tour together; Ben had just bought the first new car of his life, a top-of-the-line Cadillac, and as his relationship with Byron cooled, he began to spend more time in the company of another fellow Texan,

Jimmy Demaret, a lighthearted, snappy-dressing crooner from Houston.

A first-rate player who would win the Masters three times, Jimmy Demaret's court jester personality turned out to be a more comfortable fit for Hogan's dour determination than Byron's happy, earnest warrior. Demaret owned a tremendous all-around game, and as their relationship developed, he and Hogan formed an effective best-ball team for the better part of the decade, but Jimmy never challenged Ben's alpha male status off the course, content to defer to the Hawk as a superior talent and presence outside the ropes. A talented singer who might well have chosen show business over golf, whatever ambitions Demaret held for his own considerable abilities he concealed behind his joker's loud wardrobe and a machine-gun diet of quotable quips. As part of his status as the tour's class clown, Demaret also became one of the only men whom Hogan ever let poke fun at him without taking offense.

The day the Japanese attacked Pearl Harbor in December of 1941, priorities changed instantly and drastically on every domestic front. Every able-bodied man on tour under the age of thirty-five knew service in the armed forces lay in his future, and along with Hogan and Nelson, most registered for the draft before the month was out. The USGA announced early in the new year that they would be suspending all their sanctioned championships for the duration of hostilities, as the R&A had done in Great Britain since England entered the war in 1939. That left only the 1942 Masters—which Jones and Roberts had already told the press would be the last invitational they held until the war was over—as Ben Hogan's last opportunity to capture a major title before getting his call from the draft board, something he had been told to expect before season's end.

Ben won two of the year's first three events, at Los Angeles and San Francisco, with Byron sandwiching a win in between them at Oakland. In March Hogan won his third title at the North & South, with Byron finishing third, and then his fourth just before Augusta, capturing the Asheville tournament for the third year in a row. When they arrived at the Masters, for the first time at any major championship Ben Hogan came in ahead of Byron as the pretournament favorite. Determined to make his own statement about who was the better man, Byron played brilliantly and cruised to an eight-stroke lead over Hogan and the rest of the field after the first two rounds.

When howling winds kicked up during the third round, Ben Hogan needed every bit of his hard-fought mastery over the golf ball to maneuver around Augusta with a stunning 67. Byron managed the fourth best score of the day, an even par 72, but his lead over Hogan had shrunk to three heading into the final round. Their long anticipated showdown in the final round of a major championship was finally at hand.

With Hogan playing a few groups ahead of him, Byron began cautiously trying to hold his lead, a tactical mistake that led to three consecutive bogeys on the front nine. He birdied the long, difficult par four ninth to stop the bleeding and learned that he and Hogan now stood in a flat-footed tie. Hogan finished first with a 70, and Byron arrived at the last hole knowing he needed par to force a play-off. When his right foot slipped on the wet tee box he pushed his drive deep into the pine woods on the right, but his ball somehow ended in a decent lie with a clear opening to the uphill green. He hooked a running five iron around the trees that kicked up the hill and onto the front of the green. Narrowly missing a fifteen-foot birdie for the outright win, Byron tapped in for par and forced a play-off, in those days a full eighteen holes to be played the next day.

The pressure appeared to rest entirely on Ben Hogan, but it was Byron whose nerves betrayed the most obvious wear and tear. He spent a ghastly, sleepless night, violently sick to his stomach, and promptly threw up his breakfast the next morning. When they arrived at the clubhouse for their afternoon showdown, Hogan got word that Byron had been ill and in a characteristic display of sportsmanship offered to delay their play-off until the following day.

"No," said Byron. "We'll play."

Clearly not himself, Byron hit his first drive into the woods and double bogeyed the opening hole. Hogan started out steady and controlled, apparently ready to break the hold Nelson had forever held over him, opening a three-shot lead through four holes. But Byron began to find his legs and fought his way back, eagling the par five eighth to square the game. The momentum quickly shifted to Byron, and after he nearly aced the terrifying par three twelfth over Rae's Creek, Nelson opened up a three-stroke lead.

Byron's lead stood at two when they reached the final tee. Both men hit solid drives, but the pressure showed when Hogan misjudged or over-clubbed his second, sailing it over the flag set on the lower tier, to the very back of the green. Playing safe, Byron laid up short of the green and the treacherous front bunker, content to pitch up for his third near the pin. Hogan's long putt from the back edge failed to fall, and he settled for par. With a stroke in hand, Byron missed his par putt and won their play-off by one slender stroke with a bogey five.

Bob Jones and Clifford Roberts were so delighted with the tremendous duel the two men had conducted that they threw in a $200 bonus check for each of them on top of their winnings. They shook hands and smiled for the cameras at the trophy ceremony, although most reporters noticed they both looked stiff and uncomfortable, the tension between them unresolved. The gap between the old rivals' skills had closed to a hairsbreadth, but Ben Hogan had missed his best chance yet for a major. And he had still never beaten Byron Nelson man to man.

Two months later, at Ridgemoor Country Club outside Chicago, Ben Hogan would win the Hale America Open, the event that served as the stand-in for that year's canceled U.S. Open. They even handed him a gilded medal identical to the one the USGA had been giving to its Open champions for over forty years, but the world at large never accounted this victory as a major. Hogan privately thought of it as such, although his vote didn't count. Byron lost in the finals of the PGA Championship, the season's final event, to Sam Snead, the Slammer's first major victory, and another blow to Hogan's pride.

If Hogan and Byron had recently grown estranged, Hogan had never cared for Sam Snead, from the moment he showed up on tour in 1937, and made little secret of it. Dignity and understated pride were qualities that had seldom been associated with the lower caste legacy of the golf professional, and both were of paramount importance to Hogan. He saw Snead's hillbilly persona as a clownish PR conceit that pandered to the press and the public and undermined the pro golfer's aspirations for acceptance at the wider social level that stars in established sports like baseball already enjoyed. For both personal and professional reasons, Hogan had modeled his public persona after Bob Jones, the gentleman lawyer, consciously trying to transform the professional's hangdog, working-class image into something closer to the classic amateur ideal. Hogan's campaign for personal and professional legitimacy continued when he won the 1942 money title for the third straight year, playing an abbreviated schedule in deference to the war effort.

Ben Hogan reported for duty in March of 1943 as a rank-and-file private in the U.S. Army Air Corps. But when Byron Nelson underwent his physical for the draft board when his number was called, they discovered he suffered from a previously undetected and mild form of hemophilia, called "free bleeding." That earned him a 4F physical exemption, so while Hogan underwent training as a pilot, the reluctant civilian Nelson volunteered to play exhibitions for the USO and the war bond campaign, over a hundred of them in less than a year, without pay, his equipment company picking up expenses. Bing Crosby and Bob Hope participated in dozens of the same events, and Byron's friendship with both men deepened. Rising quickly to the rank of lieutenant, Hogan faced down his fear of flying, piloted a number of logistical missions, and was occasionally given leave from his base near Fort Worth to play in Red Cross benefits, as was Sam Snead, stationed at the navy base in San Diego. With the PGA Tour all but canceled, Byron played in only four events in 1943, and placed in the money just once, working the rest of the season, when he wasn't on the road playing exhibitions, in his pro shop at Inverness.

As hostilities overseas drummed on, and citizens began to express a need for relief from its unrelenting tragedies, many institutions that had curtailed their prewar escapist entertainments out of deference to the war effort felt free to normalize their products once again, and so the PGA Tour resumed in abbreviated form in 1944, with twenty-three official events. Byron played in twenty-one of those tournaments and won ten of them. He shot only three rounds over par all season and dominated the money list with nearly $38,000, twice what any player had ever won in a single year on tour before. Ben Hogan impatiently sat out the entire season in Fort Worth, mustered out of active service but held in limbo by red tape while waiting for his official discharge. Sam Snead beat Hogan in the race to get back out of uniform, in time to defend his title at the '44 PGA Championship, the year's only major; Snead was never a factor, and Byron finished as the runner-up to an unknown winner, Bob Hamilton.

When the season concluded, the Associated Press named Byron Nelson their Athlete of the Year, the first time that honor had been accorded any golfer since Bob Jones's grand slam. Byron at last possessed the confidence and growing financial freedom to sever his ties with Inverness and venture back out on tour as a free agent, a liberating moment for a man who always aimed to please and whose primary job as a club pro had forever been about serving others. Now he could concentrate all his efforts on playing for his own future. When they added up the numbers in his Little Black Book, Byron and Louise realized that a few more seasons like the one he'd just turned in and their dream of buying a ranch, for cash, would be within their reach. With that prize dangling in front of him, both his physical game and his mental approach to it peaking simultaneously, Byron went out and rewrote the history books.

The 1945 PGA Tour season began in Los Angeles with a win for Sam Snead, a stroke ahead of Nelson. Byron won the following week in Phoenix, and after two straight runner-up finishes, he won twice in a row, at Corpus Christi and New Orleans. Sam Snead fired right back at him with three straight victories, with Byron placing second in two of them, one an eighteen-hole play-off at Gulfport, Mississippi. He dropped to sixth in the third of Snead's wins, at Jacksonville, and Byron felt so furious at himself for that sorry performance he cranked up his game to dominate a four-ball match play tournament with his partner Jug McSpaden in Miami the following week. The week after that he narrowly edged Snead in a two-day, double eighteen-hole play-off to win in Charlotte.

Of the season's first eleven events, nine had been won by either Snead or Nelson, with a razor's edge to Byron, five to four.

Then, the deluge: Byron Nelson won the next nine tournaments in a row to extend his streak to eleven straight PGA Tour victories.

During the streak, he was, first and foremost, remarkably consistent, recording over forty rounds under par. He was more than often brilliant and on most days downright untouchable. His swing appeared as powerful and repeatable as a piston on a V-8 engine. He was on occasion the beneficiary of what might in other circumstances be considered luck, but not during this stretch; Byron's utter domination of his sport in 1945 was the magnificent summing up of a lifetime's hard work. Recalling the glory days of Jones, he put golf back on the front pages of every newspaper in the country. He managed all this while in almost constant pain from a problematic back painful enough to send him to the Mayo Clinic, and under steadily mounting pressure from the press and public with every passing week: Greensboro, Durham, Atlanta, Montreal, Philadelphia, Chicago, his fifth major in the match play PGA Championship at Moraine Country Club in Ohio, the Tam O' Shanter tournament in Chicago again—where Ben Hogan made his first return to action on a weekend pass, finishing a distant second, eleven strokes back—and then finally the Canadian Open outside Toronto.

Only one man in their sport, Johnny Farrell, had ever won as many as four professional tournaments on tour in a row before. After five, they put Byron on the Wheaties box, for $500 and all the cereal he could eat. No man had ever won more than eight tour events in a single *year,* the record Byron had set in 1944, until he blew the doors off that number before the end of June. By the time he reached eleven in a row, the press stopped tossing superlatives around and simply called him "Mr. Golf." Most of his wins came on courses he'd never played before. His approach was simplicity itself: step up to the tee, hit the fairway, hit the green, and make the putt. The press said it was almost monotonous to watch him. Byron responded: "It may be monotonous, but I sure eat regular."

During the streak, the angle that Byron was saving up money to leave the PGA Tour one day and buy a ranch found its way into the papers; neither Byron nor Louise made any secret of it. When he got on his roll, every time a ball dropped Byron just said to himself: "There goes another cow." Throughout, he withstood all the tension and scrutiny and growing hysteria around him with grace, gentle good humor, and homegrown humility that would be unrecognizable in the modern world.

The week after the Canadian Open, Byron extended his winning streak to twelve, but because it was a non-tour event in Spring Hill, New Jersey, it's not included as part of his record. He finally fell back from this impossible standard the following week when he tied for fourth place at a tour event in Memphis. Nearly exhausted, he afterward admitted feeling nothing but relief that the streak was over. Then, admitting later he was angry that he'd finally lost, he went right back out the following week and won again in Knoxville, beating Ben Hogan, now officially a civilian again, by ten strokes. The week after that, in Nashville, Hogan turned the tables and won a professional tournament for the first time since he'd left for the army in 1942, besting Byron by four shots. Now their battle for supremacy on the PGA Tour, postponed for three years by real-life events, was finally joined again, with Sam Snead making it a three-cornered fight.

Snead took the next two tournaments, in Dallas and then Southern Hills in Tulsa. When the tour shifted to the Northwest, Byron won again in Spokane. Earlier in the season, at Atlanta, Byron had broken the seventy-two-hole scoring record for a PGA tournament with a 263. The week after Spokane, in Portland, Hogan won again and bettered Byron's scoring record another two strokes to 261, beating Nelson in the process by fourteen strokes. Immediately afterward, according to Jimmy Demaret, when Byron went to congratulate him, Hogan let his true feelings slip: "I guess that takes care of this 'Mr. Golf' business." Their fierce rivalry, more than ever before, had taken on an openly personal tone. With one chance in the regular tour season left to answer Ben's challenge, Byron fired back with a resounding victory the next week in Seattle, breaking Hogan's two-week-old PGA tournament scoring record with a 259.

Like fighters needing a rest between rounds, they went their separate ways for a while. Hogan and Snead followed what was left of the tour season back east, while Byron headed home to Fort Worth. But the two old caddie mates would face each other one last time that season. Byron and Ben's childhood stomping ground, Glen Garden Country Club, held its inaugural Invitational Tournament the week before Christmas in 1945, and so they went out to fittingly conclude the year on the course where they'd played their first face-off eighteen years earlier.

The stage was set, but the weather refused to cooperate, barely rising above freezing, and showering the course with snow flurries. Their hotly anticipated showdown never materialized, when Byron ran away from the field, broke his own Glen Garden scoring record in the third round, and beat Jimmy Demaret to win by eight strokes. Hogan finished a disinterested and disappointing sixth. The elegant and gainfully retired Walter Hagen, a gentleman of leisure at last at fifty-two, had been persuaded to attend, but not compete, for a hefty appearance fee, and he presented Byron with the final winner's check of his extraordinary year. During the ceremony, Lord Byron recalled his first encounter with Sir Walter as a young boy in the eighteenth fairway at the 1927 PGA Championship in Dallas. Hagen, graciously, and perhaps fictitiously, claimed that he remembered it well.

When the dust settled, Byron had won eighteen out of the thirty tournaments he entered in 1945. His streak of eleven tour wins in a row is one of the only records in any sport that one can to this day comfortably assert will never be broken. He established a new low scoring record for the season of 68.3, a standard that would hold up for nearly sixty years. He obliterated his own year-old money record by winning over $60,000, although since he patriotically accepted most of his prizes in war bonds that necessity forced him to cash before they reached maturity, the actual figure was closer to $47,000. (In today's money worth over half a million, still only a fraction of the amounts being won today.) At season's end, for the second time in a row, a feat not even Bob Jones had ever managed, the Associated Press named Byron Nelson their Athlete of the Year.

There would later from some quarters come gripes that, with many of the tour's best players still in uniform, Byron had accomplished all this against less than a full field of competitors, but Sam Snead had been there every step of the way, the most winning golfer of all time, notching six victories of his own, and Hogan returned for nearly half the season, winning five events. That argument also doesn't account for the fact that, excepting the rare match play tournament, golf isn't a game played by any one golfer against another, but by each individual contestant against the golf course and what Bob Jones used to call Old Man Par. In that regard, no one, not even Jones during the grand slam, had ever come close to equaling the sustained brilliance of Byron Nelson in 1945.

His bountiful season allowed Byron and Louise that winter to accelerate the financial timetable for buying their ranch, and they began actively looking for the right piece of land around Fort Worth. When the 1946 tour season started a few weeks later, Byron picked up right where he'd left off with two straight victories, his first ever at the Los Angeles Open at Riviera, a coveted title that had forever eluded him, and then at Olympic in San Francisco, where he beat Ben Hogan by nine and made his first, fleeting acquaintance of a cheeky teenager in his gallery named Kenny Venturi. Spanning back to December, that made another four PGA tournament wins for Byron in a row, a streak that, in the light of what he'd done the year before, went hardly remarked upon.

And with those two winners' checks in the bank, and his first instructional golf book hitting the national best-seller lists, suddenly the numbers in Byron's Little Black Book hit critical mass. He abruptly withdrew from the following week's tournament and returned home to Fort Worth. During a three-week break from the tour, Byron told Louise and his primary off-course sponsor, MacGregor, that he had determined that 1946 was going to be his last year on the professional circuit. He'd had more than his fill of living on the road, and the competitive strain generated by his record-breaking year had started to adversely affect his health. He could feel that his nerves were nearly fried by the constant pressure; he was often sick to his stomach now before going out to play in a tournament, the same grinding anxiety and tension that had driven Bob Jones from the game sixteen years earlier. If he didn't step away soon, the opportunity to leave the game on his own terms might be lost forever. Almost immediately afterward, the Nelsons made an all-cash bid of $55,000 on the ranch they wanted to buy, a gently rolling 650-acre spread in a tiny town called Roanoke, twenty miles north of Fort Worth.

A competing bid had already been placed on the property, so while waiting to hear if their purchase would go through, Byron returned to the tour and that week's tournament in New Orleans.

Trailing Hogan at the start of the final round, eager to bag another first place check to pad the Nelsons' account, Byron birdied the first six holes in a row and ended up roaring past Ben to win by five strokes. The following day the Nelsons learned their offer on the ranch in Roanoke had been accepted; they were in escrow. The rest of Byron's last competitive year would split his attention between closing the deal, getting the ranch ready to live on, and winning enough on tour to underwrite the effort. He would win six times that season, losing a play-off in the first postwar U.S. Open at Canterbury, Ohio, to tough returning veteran Lloyd Mangrum, who'd been wounded at the Battle of the Bulge. Byron would play in only one more U.S. Open, and not until 1955.

Ben Hogan just missed joining their play-off when he three-putted the final green, exactly as he had done a month earlier to lose the 1946 Masters to a journeyman pro, and former undertaker, from Missouri named Herman Keiser. After fumbling away two straight chances to win the major he so desperately wanted, the dreadful word "choker" began to attend Hogan. After these grave disappointments he abandoned the tour for a few weeks, heading back to the drawing board in Fort Worth to institute yet another swing change, trying to banish once and for all his troublesome hook.

In Byron's final major that August he reached the quarterfinals of the match play PGA Championship in Portland, Oregon. Right after he lost that match to Porky Oliver, knowing it was his last as a full-time tour player, Byron began driving back to Texas, and later recalled it as the happiest day of his life. With Byron out of the running and his newly fine-tuned swing under complete control, Ben Hogan finally broke through and won that tournament over Oliver for his first major championship. Trophy in hand, he was ready at last to challenge Byron Nelson's claim as the game's greatest player. But a few weeks later, before an exhibition he'd committed to in Chicago, Byron announced his official retirement from the tour, calling it quits at the pinnacle of his success, creating nearly as many shock waves as Bob Jones had with the same news sixteen years earlier. After he and Louise moved out to their ranch that fall, Byron played his last official PGA event in December back where it all started, at Glen Garden Country Club, as defending champion of the Fort Worth Open. He finished seventh and dutifully wrote down $550 in the final entry of his Little Black Book.

Byron packed up the tools of his erstwhile trade, shipped them back to MacGregor in Chicago, with instructions not to return his clubs unless and until he specifically asked. Then he broke out a more traditional set of tools and went to work repairing the ramshackle fences that bordered the Nelsons' new spread. Byron Nelson had made the cut in the last 113 golf tournaments in which he played, another record that would stand for over half a century, and then walked away from the pro game, cold turkey. For all his recent success, after paying cash for their ranch, the Nelsons had only $2500 left in the bank, just enough, they figured, to get their first animals to market in the spring.

Ben Hogan won thirteen tournaments in 1946 and also took the scoring title. Fresh corporate money was flooding into the coffers of the PGA Tour, in no small part because of what Byron had accomplished in 1945, raising every purse to previously unimagined levels, and Hogan was once again the tour's leading money winner with over $42,000. Ben's future, especially now that his perpetual adversary had left the stage, looked like nothing but blue skies. But he had never beaten Byron straight up, and he never would. Both men were thirty-four years old. They would never challenge each other in an important competition again.

Back to the Sea

The four men stood on the elevated fourteenth tee box, staring out at the fairway and the blue Pacific to their right. A swarming crowd now surrounded them and lined a large portion of the fairway ahead. Watching through field glasses from near the clubhouse above and to the left across the road, caddie master Joey Solis estimated there may have been somewhere between five and ten thousand people on the grounds at Cypress Point by now. None of the players later recalled their gallery being that large, but they were now so fiercely intent on their match, and all were so used to playing in front of big crowds, it's a wonder they even noticed anyone was there at all.

Hogan and Nelson had hardly spoken a word to each other all day, and their silence highlighted a curious paradox: each was closer to both of their younger competitors than they were to each other and clearly would have preferred their company in any other situation, social or professional. But that hadn't for one second stood in the way of the two old pros playing their guts out as a team representing their side of the game. Byron had come out on fire at the start of the round, four under through the first six holes, and as soon as his brilliance flickered, Ben stepped up and took over; eight under in the last ten.

Like each other or not, they were still men from the same town, the same state, the same generation, and they'd both endured the deprivations of poverty and the hardships of an impossible profession, often together, to achieve greatness and lasting fame. Circumstance had pitted them against each other, reluctant gladiators, and because they were the two best players of their time, the individually combative nature of their sport had finally driven them apart. Though they were utterly opposing personalities off the course, their characters as champions between the ropes were indistinguishable; each had been too strong, too good, too unyielding to ever give ground to the other. Although their wives remained close friends, they hadn't played together as a twosome in a best-ball match, as near as either could remember, for nearly twenty years.

And yet on this day, with nothing more than their professional pride on the line against two great amateurs, that was more than enough to bring out the lionhearted best in them. They had once stood together in the front rank of men who, having run out of ways to put food on their tables, driven by nothing less than poverty and despair, had single-handedly turned the shabby, tumbledown professional game into a mainstream attraction and a way to craft an honest living. As they tested their hard-earned skills in the tour's primitive, ill-attended arenas, pushing each other to the limit, they had captivated the public's imagination and transformed their sport from a half-forgotten relic of another age into a powerhouse of postwar American culture. Both did great things and both had become great men, but their long friendship bore the burden and finally paid the price. Now, in the last hours of Hogan's playing career, and ten years after Byron had left the stage, facing the best young talents from the next generation, they could still inspire each other to turn back the clock and make one last stand against the dying of the light.

Only a few hundred, at most perhaps a few thousand, lucky souls were now on the grounds that day to witness it.

Ken and Harvie were conscious of being in that number, and in years to come would count themselves fortunate for it, but they also had no less a surplus of pride, and a lot more to prove. These two ambitious young talents hadn't lost a best-ball match to any other team anywhere in the world during the four years they'd been playing together, and they had played hundreds of them, in every imaginable circumstance. Harvie later calculated that he hadn't posted a single round higher than 68 in any of their matches during that entire stretch. Just as Ben had done for Byron that day, Harvie had come on strong after Ken's blistering start. That's the way great partnerships played this unique variation of the sport, a tag team, one drafting off the other as he hit a streak, stepping up to shoulder the load again whenever the other faltered.

Ward and Venturi were also both committed career amateurs, in the lineage of Ouimet and Jones, gentlemen who for two generations had dominated the sport, and still regulated it, a tradition now threatened by the emergence of the professional tour, where Byron and Ben had led the charge and made their fortunes. So what if Ben Hogan and Byron Nelson represented a living history of the game; the rules of life, and sport in particular, dictate with ruthless inevitability that youth must be served. The game wasn't played in a museum, and someone had to come along and tear down those marble statues eventually. As far as Venturi and Ward were concerned, it might as well be them, and it might as well happen today. If the amateur side of the game was ever to regain its supremacy, or even hold its own again as the pros continued to gain ground, it had to start here and now.

At 388 yards, the fourteenth asks for a long and accurate tee shot, up a softly sloping hill, and then the fairway turns sharply right to a small green perched on a plateau set even higher. Ghostly stands of cypress trees close in and pinch the fairway a hundred yards out from the green, making paramount the placement of the tee shot, punishing any drive that doesn't hew to the right line.

For the first time all day, as if they'd all sensed the magnitude of what they were in the middle of, all four men played cautiously for the middle of the fairway. The hole had been cut at the back right corner, and the ground falls away precipitously just behind the green, sloping down toward the ocean. All four played equally guarded second shots to the middle of the green, with Byron finishing just off the front; no one challenged the treacherous back flag, where the slightest misjudgment could lead to disaster. Nelson's chip finished well short, and after Hogan lagged close for their par, Byron picked up, taking a bogey five. Venturi and Ward both missed their birdie attempts and took fours to halve the hole. So they'd had their breather now. It would be their last.

Pros still one up over the amateurs, with four holes to play, and Cypress Point's dramatic third act was about to begin.

The walk down to the fifteenth tee descends the hill behind the fourteenth green, crosses the Seventeen Mile Drive again, and all of a sudden brings you face-to-face with the rugged coastline. The sight of it so close after seeing it as a distant backdrop for much of the day comes as a vivid shock: sculpted rocks, foamed inlets, tide pools and roiling sea, underscored by the roar of crashing waves just below the crushed shell path. The briny sharp smells kick up, a pungent surprise; a fine spray aerosols your skin; the afternoon light dazzles off the water; every sense feels suddenly assailed, heightened and alive. The path skirts above a tidy sheltered crescent of beach, and as they passed it, Harvie exchanged a knowing smile with Ken, nodding down toward the beach with a raised eyebrow; Ken had heard the stories and knew Harvie had made more than one amorous afterdark conquest in that sandy hideaway, perhaps, given his reaction, as recently as last night. Harvie, the naughty boy scout, couldn't help but confess.

The laugh helped buffer Ken's tension as they turned left around the corner onto the lower fifteenth tee, and the soul-refreshing view that opened up reduced them all to a private state of wonder. The fifteenth hole is a jewel box, a 113-yard par three, slightly downhill across a narrow, deep, diagonal cove to a green nestled atop the rocks, an island of grass surrounded by ancient cypress stands and six of MacKenzie's rough-edged natural bunkers. A second tee box sits on the hill above the first, and that was where the gallery formed in around them. The fifteenth's overwhelming beauty can stagger the hardest of hearts, but there are no tricks, no camouflage, no other defenses except the wind off the sea, which can render it nearly un-playable on any given day but on this occasion was nothing more than a mild breeze. A small tongue of green bulges out to the right from the center, toward the edge of the rocks and the water below, between the two largest bunkers, and that was where the flagstick had been set, the most difficult position to shoot for.

Playing first, Hogan went straight for the flag with a controlled nine iron. The sharp grooves on his iron nipped into the ball with a satisfying click. Perfectly judged, it dropped from the sky like an ar-row and stuck less than two feet from the hole. Byron played a simi-lar shot, pulling it ever so slightly, eight feet to the left, well inside birdie range. Both men turned to the amateurs and smiled.

Your turn, boys.

Harvie took the tee. Perhaps the memories stirred by the cove be-low had proved a trifle too stirring; he flushed a wedge right on line to the flag but clear over the green and into the light rough beyond. The pressure shifted squarely onto Ken, knowing they could ab-solutely not afford to go two down with only three holes left to play.

So he hit a wedge that nearly went straight in the hole and landed inside of Ben's ball. A tap-in birdie. Now it was Ken and Harvie's turn to smile. The crowd erupted above them—this was better than any tournament finish in recent memory, with a lot more than money at stake—but the players paid no attention. Their long, winding walk around the cove to the green passed in silence; Harvie glanced down at the beach below there as well, giving no indication that it was the scene of another romantic escapade. But the chances were good.

As they walked out onto the green, Hogan said: "Pick 'em up, fellas."

Halved with Hogan and Venturi's birdies, the pros remained one up with three to play. Even before they began their next walk through a vale of twisted cypress, every pulse in the group quickened. The moment you wait for, in either anticipation or dread, during all of any round at Cypress Point had arrived.

The sixteenth.

Hogan Alone

With Byron's official retirement from the PGA Tour, in 1947 Ben Hogan stepped into the breach. He won the season's first event, the Los Angeles Open at Riviera, followed it with another win at Phoenix, and, with Jimmy Demaret as his partner, soon after took the annual best-ball event in Miami. But Byron returned for the Masters, aside from Bing's Clambake his only appearance on tour that year, out of courtesy to Bob Jones, and he showed that precious little rust had formed on that timeless swing. Byron finished second to Jimmy Demaret, but his lack of compelling internal interest during the final round and its outcome provided final confirmation that he was done with the demands of the regular tour, and he went home happily to tend his ranch.

To his disgust, Ben Hogan finished in a tie for fourth, behind his friend Demaret, a retired Nelson, and even more galling, the upstart peacock amateur Frank Stranahan, making his first national splash. Another disappointment followed at the 1947 U.S. Open, when Hogan faltered down the stretch and ended up in sixth place, while a journeyman club pro named Lew Worsham went on to improbably defeat Sam Snead in a play-off. Hogan's failure to win an Open, soon remedied, would eventually be forgotten in light of Snead's tragic/ comic record in the event; from 1939 on, six times in fifteen years the championship appeared to be firmly in his grasp during the back nine of the final round, and on every occasion some mental slip or incredible ill fortune seized it from his hands. The title of U.S. Open Champion would forever elude, and haunt, him.

Ben won seven tournaments during the '47 season, but his campaign in the year's majors ended unhappily a few weeks later, when he was eliminated from the PGA Championship in the first round. The golf year culminated with the revival of the Ryder Cup, the first time the event had been held since 1937. Hogan captained the American team, which included by special invitation the retired Byron Nelson, and they routed the British, 11 to 1.

The 1948 season began in identical fashion, with another win for Hogan in the Los Angeles Open at Riviera, where the U.S. Open would also be held for the first time later that year. After another mediocre showing at the Masters, by his standards, Hogan won his second major at the match play PGA Championship and arrived for the U.S. Open at Riviera—which after his second straight win in the Los Angeles Open earlier that year a reporter had memorably nicknamed "Hogan's Alley"—as the prohibitive favorite. Now thirty-five years old, the most established and feared star on the pro tour, Hogan played a relaxed final practice round with his pals Jimmy Demaret and Bing Crosby. Three days later, Hogan and Demaret began the fourth and final competitive round as the two front runners, with Ben holding a two-stroke lead. Playing a few holes ahead of Hogan, Demaret carded a sterling 69 to break Ralph Guldahl's decade-old Open scoring record. Demaret's possession of that record lasted exactly half an hour, when Hogan roared home to match his 69, lop two more shots off the championship's scoring record, and cruise to his first win in the U.S. Open.

Twenty-one years removed from his first play-off with Byron Nelson at Glen Garden, Ben Hogan had at long last achieved the summit.

He roared on from Riviera to take five more tournaments in a row after the Open, including the Western, still considered a major. Endorsements in excess of six figures flowed in his direction, solidifying the Hogans' finances and allowing them to buy their first real home in Fort Worth. He could afford to dress like landed gentry now, and he took meticulous pride in it, the Irish urchin who'd made good in bespoke tailored English tweeds and silks. Equally as gratifying, both press and public now crowned him the king of his sport, granting him sole occupancy of Byron's vacated throne. His first golf instructional book soared up the national best-seller lists, surpassing Byron's sales, another confirmation of his newly risen status. Dignity, respect, ten wins, three majors, and both the scoring and money title for 1948 were all his.

A few national columnists still grumbled that Hogan's bluntness, cold and mechanical demeanor on the course, and relative lack of social grace in interviews left a great deal to be desired when compared to their memories of the gentlemanly Nelson and the aristocratic Jones. One dismissed him as the "Frigid Midget," and many others were even more unkind. His closest friends were constantly being quoted on the defensive, affirming Ben's personal warmth, loyalty, and good humor, but few reporters or people had or ever would gain access to the small circle he allowed to share those qualities. For the public at large he remained a forbidding figure, a man on a distant mountaintop, admired but hardly loved.

His friends in Texas organized a hometown hero's dinner for the Hogans at Colonial Country Club late in the year, honoring his achievements. Ben appeared in high spirits, fulfilled and relaxed in their company that evening, a man who had stared down the worst life could throw at him and come through it to fulfill his dreams. Everyone loves a happy ending, and Ben Hogan's story, everyone could agree, offered one of the most remarkable in memory. So many doors were being opened to him now, through his relationships with serious millionaires like George Coleman and Marvin Leonard, that there were rumors down the wind he might soon follow Byron into re-tirement. He admitted that the travel on tour was wearing him down, just as it had Nelson, and it was clear the broader social legitimacy he craved lay within his grasp now if he never hit another five iron. Un-like Byron, he had no interest in a retreat to the simple rural life he'd worked so long and hard to outrun; Hogan was an urban creature and had his eye on the hard-nosed competitive world of corporate America, his keen mind hungering for more grown-up and satisfying challenges.

But he wasn't ready to abandon his first arena just yet. He mo-tored out with Valerie to the West Coast in their new Cadillac for the start of the 1949 season. After an uncharacteristically indifferent eleventh place finish at the LA Open, they rambled up the coast to Monterey for the Crosby Clambake, staying as houseguests of the Colemans near Pebble Beach. Determined to make a good showing, during his Tuesday practice round with George at Cypress Point Hogan fired a flawless 63 and established a new course record. By-ron Nelson was with his now regular playing partner, Eddie Lowery, on the grounds at Cypress that afternoon as well—one of only a few tournaments, at Eddie's insistence, for which Byron was willing to leave the ranch. The two champions from Texas barely spoke when they met briefly in the Cypress clubhouse after their rounds; Byron offered his congratulations for Ben's victory in last year's Open. The Nelsons hadn't been invited to Hogan's celebration the previous fall at Colonial, and Byron hadn't seen him since. Ben said thank you. Both moved on.

After two rounds of the Crosby, Hogan trailed the game's top am-ateur Frank Stranahan by a shot, but Ben threw down a 70 at Pebble Beach on the final day to capture his first Clambake by two strokes and accept Bing's winner's check for $2000.

Hogan won the following week's PGA tournament back in South-ern California as well, beating his pal Jimmy Demaret in a play-off, and they exchanged places in another play-off at the Phoenix Open the weekend after that. As they relaxed over cocktails afterward, when Hogan announced he would skip the next tour event in Tucson in order to drive home to Fort Worth for the long-awaited move into the Hogans' new home, Jimmy teased Ben that he finally had him on the run: "I beat you in one play-off and you duck the rubber match."

Two days later, Wednesday, February 2, at eight thirty in the morning, as the Hogans picked their way east from El Paso on a fog-bound two-lane highway, a Greyhound bus trying to pass a freight truck on a small bridge crashed head-on into the Hogans' Cadillac at over fifty miles an hour. A split second before impact, Hogan threw himself across the front seat to protect Valerie, and in trying to save her life saved his own. The steering column rocketed backward through the driver's seat he'd just vacated and would have killed him instantly.

Horrific confusion plagued the aftermath of the accident. The passengers of the bus, disembarking and milling about, quickly realized whom they'd hit, and a few did what they could to help, while most of the others rubbernecked. Initially denying he was hurt, Hogan descended into shock, while Valerie, who had survived with hardly a scratch, tried to comfort him in mounting panic. Ben's clubs had been scattered across the highway, and he fretted about having someone gather them up as he slipped in and out of consciousness. It took an hour and a half for an ambulance to reach their remote location, and four hours to transport him to an El Paso hospital, where he arrived in critical condition. His pelvis was fractured in two places, left collarbone shattered, left ankle and two ribs broken, but his strong athlete's body rallied to survive the initial shock and doctors were quietly optimistic he'd survive.

Few news bulletins hit the public with more jolting impact than the death or injury of a celebrated athlete cut down in his prime. After photos made all the newspapers of Hogan in a body cast, lying broken in his hospital bed, an enormous outpouring of support and concern rolled in from across the country. As James Dodson points out in his excellent, exhaustive biography of Hogan, for a man who had always appeared so invulnerable and self-contained, it took a tragedy of this magnitude to bring him the sympathy that transformed him from a stony figure the country had only admired from afar to a flesh-and-blood man they now embraced with all their hearts. Unconscious action had revealed the deepest part of his character, and in that desperate moment, confronted with instant obliteration, his only response had been to protect the woman he loved. This one unselfish act, more than any display of iron-willed prowess on a golf course, transformed the world's perception of Ben. When it appeared Hogan would physically survive, their concern, and his, collected around a second, sobering form of death: the prospect of him ever walking again, let alone playing championship-caliber golf, remained uncertain at best.

Less than two weeks later, Hogan was closer to death than he had been on the morning of the accident; a blood clot from his injured leg had migrated to his lungs, triggering a pulmonary embolism that nearly finished him. When two more clots were identified traveling in the same direction, and the doctors' initial attempts to dissolve them with drugs backfired, Hogan spiraled down toward the brink. Newspapers updated his obituary, on a deathwatch, standing by for immediate release. After consultation with experts from around the country, a specialist was flown in and radical, emergency surgery performed to tie off the vena cava, the thick primary vein returning blood to the heart from the lower body. That prevented the clots from killing him, but this procedure was not reversible; the circulation to his lower body, particularly the severely damaged left leg, would never be the same. Hogan's legs were the engine of his golf swing, and for the moment and foreseeable future they had been reduced to ruin. His long-term prognosis offered little more than a severely curtailed physical existence, etched with constant pain.

Hogan made the expected tough-guy pronouncements to the many friends who flocked to his bedside. "I'll beat this thing," he told

Jimmy Demaret. "I'll be back out there playing real soon." He was painfully gaunt, almost skeletal after his terrible ordeal, and when his friends saw him brought so low in the flesh, reduced to a phantom of his vital self, no one else in his life but Valerie could second that conviction with any certainty.

Ben Hogan left the hospital two months after he'd arrived, in a rolling bed, not even able yet to travel in a wheelchair. Train and then ambulance delivered him at the doorstep of the new home he'd barely set foot in, as an invalid. As the shock of his loss to the game wore off—his logical successor, Sam Snead, won the 1949 Masters in Ben's absence—the debate about whether Hogan could ever return to the game dominated the national discussion. Even if he managed it, most concluded he'd be lucky to ever break 90 again. The doctors had told him it would take at least six months for the swelling in his legs to subside and for them to return to their most rudimentary function. Even social golf, if it would ever again be possible at all, lay years out of reach. What Ben Hogan now willed himself to do in response would become the template for every subsequent Hollywood cliché about a sports hero standing tall against physical adversity and refusing to give up, including the eventual hokum movie version of Hogan's own story.

Within a week Ben forced himself out of bed and began walking laps around his living room carpet, tortured, painful steps taken with the aid of a walker. Within a few days he went into the Hogans' backyard, grass under his feet again. Two weeks later, on Easter Sunday, he made it halfway around the block using only a cane. He soon switched to a golf umbrella, feeling it suggested less infirmity, and gradually extended the distances he covered, but he was often forced to sit on the curb and wait for Valerie to come pick him up in the car after his legs gave out. But he never quit.

By June he was back on the putting green at his home course, nearby Colonial Country Club, and then the driving range a few weeks after that. He mailed in his entry to the U.S. Open, just in case, even though he was months away from walking unaided. His swing looked like a cruel parody of his old peerless form, an upper body lurch wobbling around a feeble, unsturdy base. He took to wrapping both legs from hip to ankle in elastic bandages, a practice that would continue to the end of his playing days, to quicken circulation and encourage any feeling, or illusion, of solidity. By September he was far enough along to serve again as a nonplaying Ryder Cup captain, crossing with the team on the *Queen Mary* to England, where he drove his men hard and served up enough inspiration in his speeches, and just by being there, for an unlikely comeback victory on the final day. After watching Hogan battle bravely against the enormous difficulties that simply getting through an ordinary day now provided, Jimmy Demaret said the American team felt too ashamed to lose.

He played his first full round in December, only ten months after the accident, still swinging gingerly, and riding the course in a motorized buggy. In constant pain, he refused to ever medicate it with anything stronger than a single aspirin. After the round, he went straight to bed, exhausted. It took a week before he had the strength to try to play again, but the results were slightly more encouraging, and less taxing. Hogan let it be known he might try to make it out to the West Coast, putting his name in for the LA Open and also Crosby's Clambake, where he planned to play a practice round or two and, if he felt up to it, enter the early season tournaments. By the time he reached Riviera, a deal was in the works with nearby Twentieth Century-Fox for a movie version of his life. But privately Ben decided he first needed to provide a happier ending.

He shot 69 his first time around Riviera. He broke par again in his three subsequent practice rounds. When the tournament began, fighting fatigue, foul weather, and his sluggish legs every step of the way, followed by the largest galleries Riviera had ever witnessed, Ben finished the tournament tied for first with the longtime rival who in his absence had finally seized the spotlight as the tour's number one player, Sam Snead. Hogan would lose their subsequent eighteen-hole play-off, but in the process he won something more important: the undying affection of sports fans around the world. The dean emeritus of American sportswriters, Grantland Rice, now seventy and in the twilight of his own career, summed up Hogan's memorable performance at Riviera this way: "His legs weren't strong enough to carry his heart around."

From Los Angeles, Ben and Valerie took the train north to Monterey for the Crosby Clambake, where they spent time socially with Bing and Eddie Lowery, who again played with Byron Nelson in the Pro-Am. Hogan finished nine strokes out of the lead behind another emerging young Texas talent named Jack Burke, Jr., but galleries now cheered Ben wherever he went, providing a level of emotional support he'd never experienced before, and that, many came to believe, finally began to dissolve the famous cast iron Hogan reserve. He even started to let down his guard with reporters, a group he'd never been able to trust, and a warmer, more engaging side of Hogan began to emerge in the many interviews he gave.

Feeling he might be ready to compete in the majors again, Hogan spent almost a month in Florida with George Coleman at Seminole Golf Club, the exclusive Donald Ross–designed Palm Beach enclave that he always felt best prepared him for the demands of Augusta National. He would finish fourth in the 1950 Masters behind his pal Jimmy Demaret. A few weeks later Ben won the first PGA Tour event of his comeback at the Greenbrier in West Virginia, Sam Snead's home turf. Snead had already captured six events in the season's early going, and Hogan took evident pleasure in slowing the Slammer's momentum by beating him in his own backyard. Snead returned the favor at Hogan's home course, Colonial Country Club in Fort Worth, a few weeks later, setting up a much anticipated showdown between the two best players in the game at the fiftieth U.S. Open in June at Merion.

One of the cornerstone clubs of golf history, Merion had provided the battleground for many of Bob Jones's heroics during the 1920s, including the final leg of his grand slam in the 1930 U.S. Amateur. For all its tremendous importance to the history of the American game, this was only Merion's second Open, and first in sixteen years, and Ben Hogan would make it one for the ages. Fighting through his injuries, on the verge of quitting the field at least twice when his legs seized up while climbing Merion's sharp ascents, Hogan lost a three-stroke lead in the final round to drop back into a three-way tie for first, setting up an eighteen-hole play-off with George Fazio and a fierce and resolute Lloyd Mangrum. Most observers on hand, Hogan included, didn't think he could find the strength to even show up for the play-off, let alone win it. Summoning the will to overcome his physical shortcomings with a mental discipline no other man in the game had ever displayed, Hogan did both, capturing his second U.S. Open title by three shots.

When it came time to hand out the Player of the Year award at the end of 1950, Ben Hogan's emotional Open championship trumped Sam Snead's eight wins, and both the money and scoring title. Populist, man-of-the-people Slammin' Sammy had enjoyed the greatest season of his career, and some part of him would never get over this slight. The idea seemed unimaginable to more than him alone; unsmiling Ben Hogan, the self-contained, graceless, mechanical man, had become their sport's, and the nation's, sentimental favorite.

Ben's injuries would continue to plague him, and his recovery was never complete, severely curtailing the number of tournaments he could enter, but Hogan's personal life, and golf game, now entered the longest sustained period of excellence and satisfaction he would ever know. He finally won his first Masters in 1951, edging out Snead again, and then his third U.S. Open later that same summer, at Oakland Hills outside Detroit, Walter Hagen's original stomping ground. He recorded a final-round 67 on one of the hardest courses in the world to overcome a five-stroke deficit, and even Hogan admitted afterward it was the finest round of golf he ever played. His peers named him the game's Player of the Year for the third time in four years.

Hogan turned forty in 1952, a time when the games of even most golfers who haven't suffered catastrophic injuries begin to naturally weaken. He played in only three tournaments that year, and won only the Colonial, close to home. One of the more devastating effects of the crash now turned out to be damage to the optic nerve of his left eye, which began to affect his ability to focus on the ball while standing over it to putt, and slowly turned that part of the game into a torment for him. More than a few fans and reporters began to wonder what Ben Hogan had left to prove on a golf course.

The big wide world was calling now: business opportunities, investments in oil wells and hotels, countless commercial endorsements and endless demands on his time and energies. In other words, all the opportunities and privileges of fame and wealth he'd dreamed of beyond his playing days had now been delivered into his hands. The movie of his life, *Follow the Sun,* opened that year, and starring an unpersuasive Glenn Ford, it turned out to be a sentimental and utterly conventional Hollywood biopic that nonetheless touched many hearts and carried Hogan's notoriety to another level. He was on a first-name basis with presidents now: General Dwight Eisenhower, the passionate golfer he'd come to know well at Augusta National, had won the White House that fall. In conversation with Marvin Leonard, George Coleman, and Eddie Lowery, the idea of Ben forming his own equipment company began to germinate, took root, and would soon become the centerpiece of his off-course activities. Hogan now had at least one eye on the door, but also felt he had one last run at greatness in him, and 1953 turned out to be his year.

Hogan began his campaign with his second Masters victory. Fulfilling a ceremonial role, one that he'd grown to enjoy as a replacement for the ailing Bob Jones, Byron Nelson now played the final round of each Masters paired with the third-round leader, and he watched from the best seat on the grounds as Ben broke the tournament's scoring record, holding back a charge from the next generation of players, which now included that year's low amateur and his new friend, Harvie Ward. The following month, in the U.S. Open at Oakmont outside Pittsburgh, another of the country's first and foremost tests of golf, when a snakebit Sam Snead faltered once again down the stretch, Hogan won his country's national championship for the fourth time in the last six years, tying Bob Jones's longstanding record.

One last mountain remained to climb. Hogan had never played in his sport's oldest tournament, the British Open. Travel there from the States still added up to an ordeal that cost more than the prize money for first place, and tradition alone usually wasn't enough reason to lure the top American pros overseas for the amount of time, cash, and energy required. British links courses and the low bump-and-run style of play they demanded also remained extremely foreign and strange to American players at that time. Men who appreciated the subtleties of the game, like Harvie Ward, who'd won the British Amateur the year before, cherished the whole experience, but he was a notable exception. (After winning the Open at St. Andrews during his only trip overseas in 1946, Sam Snead infamously said afterward that he didn't understand what all the fuss was about.) During Hogan's last great summer, a number of the game's best players, Walter Hagen, Gene Sarazen, Bob Jones, and Harvie Ward among them, all reached out and pressed Hogan to make the trip and play in the Open at least once in his life. That year, he finally took them up on it.

Carnoustie has long been the toughest golf course in the British Open rota, a rough, long, muscular patch of working class ground north of St. Andrews and the Firth of Tay in Scotland. This is all Hogan did once he got there: after a handful of practice rounds to acclimate himself to the completely unfamiliar rigors of links play, and suffering from a flu that bordered on pneumonia, he stood up to a final-round charge from Frank "Muscles" Stranahan and on that day broke both the one- and the four-round scoring record at Carnoustie and set a new Open scoring record, on his way to winning the game's oldest championship.

The British public embraced Ben Hogan throughout with a passion and reverence that stunned him and won his heart in return. He'd been all over the map, but never traveled quite so far from Dublin, Texas; with the Claret Jug in hand, he and Valerie were invited to an audience at Buckingham Palace with the empire's newly crowned monarch, young Queen Elizabeth the Second. This was the first time any man had won both the British and American Opens in the same year since Bob Jones sailed back across the pond with the first half of his grand slam in 1930. When Ben and Valerie returned to New York, the city and country greeted him with one of the last ticker tape parades down the canyons of Broadway, another honor that hadn't been accorded a golfer since Jones's triumphant return from England twenty-three years earlier.

Hogan had tears in his eyes when he addressed a national radio audience that day, and again when they paid tribute to him at a dinner thrown for him that night by the USGA, attended by everyone who'd ever mattered in the history of American golf, from Francis Ouimet and Eddie Lowery, to Bob Jones and Walter Hagen, to young greats in waiting like Harvie Ward. In his concluding speech, Bob Jones pointed out that if that year's PGA Championship hadn't been scheduled the same week as the British Open—an oversight that would soon be remedied for just this reason—Ben Hogan would undoubtedly have made an unstoppable run at winning all four of the modern major professional championships in the same calendar year: the modern professional's version of the grand slam, an achievement that is still waiting to meet its match.

Here at last, the world at his feet, Ben Hogan stood on the mountaintop, now a beloved and no longer distant figure; nine major championships in six years, with three taken in the last season alone.

Return to Ben Hogan five prime years lost to a world war and crippling injury, and that number might well have been posted at a level left completely out of reach. A man self-made from a handful of dirt, stalwart in the face of unimaginable physical tragedy and private emotional torment, he had now surpassed them all, towering over the fading memories of the first great American professionals Hagen and Sarazen and every player of his own generation, including even his greatest contemporary, Byron Nelson. From this point forward, only Bob Jones could ever even be talked about in the same breath.

Ben Hogan would never again play a full season on tour or win another major. He came agonizingly close again at the 1954 Masters, losing a play-off by a single stroke to Sam Snead, and at the U.S. Open at the Olympic Club near San Francisco in 1955, falling in another play-off—in what some considered the greatest upset since Ouimet and Vardon—to an unknown, wide-eyed, thirty-three-year-old public course professional from Iowa named Jack Fleck. Harvie Ward, who lived just across the street, held the halfway lead in that Open, finished as the low amateur, and stayed around to watch those amazing events unfold. Sergeant Ken Venturi, stationed in Austria, had to read about the results a few days after the fact in *Stars & Stripes*.

Hogan's full game showed no decline in either of those tournaments or for years to come, but the damage done to his eye in the accident continued to worsen, and it wormed away at his confidence on the greens, and so his scoring slowly, inevitably deteriorated. The Ben Hogan Company opened its doors in 1954, with key investments coming from all those businessmen he'd befriended over the years, Marvin Leonard, George Coleman, and Eddie Lowery chief among them. He would prove to be an expert, hands-on chief executive, involved in every aspect of his business from design to manufacturing to marketing, applying the same diligent and relentless intelligence and energy with which he'd attacked the game.

There was little question now that he had started down the other side of the mountain. Although saying he still intended to play in the Masters and the U.S. Open, Hogan had more or less announced his retirement from the PGA Tour after losing the 1955 Open, and he didn't appear at another tour event again until the Los Angeles Open in January of 1956, where he played in a one-day celebrity match, a farewell of sorts to Riviera, the course where his career had reached its memorable first-act climax at the U.S. Open eight years earlier. The following week, as a favor to his old friend Bing Crosby, Hogan traveled north to play in one last Clambake as Bing's partner, his last go-round at the world's most popular pro-am.

And then, on Tuesday evening, January 10, 1956, George Coleman called after dinner to invite him out for a casual practice-round match with Byron against the two kids at Cypress Point.

The Finish

Two hundred and twenty-two impossible yards across turbulent open water, the green rests above the craggy, bleached, sheer face of a forbidding cliff rising straight from the sea. An elevated, rocky promontory—perfected by geologic chance, surrounded by ocean on three sides, linked to the land by a narrow spit of ground to the left, where a lone cypress splits a swath of fairway—the green, broad, squarish, and flat, looks the size of a dinner plate from the tee, surrounded by five bunkers that compound its inspired and terrifying prospect.

The most spectacular hole in golf, the sixteenth at Cypress, deserves its reputation but, more than any other part of the course, wouldn't have fulfilled the severity of its convictions without the direct intervention of the club's original founder, former U.S. Women's Amateur champion Marion Hollins. She had singled out this spectacular location for a three par during her earliest interest in the site, but her first architect, Seth Raynor, had tried to dissuade Hollins that the carry could ever be mastered; players might be struck dumb by its savage beauty, but would only fire one wasted bullet after another into the unforgiving sea. Hollins promptly teed up three balls in a row in the rocky ground and drove them all to the middle of the green she envisioned across the cove. Case closed.

When he came on board the project, Dr. Alister MacKenzie immediately grasped the genius of the hole that Hollins proposed, but he first envisioned it as a par four, with a tee box planted another hundred yards or so back toward the clubhouse. When Hollins insisted that sixteen remain a one-shotter, that this was what made the hole unique and special, MacKenzie suggested an acceptable compromise: an alternate route to the green for the fainter of heart, built near the lone cypress atop the crowned ridge to the left, an abbreviated stretch of fairway that narrowed as it neared the green. This was still a blind shot, up and over the sea cliffs closer to shore, fraught with hazards that included another beached cove just out of sight to the left of and below the green. MacKenzie's compromise offered a more guaranteed route than a frontal assault at the flag, but at the cost, on average, of a half-stroke penalty.

Ben Hogan never believed that the possible rewards of a tee shot taken straight at the sixteenth green justified the risks. From a man who calculated every angle of every last variable on a golf course with the precision of a geometry professor, this constituted a powerful argument for leaving your earthly pride in the bag beside the driver and slapping a four-iron toward the twisted tree.

On this day, as they emerged from the tangle of gnarled cypress and approached the sixteenth tee, spikes crunching on the crushed shell path, Hogan spoke to his caddie, Turk, before they arrived.

"Driver," he said.

That perked everyone's ears up. Venturi watched closely as Hogan teed up his ball, suddenly and vibrantly aware that his young life had come full circle; here he was at the very spot where he used to idly dream of playing his boyhood heroes, and there they both were, Hogan and Nelson, matched against him in the battle of his life. He nearly had to pinch himself.

Silent and taut, the slight, sinewy Hogan took his stance, staring across at their uncompromising target. Then a flash of efficient, explosive action, and all eyes found the ball, piercing the sky, rising in a promising arc—eyes darting down to find the cliffs, mind racing to unconsciously measure the odds, back up to the ball—to watch it drop so much farther away than it appeared, yes, safely, in front of the green.

Hogan watched his drive all the way in, eyes squinting, then gave the slightest nod of satisfaction. The risk taken, the bet cashed. Putting for birdie, about thirty feet to the flag in the center of the green.

Byron took out his driver as well. Neither man still played the twin drivers they'd shared at Pinehurst sixteen years earlier. Ben had eventually snapped the shaft of his heavy war club after years of demanding use, and Byron played with newer clubs that MacGregor continued to build for him; bearing his signature label, they remained an important part of the company's catalogue and still sold in solid numbers. While only seldom called upon to leave his ranch, Byron had reached a satisfying compromise with the expanding economic advantages of the game, much of it as a result of the aggressive prompting and advice of Eddie Lowery, in which he played just enough high-profile tournaments and exhibitions to keep his name-brand value alive in the marketplace.

Now, with his "Byron Nelson" driver in hand, Byron uncorked his finest tee shot of the day, a flag-seeking missile that cut through the mist, pitched in, and rolled to a stop less than six feet from the hole.

This time Venturi refused to meet either of the older men's eyes as he took the tee. Another make-or-break moment. His drive cleared the water handily, but settled on the far left side of the green, and any prospects for the birdie they now needed had to be treated as remote.

Harvie knew what he had to do. He much preferred the Hogan route at sixteen and had once ruined a potentially record-breaking round here—seven under to this point—by hitting a driver onto the beach to the left, where he was forced to time his recovery shot back up to the green between incoming waves; he ended up taking an eight and falling out of contention. Harvie slowed down when he was under pressure, and he breathed deeply as he stepped up to take his turn, drinking in the sea air for his full ten seconds of allotted concentration. Ten seconds after that, his ball was resting inside of Byron's, five feet from the birdie they had to have and were now almost assured of collecting. He turned and gave Ken a cockeyed grin and a slight roll of the eyes: *How does he do it, folks? Even he doesn't know.*

They walked in weighted silence around the cove and out along the promontory to the sixteenth green. The weakened winter sun had now slipped below its apex to the south, toward the shadowy headlands of Big Sur. Sea mist filtered the air with a pearlescent sheen, dazzling light dancing off foamy white blue waves as they sounded off the rocks. The emotional state typically induced by the immersion in nature and ravishing vistas at sixteen comes close to reverence; they all felt it along that walk and knew that today the feeling added up to more than the sum of the weather and scenery. The crowd stopped short of the green, sensing the mood between them somehow as well, as if to follow them any farther would intrude on a private moment.

Neither Hogan nor Venturi dropped their long birdie putts, but both finished close enough to pick up with pars and quickly cleared the stage. Byron's ball sat slightly away, maybe six feet from the cup. He never made any secret of his spiritual nature—when it's that genuine, you don't need to—and in that heavenly setting, at that moment it almost seemed foretold when his putt found its way into the hole for a birdie two. But the more material instincts of youth can find their own paths to earthly rewards, even if doled out in sparing ten-second increments, and so Harvie Ward followed in right afterward with a sure-handed, hard-earned birdie of his own.

Their remarkable assault on Cypress Point continued with another hole halved. The pros were still one up with two to play.

The seventeenth tee rests on a slight rise behind the sixteenth green, a long, narrow plateau, pointed like a runway back toward the mainland. The view here from the westernmost reach of the promontory encompasses a panorama offered nowhere else in the world, stretching up and down the rugged coastline, the whole of Cypress Point and the Monterey Peninsula spreading out before you, and the shrouded headland of Big Sur looming to the right; earth, water, land, and sky. The four men surveyed the fairway, slanting away from them to the south back across the sea, sunlight nearly blinding as it angled off the churning waters below.

The choice MacKenzie offered them here was perhaps his most difficult and ingenious on the course: slightly over three hundred yards, as the crow flies, to a green clearly visible on the next rocky outcropping to the south; but the actual fairway lies back across the water, canted at almost a ninety-degree angle from the tee box, and the cliff face pinches it inward as it runs away from you. That creates a two-shot route of nearly four hundred yards, but the distance you bite off with your drive can greatly reduce the severity of the second shot if you're willing to flirt with the rocks. The other choice is to play safely to the left, where a tall, dense stand of cypress occupies the right center of the fairway—a reprise of the first hole—wreaking havoc with your subsequent line to the green. To play past the cypresses on their left side, where the line to the green opens up again, requires a drive of nearly three hundred yards.

They could see the flag waving in the breeze, positioned at the left front of the green. Hogan again led off, the shape of the fairway a perfect fit for his power fade, and he found the springy rough short and right of the cypress trees. Byron played the same shot, but straighter and a little deeper, soaring over enough of the rocks that the crowd gasped at the boldness of the line when it landed safely. Ken could see Harvie engage with the challenge more avidly than at any point in the day, eyes focused in fierce concentration. He followed Byron's line and went one better, challenging the rocks even more aggressively, and he was rewarded with an even better result, less than a hundred yards from the green. Ken decided to take his ball left with the draw he slightly preferred and could hit harder. He drew another gasp from the gallery as his ball nearly clipped the cypresses as it turned left, kicked, and bounced past them.

George Coleman, Paul Shields, and some of the other Cypress members in attendance smiled and shook their heads; they could hardly remember seeing anyone pass those trees from the back tees before. Eddie Lowery couldn't think of a thing to say to his young charge, and that was news in itself.

They made the long walk back across the neck of the promontory to the seventeenth fairway, their gallery scattering ahead of them to frame the green. Trailing the others as he had most of the day, Hogan lit another cigarette—his habit had long ago been set at three packs a day. Harvie hung back to bum one off him, and as they walked along, he got a flash of the famous Hogan sunbeam smile at something he said softly to him. Byron and Ken looked at each other from across the fairway as they walked ahead and smiled warmly at each other, no quarter asked for or given in it, but a brief acknowledgment of the wonder they were all experiencing.

Hogan stopped by his ball and tossed his cigarette down onto the rocks below; that's how close he'd cut his drive to the edge of the cliff. He used an eight iron, lofting his ball over the corner of the rocks and water for the second time on the hole, to find the middle of the green, a safe guarantee for par, deferring to his partner to make the aggressive play now. A one-hole lead on seventeen in match play means nothing if you squander it with a strategic mistake, and Hogan had, as usual, made the textbook call.

Byron, back in the sharp command of his game with which he'd bolted from the gate, nipped a nifty wedge from 110 yards straight at the flag, where it bit, danced, spun, and backed up, seven feet right of the cup. As he handed the club back to his caddie, Hogan, passing on the left, just nodded his head and smiled at him; from

Ben that almost amounted to a hug, and Byron grinned apprecia-
tively.

Harvie kept his eye on his own ball from the moment Byron
swung, unusual for him. He never even looked at the green to see
where Byron's ball had landed; he knew it was going to be close, and
he had to better it. He pulled his wedge as he walked into his stance,
the shot already firmly pictured in his mind, and he set up and
swung inside of seconds. And for the second time in a row he landed
his ball inside Byron's, leaving five feet for a birdie three.

Ken watched all this transpire from beyond the stand of cypress.
He couldn't quite make out where Byron and Harvie had landed on
the green because of a small mound set before its front right corner,
so his caddie stepped quickly forward to spot them and returned
with the news. With Harvie safely in so close, Ken knew he could afford to gamble, and the way to do that here was to try and feather the
ball in on the front edge just over the small mound, between where
it ended and the flag. He went for that spot with a half wedge, from
only ninety yards out, but knew at impact he'd shaved it a little too
fine; his ball struck the descending side of the mound—which of
course MacKenzie had placed where it was for exactly this defensive
purpose—and skittered about fifteen feet past the flag.

As they moved forward, their breathless gallery circled around the
mouth of the green on the outcropping's landward side, like a crowd
in an amphitheater. Hogan's ball was away and he moved to it. An
unanswered birdie here could secure the match for them, guarantee-
ing no worse than a tie if the youngsters made one of their putts. Ben
again stood over the ball for what seemed an eternity—no one else
among them knowing that he was locked in battle with his obstinate,
injured left eye to bring the ball into focus before he took it back.
And then he did, and stood frozen, watching, as the ball lipped out
on the high side. He bent down to pick it up, hesitant, a catch in his
knee, and Ken thought the effort of hiking Cypress on his weary legs
showed through. He followed Hogan with his birdie effort—a

chance to square the match if Byron failed to cash in—but the ball took a wayward turn at the hole.

Now it was Byron's turn to try to increase their lead. He hesitated, unusual for him, after he took his stance, standing upright again to have another look at the line—something Ken's ball had done had given him a second thought. Then, satisfied, he bent back down and banged it straight into the hole for his birdie.

The air tightened like a guitar string. The crowd stood as silent as a congregation. All you could hear was seabirds, wind, and the surf crashing against the rocks below. It was simple now; if Harvie missed his putt for birdie to equal Byron's birdie, the match was over.

Harvie's eyes opened wide in concentration, unblinking, as if he could take in more information that way, and he briskly walked around, then behind the ball. He looked up and down his line to the hole, just as he used to do on the sand greens back home, and when he took his stance, he paused ever so slightly, as if waiting for a certain feel or magic to come into the blade of his old rusty putter.

Then he made the putt look easy. Birdie three.

So they would play the eighteenth, with the pros holding on to the same slender one-hole lead they had protected, but failed to extend, with six birdies in the last seven holes. It was a short walk to the tee box just south of the green, behind it another magnificent vista of thrusting rocks and turbulent sea. Although he had once briefly considered building a bridge to a tee box perched out on those rocks, Alister MacKenzie abandoned the idea as impractical and concluded his Monterey symphony with a bold forte; no camouflage, no strategy, no alternate routes. A straightforward and demanding four par, routed back toward the clubhouse, that demands accuracy and agitates the unfamiliar eye. The tee box points you directly toward a stand of tall cypress; a brief gateway opening between the two largest of them to the right says "this way." Bunkers and more trees guard that right-hand side before it doglegs to the right, and the fairway opens on the left once you fly the initial row of trees, but the experienced know the only way to reach the small, canted green in two, up the course's steepest hill, is by placing your tee shot on an ungenerous patch of that right-hand side. Drift even a few yards to the left of that target and you're forced to contend with a stand of towering pines atop the hill that fiercely guard the left side of the green. Come up short of the turn with your drive and the encroaching forest on the right-hand side will block you out entirely. The hole was not long, a little short of 350 yards, although the hill lengthens the second shot considerably. Some critics, besotted by the abundance of strategic options already on display, have complained over the years that this finishing hole represents the only weakness on the course.

They're missing the point. MacKenzie is saying: *I've offered you options and bailouts all day long. Enough. Deal with it. Put it where I tell you to or take your just punishment.*

So it is a hole designed specifically to test one's steel under duress, and decide matches that still hang in the balance.

Three wood for Ben Hogan off the tee, over the first tall cypress on the left, applying the slightest touch of fade to steer it to a soft and ideal landing. They could have placed a bull's-eye on that circle of fairway and he would have hit the black. Byron played his three wood only a few yards shorter and to the left of Ben's, but even at that he knew the trees along the left would make difficult his approach to the center-cut flag. Harvie's drive, a hammered four wood, left him squarely between the two pros, with a clear shot at the green. Playing the final tee shot of the round, Ken airmailed his ball over the left cypress tree, the same line as Hogan, and just short of him. The perfect play; he joined Ben in the mayor's office.

The gallery swarming ahead of them was now joined by another wave of people who had assembled at the top of the hill—the parking lot was jammed with latecomers who'd heard the news about the match—and by the time the four men came into sight below, they had lined the back of the green above. Exactly the kind of crowd Hogan had been hoping to avoid, and in truth it had been with them now for the last five holes, but it was as if Ben were seeing the gallery for the first time as they made their way onto the final fairway. Byron played first, to the front right edge of the green. Then Harvie reached the green almost right on top of him, leaving him an uphill birdie putt of twenty-five feet. Ken played an eight iron, a beautiful, soaring arc that landed just below the hole and backed up to about twelve feet.

The entire shifting panorama stilled like an oil painting. Hogan focused, sighted, and fired an eight iron straight at the top of the flag. His ball settled to the right and above the cup, ten feet from birdie, a certain par. Either Ken or Harvie now needed to make their putt for birdie to win the hole and extend the match, but if Hogan made his it was over.

Now all four of the men walked up the hill toward the final green together, Ken, Harvie, and Byron slowing their pace to keep in step with Ben, everyone else in their party trailing well behind, yielding them the stage. And the educated crowd around them broke into spontaneous applause, in recognition of the moment, of the men, of what this gathering between the two branches of the game meant and how they'd played that day. Gratitude. Respect. Knowing they would never witness anything of this sort again.

The four men drank it in as they climbed. Harvie grinned from ear to ear and gave a cheerful little wave. Ben and Ken tipped their caps; Ken wore a duplicate of Hogan's white linen, a form of tribute. Byron doffed his, making warm eye contact with many of those he knew in that crowd and some he didn't. Behind them, Eddie Lowery, that most unsentimental of men, wiped a tear from his eye.

Once they'd settled, Byron putted first, dutifully lagging up for their par, and once that was secured, he picked up, then walked over to where Ben waited.

Par here meant nothing now, so Harvie made a serious run at birdie from twenty-five feet, contorting with dramatic disappointment, and getting a laugh, as the ball scooted just past the uphill side of the cup. He spanked it off the green as punishment, and got another chuckle.

Ken stared down his treacherous twelve-footer for birdie; it would slide at least two feet from right to left as it sped down toward the cup. Once he set it rolling, the green's severe back-to-front slope would do the rest, but the line and pace had to be judged with a watchmaker's precision. Ken relaxed the pressure in his hands on the grip, just as Byron had once taught him to do in these situations, and tapped the ball ever so gently.

Starting on the line, it took the slope, tumbled down the fall line, and dropped in the hole for the birdie three they'd needed. Ken stepped to pick it out, took his cap off to the crowd, then joined Harvie, who feigned a heart attack and leaned on his friend for support, and got another laugh.

Byron and Ben, two tough old Texans, looked at each other.

"Okay, Ben, knock it in. We can win."

Hogan had a twinkle in his eye. "I'm not about to be tied by a couple of damn amateurs in front of all these people."

Then he turned to Ken and Harvie and winked, just as Harvie had done to them on the first tee. *See you, and raise you, kid.*

Ken found himself, in that transported moment while Ben took his stance over the ball, strangely hoping that Hogan would make the clinching putt to beat them. He even knew why.

Because he was Ben Hogan, and it was just past twilight, and his like would never pass this way again.

Ben didn't hesitate over the ball this time. Firm and assured, he rolled it straight into the heart of the cup for the winning birdie.

The match was over. The men doffed their hats and shook hands all around, smiling broadly. Ken and Harvie threw their arms around each other's shoulders, their first loss as a team in four years, but considering the circumstance, they were happy in defeat; they had held their own against the two greatest pros of the age, and there was no shame in that. If anything, they had affirmed Eddie Lowery's conviction that as amateurs they could still be the best in the world. Dozens of friends pressed forward with words of thanks and congratulations. Eddie and George joined the circle, expressing their wonder and amazement, scorecards in hand for anyone to see. The crowd hovered around them, buzzing, as word spread about the rumored scores. They soon learned that the facts were these: Ben Hogan had tied his own course record at Cypress Point with 63. Ken Venturi had shot 65, Byron Nelson and Harvie Ward 67. Between them, in their eighteen holes, the two teams recorded 27 birdies and an eagle.

The pros had won their match one up, with a net score of 58, fourteen strokes under par. The amateurs had shot thirteen under par, a net of 59. The margin of victory remained that eagle Hogan had holed from eighty-five yards out at the tenth, and it had stood up through the entire back nine.

The foursome made their way toward the clubhouse while the crowd milled blissfully around them. Joey Solis had come out of his caddie shack to watch the finish, and he thought as many as five thousand people had collected around the final green by this time. Head pro Henry Puget came forward to shake each of the players' hands, as did dozens of the pros and amateurs in the Crosby field who had gathered to watch the finish.

The aura of happiness and satisfaction that attends any good round trailed them all the way into the locker room, where they changed their shoes, put on coats and ties, and made their way into the clubhouse for drinks. The lively room lit up with members and guests who wanted to hear the blow-by-blow, but for the moment they let the players sit at a table alone together, like any foursome after their regular outing, reliving the day, relishing the memories, and settling accounts.

When Harvie and Ken took out their wallets to pay their bet—they had lost two out of three ways, the back nine and the match—Ben and Byron refused their money. Their wager was forgotten. No one argued about it. They all knew they had something better in its place.

Eddie and George sat at the next table hunched over their score-cards, attesting and comparing. No one knows for certain whether their bet was ever settled. Neither mentioned it to anyone, or ever wrote about that part of the match; the issue remained private between the two of them. George Coleman once hinted that in the wake of the events they'd witnessed, they had come to a mutual decision that the only gentlemanly thing to do was forget about their wager, whatever the amount they'd eventually settled on, unwilling in the aftermath of such an occasion to sully it with any taint of commerce. But its actual resolution remains one obstinate detail lost to time and memory. For years the original scorecard of the match was posted on the wall of Henry Puget's Cypress Point pro shop, and George and Eddie supposedly kept their copies as well, but all three have since vanished into the vast inventory of their large and complicated lives. Not a living soul has seen them since.

Byron drank lemonade and iced tea, Ken had a beer, Ben and Harvie Scotch on the rocks. One drink apiece. At one point, Hogan leaned over to Ken and put a hand on his shoulder.

"I'll tell you one thing," he said, smiling. "I didn't want you to know it, but we wanted to beat you guys so bad."

"Oh, we knew," said Ken.

"We sure as hell did," said Harvie. "Don't think for one second we weren't dying to beat you like a tied-up goat. And we would've, too, if I'd had another damn hour of sleep."

"One more hole and we would have gotten you," said Ken.

"That's why we only played eighteen," said Ben, and they all laughed again.

"That was some kind of fun, wasn't it?" said Byron, beaming.

"Boys, that's as hard as I can ever remember playing," said Ben, and Ken could see that he meant it. "I didn't want that round to end."

Ben held out his drink. The other three raised theirs and touched glass. Nothing else needed to be said.

A short time later, the room emptied. The four players, and George and Eddie, shook hands again outside around predictable and casual banter about a rematch, then parted and drove off along their separate ways into the golden, dappled light of a perfect January afternoon at Cypress Point on the Monterey Peninsula.

The amateurs had stated a strong case for their claim on present greatness, but the old warriors had defended their ground, holding off the changing of the guard for one last glorious round. Recent history indicated that the game's future appeared to belong to the rising professional player, but Venturi and Ward had made it clear they would have plenty to say about that as career amateurs; there wasn't another pair of pros on the planet who could have beaten them that day. The two competing sides of the game, pros and amateurs, had met at the summit, the difference between them as razor thin as a single fortunate bounce on a Ben Hogan wedge shot.

The four men would never play another round together again. Each man's most relentless personal opponent, time, would begin to collect its inevitable toll. During the next few months, in the personal destinies of Ken Venturi and Harvie Ward, the futures of the amateur and professional game, and the sport itself, were about to cross the great divide.

The 1956 Clambake

The perfect weather on the Monterey Peninsula didn't hold. It rained Thursday night and turned cold and damp by the time they began the first round of the Clambake Friday morning. Playing at Cypress Point, the team of Ben Hogan and Bing Crosby—with the help of Bing's six strokes—turned in a best-ball score of 60 to lead the Pro-Am field, with the largest gallery of the day following them, over five thousand adoring fans. Ben had recorded a sterling 67 in his practice round at Pebble on Thursday, the day after The Match, and he repeated the performance with his own ball on Friday back at Cypress Point, solidly in contention for the pro side of the tournament.

But it rained hard on Saturday, then poured wretchedly all day Sunday for the third and final round at Pebble Beach, washing Bing and Ben out of the running in both the regular event and the Pro-Am. Hogan shot an 81 in that final round, nineteen strokes off the record winning number posted by Dr. Cary Middlecoff, the Tennessee dentist and winner for the second straight year, but two strokes in front of his former fellow caddie from Glen Garden, Byron Nelson. Hogan's spirits remained high, despite that unsightly final-round score, as crowds, knowing it might be the last chance they had to see the Hawk in action, cheered his every move.

Harvie Ward and his partner, a Seattle pro named Bud Ward—no relation—finished in fourth place of the Pro-Am, just one stroke ahead of Pebble's head pro, Art Bell, and his partner, Ken Venturi. George Coleman and his pro partner, young Jack Burke, Jr., failed to make the final Pro-Am cut. So did Byron and Eddie Lowery, the defending Pro-Am champs; Eddie and George watched the final round at Pebble from the sidelines.

But Hogan mounted one last charge for the soggy fans at Pebble Beach that day. He birdied the fourteenth, then the fifteenth, then chipped in for a third straight at sixteen; their gallery went mad, with Bing dancing around on one leg, leading the cheers, waving his putter over his head. At the final hole, Hogan's birdie attempt finished two inches short. In the pouring rain, their gallery and the crowd assembled around eighteen stood up and gave Ben Hogan and Bing Crosby a standing ovation as they walked off the game's great stage for the final time together.

Afterward

Two months after The Match, Ken and Harvie squared off against each other in the match play finals of the San Francisco City Championship. Ken had won this prestigious amateur title once before, four years earlier, and Harvie was defending champion; ten thousand people showed up to watch the city's two best players settle the issue at Harding Park. Venturi got the better of his friend and partner that day, winning the championship on the thirty-second hole, 5 & 4. Afterward, Harvie told the press that Ken had now become "the best amateur I've ever played; better than Frank Stranahan in his prime." Later that same night after their pitched battle, Ken's first son, Matthew, was born, and Harvie spent the better part of the night with him in the maternity ward waiting room. Ken Venturi and Harvie Ward would never face each other in an amateur event again.

One month later, emboldened by their success against Hogan and Nelson, twenty-four-year-old Ken Venturi made his second appearance at the Masters, sharing a house with Harvie Ward in Augusta, rented by Eddie Lowery. A series of practice rounds with Byron and Harvie rounded Ken's game into peak condition as the tournament began. Venturi didn't know it at the time, but Eddie liked what he saw from Ken on the course so much he placed a $1000 bet with a bookie across the board for him to win, place, or show.

Eddie's faith was not misplaced. Ken stunned the world by shooting a 66 in the opening round, the lowest score ever recorded by any amateur in the tournament's history. He stood alone on top of the leader board, above the best names in the sport. Playing with three-time Masters champion Jimmy Demaret, Venturi followed with a 69 in the second round that tied Byron's record for the lowest halfway score in Masters history. High winds affected the third round, blowing up scores, but even with a 75 that day, Ken Venturi entered the final round on Sunday holding a four-shot lead.

A ceremonial Masters tradition since Jones had stepped aside paired the tournament's third-round leader in the final round with Byron Nelson, and that twosome had already been announced to the press. But that Saturday evening Jones and Cliff Roberts had second thoughts, worried that given Venturi's mentor-student relationship with Byron, the pairing might appear improperly favorable to him. They didn't want the first amateur ever to win the Masters to have to contend afterward with unfair accusations from the press that playing alongside his teacher had given him an advantage or "a hollow victory." Venturi had no choice but to agree and, when given a choice, asked to play with Sam Snead, whom he knew hardly at all but respected as he did Hogan and Nelson.

When Ken reached the first tee the next day, and the full weight of what he was facing hit him, he allowed his mind to race ahead and imagine all the earthly rewards that a Masters victory was about to bring him. These siren songs of glory were impossible for any young man to resist; Ken had been given to understand that as the first amateur Masters champion, the doors of corporate America would be thrown wide open to him; he'd be set up in business for the rest of his life. There had even been talk that when Jones stepped aside from his post at Augusta, an event his advancing illness continued to hasten, Venturi might be the man to eventually succeed him in that role.

From the first shot that day these fantasies proved fatal to his game. When Harvie Ward, finishing an hour ahead of Venturi, came off the course and heard an update, he immediately grasped what was happening to Ken's round and tried desperately to get inside the ropes to settle him down as only he knew how, but Harvie's efforts were denied by marshals, who finally threatened him with expulsion from the grounds if he didn't stop trying to step between the ropes. Without his best friend's counsel, and frozen out by an ungracious Snead, who resented an amateur's very presence on the course, Ken three-putted six greens that day, shot 80, and lost by a single stroke, when a birdie failed to drop on eighteen, to Jackie Burke, one of only two men in the entire field to break par that difficult day; Burke came from eight shots back to win the tournament.

Venturi handled his devastating disappointment manfully in the aftermath, earning praise from Jones and Roberts for the dignified way he conducted himself. But the failure haunted him deeply, and as he walked off the plane back home in San Francisco the next day, a posse of reporters pounced before he'd had a chance to rebound. In search of a story and an angle, the press allowed a few of Ken's unguarded statements—about the canceled pairing with Byron, Snead's silence to him during their round, and the tournament officials who prevented Harvie Ward from reaching him—to be played up and reheated into some negative headlines that read like sour grapes.

Certain his words had not expressed that sentiment, Ken had perhaps let thwarted feelings seep through between the lines, and the reporters hadn't hesitated to connect the dots. Ken and those close to him felt that the public reaction to these sensationalized stories caused extensive damage to his reputation as an amateur sportsman. He was labeled a sore loser, a crybaby, and, worst of all, a choker. Shouldering it as a bitter lesson about life in the public eye, Venturi vowed to put the whole experience behind him, saying nothing more about it and preparing to play in the upcoming U.S. Open.

A few days later, a lengthy telegram appeared in newspapers around the country, addressed to Bob Jones and Clifford Roberts, apologizing for and attempting to explain what it claimed were completely misinterpreted statements that he'd given to those reporters. The telegram was signed by Ken Venturi. The problem was, Ken hadn't written the telegram, or ever known a thing about it.

Venturi quickly learned that Eddie Lowery had written and cabled that telegram and signed Ken's name to it without his knowledge or consent. When Ken angrily confronted his boss about it, Eddie insisted that as an elder statesman of the game and Augusta member, he was in a unique position to know that in order to avoid a compounding public relations disaster, this was the only right response to offer. He argued that Jones and Roberts had responded favorably to the telegram in their subsequent statements, but Venturi still felt a lingering sting of betrayal; if he had done nothing wrong to begin with, as he firmly believed, why should he have to apologize for it? And what authority gave Eddie the right to speak in his name without first asking permission?

Ken would continue to work for Eddie for another year, and they always remained friends, but this violation of trust, in his mind, gravely wounded their close relationship. Ken did go on to make an excellent showing at the '56 Open at Oak Hill outside Rochester, New York, finishing in eighth place, low amateur in the field, just behind the up-and-coming Arnold Palmer. Forty-four-year-old Ben Hogan made another valiant autumnal run at his fifth Open title before his failing putter betrayed him on the final holes and he finished second by a single stroke for the second year in a row, this time to Dr. Cary Middlecoff. Harvie Ward made the cut, but finished well down the leader board.

Venturi posed afterward for photographers near the eighteenth green, with Middlecoff, Hogan, and the Open trophy, and for the first time his thoughts took a serious turn toward joining the professional ranks. His recent success in the match against Hogan and Nelson, the two greatest pros alive, played no small part in Ken's decision. The tour was also changing rapidly, and expanded television coverage was beginning to make an economic impact; bigger money in tournament purses, more off-course endorsement opportunities for winners—all pointed to a coming day when pro golf might even become a desirable, if not glamorous, profession. But with a wife and new son at home to care for, was he willing to give up the safe and solid guaranteed income he could earn working for Eddie Lowery, to pursue that ephemeral dream?

Venturi entered the 1956 U.S. Amateur at Knollwood Country Club outside Chicago with that question ringing in his mind, lost in the third round, then hung around to watch his friend Harvie Ward try for his second championship in a row. Ken had failed to reel in that Masters he'd had on the hook, and now, after this early exit from the Amateur, because he was the only non-pro who could play to the same level, his friend Harvie's coronation as the country's top amateur became complete. Marching relentlessly through the field, Harvie played the last thirteen holes of his final match against an overmatched Chuck Kocsis in five under par and ran away with the championship.

If Ken's mind about turning pro was beginning to change, Harvie seemed more poised than ever to become the next Bob Jones; he reiterated to the press afterward that his determination to remain a career gentleman amateur remained resolute. When he returned home with his second straight title, the city of San Francisco threw a huge celebration for Harvie, as Atlanta had frequently done for Jones in his day. Like Jones, Harvie had become a source of civic pride, and with this victory he reached the pinnacle of his career. At the gala dinner they threw for him, Harvie sat between the mayor and Joe DiMaggio, the other crown prince of San Francisco sport. Ken Venturi didn't begrudge his closest pal that great success, but he saw it as another reason he ought to turn pro and carve out his own mark on the check-cashing side of the game.

That fall Eddie Lowery offered Ken a chance to take over the Lake Merced dealership of Van Etta Motors, a tremendous opportunity for a man in his mid-twenties that could set the course of his life. Instead, with the support of his wife, Ken declined, informing Lowery he intended to turn professional and try his luck on tour. Eddie tested his resolve, challenging him by saying he wouldn't make it, that the grind was too tough. Ken angrily insisted he was going to show the world that what had happened at the Masters was a fluke. Eddie smiled; Ken had passed the test. Eddie gave him his blessing, but assured him that if those plans didn't work out he'd always have a place to come back to at the dealership.

After winning the California State Amateur championship again that fall, Venturi announced his decision to turn pro at a press conference in late November of 1956. An archaic PGA rule then required a six-month waiting period after declaring before a player could join the tour full-time, so Ken continued selling cars for Lowery and entered a few spring tournaments through exemptions and invitations. The first came from their friend Bing Crosby. Ken had only $5000 in the bank when the season began at the Clambake; comfortable on the Monterey courses he knew so well, and in front of sympathetic hometown fans, he finished fifth in his professional debut and took home a check for $350. He finished second the following week in Palm Springs and pocketed $850. His confidence continued to build when he joined the tour full-time that summer, with another top ten finish at the Open—this one for a paycheck—and then two straight wins late in the year, the second at Milwaukee, where in the final round he stood up to a late charge, and some gamesmanship, from a prickly Sam Snead.

When Venturi's five-stroke lead had dwindled to one as they finished the eighth hole, Snead sidled up to him as they walked to the ninth tee and asked: "You ain't chokin' again, are you, boy?"

"I'll show you choking," said Ken.

Fired up, Venturi beat back all challengers this time, won his second tournament in a row, and gave it back to Snead on the eighteenth green when he refused to mark his ball and let Snead putt out ahead of him. He stood up to the intimidating Snead again a few minutes later when the older man confronted him at the scorer's tent. Snead backed down and passed the word: "Don't mess with the kid; he only plays better when he's mad." Venturi had passed his trial by fire; he was a tour player now.

Ken finished tenth on the PGA Tour's money list, winning nearly $19,000 in only sixteen tournaments, and *Golf Digest* named him their Rookie of the Year for 1957.

While Venturi was making his way out on the road, back home in San Francisco, Harvie Ward's world turned upside down. After winning his second straight Amateur, Harvie's 1957 had begun poorly, with surgery to remove a ruptured disc in his lower back, and he was unable to play for the first three months of the year. But after rehabilitation he was ready when the Masters rolled around in April, and after three rounds Harvie trailed the leader, Sam Snead, by a single shot.

All the excitement and interest that had attended Ken Venturi's near miss at victory as an amateur the year before now centered on Harvie. Snead and Ward went out and fought such a pitched battle against each other on Masters Sunday that neither of them noticed relative unknown Doug Ford coming from three strokes back to shoot a 66 and steal the championship out from under both of them. Harvie finished fourth, winner of another low amateur trophy, his best finish to date in either an Open or a Masters. Just entering his thirties, the prime years of most great golfers, he appeared more ready than ever to continue his run as the heir apparent to Bob Jones.

Then it all came undone.

A disgruntled employee from Van Etta Motors—there is specula-
tion it may have been Eddie's younger brother, after a bitter family
quarrel—approached the IRS in early 1956 with information that
Eddie Lowery might be keeping two sets of books. Still wary of the
cozy relationship between businessmen and golf after the Deepdale
Golf Club scandal the year before, federal auditors initiated a full in-
vestigation of Lowery's entire financial life. Their inquiry lasted six
months and in early 1957 resulted in the case being bound over to a
grand jury, with a recommendation that Eddie Lowery be indicted
and stand trial on formal charges of felony income tax evasion. Out-
raged, convinced he had become the victim of a vindictive witch hunt,
Lowery offered his full cooperation and vigorously contested the
charges at every turn.

When he was summoned before the grand jury, Eddie's ledgers
brought into the open details of expenses he had incurred over the
previous few years, and written off, involving his employees, most
prominently Harvie Ward. Chief among them: airfare paid for Harvie
to attend various tournaments and championships, including the
Masters, the National Amateur, and the 1954 Canadian Amateur.
The federal indictment alleged that most of this money, if not all,
had been illegally gifted to Harvie a few years earlier in the form of
what was designated by Eddie as an $11,000 "loan."

The story splashed in bold headlines across the front pages of the
San Francisco newspapers. When Harvie walked off a plane from
Fort Worth the day the story broke in early May, returning from a
trip to visit Ben Hogan and his thriving new company for a club fit-
ting, a pack of press confronted him with a hundred ugly questions.
Harvie was photographed, in shock, reading the story and learning
for the first time of these disastrous accusations, all of which he ve-
hemently denied.

The USGA, the game's governing body, had had sufficient prior
concern over these incidents to have questioned Eddie Lowery—for
the previous three years a member of its Executive Committee—

about them twice before, once in 1954 and again during the association's annual summer meeting in 1956. Eddie wrote two long letters in response, detailing and defending all his actions with regard to Harvie, Ken Venturi, and a few other amateurs he supported, which had satisfied the committee's concerns enough at the time to table the matter.

In defense of Eddie's position, no less an august presence than his old friend Francis Ouimet, now a Boston stockbroker—who counted Ken Venturi among his clients—and still active in USGA affairs, went on record that year to urge the committee to liberalize its strict policies regarding amateurs and their ability to accept expense money under certain conditions. Ouimet had run afoul of the USGA's amateur standards himself forty years earlier, not long after his groundbreaking victories in the Open and Amateur, when his business investment in a sporting goods store resulted in the revoking of his amateur status. Thirteen years later Bob Jones faced similar questions from the USGA, even after he'd officially retired from competition, when he starred in a series of instructional golf films for Warner Bros. Jones simply declared himself a "professional" rather than argue semantics. Seventeen years later Jones asked to have his amateur status reinstated, tongue firmly in cheek, and answered the standard query about whether he'd ever made any money from golf by replying: "Hell yes!"

In this instance, the USGA took no action in 1956 with regard to either Eddie or their own policies. Eddie did not seek another term on the Executive Committee after his ended that year, and when Harvie went on to win his second consecutive Amateur Championship, the entire matter appeared to be forgotten until the IRS got involved, Eddie testified, and the story hit the newswires: that two-time defending U.S. Amateur champion Harvie Ward, standard bearer for the highest traditions in the game of honor, stood accused of cheating the system. Newspapers are and always have been sold without much regard for tomorrow's conscience, and nothing peddles them faster than scandal; Harvie Ward's good name had been dragged down into the mud.

Within days, a telegram arrived from the USGA's executive director, Joe Dey, requesting that Harvie respond to questions raised by Eddie's testimony. Dey concluded: "USGA REGARDS IT AS REGRETTABLE THAT QUESTION HAS ARISEN CONCERNING YOUR AMATEUR STATUS AND FEELS MATTER SHOULD BE SETTLED AS PROMPTLY AND FRANKLY AS POSSIBLE. PLEASE TELEGRAPH REPLY COLLECT."

After seeking counsel, and speaking at length with Lowery, Harvie decided to attend a formal hearing with the Executive Committee. He told them he intended to contest these accusations and wished to personally present evidence in his own defense. A letter-writing campaign from distinguished figures in the game around the country began in support of his reputation. Eddie Lowery wrote the committee an extensive account of his version of these events, in which he went out of his way to hold Harvie blameless for what had transpired. Less than a month later, on June 7, Harvie arrived alone, without legal counsel, which he was entitled to bring if desired, for his meeting with the Executive Committee, held at Glen View Golf Club in Golf, Illinois.

Harvie intended to present a comprehensive defense: That at each tournament in question to which he'd traveled with Eddie's support, the two of them had conducted legitimate business with either car dealers or automobile manufacturers. That his job as a salesman at Van Etta Motors was not a setup to finance his amateur golf, but a thriving career that he practiced vigorously, honestly, and with unqualified success. That the "loan" in question extended to him by his boss had been given in good faith as an advance of salary so that he could invest in the stock market. That most amateurs, by virtue of economic hardship, stay with friends while competing in tournaments and that, under USGA rules, an amateur is allowed to accept that hospitality without penalty. With only two exceptions, he had traveled to all these tournaments as Eddie's guest, under assurance from his boss, as a member of the Executive Committee, who should have been in a position to know, that they were operating comfortably within the rules.

Harvie was also prepared to point out with characteristic bluntness that it was common knowledge that blurring of these lines occurred in the amateur game on a daily basis as a matter of necessity. No one got hurt; everyone knew about it and agreed to look the other way. As Ouimet had argued the year before, the purity of spirit that the USGA lived to uphold existed only in the realm of theory, not the untidy world of real life and dollars and common sense. The truth was that businessmen who played the amateur game—insurance executives or car salesmen, doctors or dentists—and competed for the USGA's title year in and year out needed to either write off their golf expenses or give up their pursuit. Men who loved the game but didn't play it for a living couldn't be expected to meet a saint's standards in order to compete for nothing more than the honor of the quest, or the day would come when they'd hold an amateur championship in which no one who wasn't a Rockefeller, Vanderbilt, or Stranahan could afford to participate.

Harvie had reason to hope that his argument might find a friendly reception before the Executive Committee. He was extremely well thought of within the game and had acquitted himself admirably as its amateur champion for two years. He knew a number of men on the committee. Encouraging signals had been sent through channels from a close friend that Richard Tufts, scion of the founding family of Pinehurst, whom Harvie had known well since winning the North-South there at the start of his career nine years earlier, was serving as the USGA's president and would also chair the meeting.

But the moment he walked through the door at ten o'clock that morning to face the fifteen men seated around the dais, and Richard Tufts refused to meet his eye, Harvie knew he was in trouble. Executive Director Joe Dey began by reading aloud to him each clause in the

Rules of Amateur Status, pausing to ask if Harvie understood each one. Harvie indicated patiently that he did. When asked if he had any questions about the rules as stated, Harvie replied that he did not.

The proceedings that followed took almost exactly two hours. Harvie's expenses for every tournament he had participated in as far back as 1947 were scrutinized, and armed with detailed records of each instance, Harvie answered in painstaking detail. With regard to expenses paid by Eddie Lowery for a number of these trips, Harvie stated that he was authorized to make sales calls anywhere in the country, which he often did while at tournaments, and that being re-imbursed for those efforts was a legitimate aspect of his job. He stated that he had also spent his own money on nearly every one of these same golf trips and never traveled anywhere exclusively at Mr. Lowery's expense. With regard to the $11,000 loan in 1954, he stated that Mr. Lowery had given it to him as a no-interest promis-sory note for him to invest in the stock market, and given that stocks had since nearly doubled in value, he could repay the loan at any time. He admitted that at one or two of the events in question he had not conducted any car business, but also said that since he be-gan working at Van Etta Motors in October of 1953, he had felt that Mr. Lowery's guidance regarding these issues would always leave him in accordance with the Rules of Amateur Status, since Mr. Lowery served on the Executive Committee and had repeatedly as-sured him that they continued to operate within the rules.

Harvie stated that although he had received many offers over the past few years to accept money from the game, he had never had any interest in turning professional, and would not do so in the future regardless of their pending decision about his amateur status. He was about to be named a vice president of Van Etta Leasing Com-pany, a new corporation organized by Mr. Lowery, and said he in-tended to proudly defend his amateur title later that summer, seeking a third, unprecedented championship in a row.

Harvie left the room at 11:50 and was invited to return at 4:30 to hear the committee's decision. By 1:15 that decision had been reached, and they broke for lunch. At 2:30 a lawyer, representing Eddie Lowery and authorized to answer questions on his behalf, appeared before the committee to offer additional testimony. At 4:40 that afternoon, after adjourning briefly so that a statement could be prepared for publication, the committee called Harvie Ward back into the meeting room.

Richard Tufts informed Harvie that he had unanimously been found in violation of the Rules of Amateur Status, for accepting expenses to travel to two British Opens, two U.S. Opens, three Amateur Championships, and three Masters during his four years in Mr. Lowery's employ. He was not found in violation for accepting the loan from Mr. Lowery. Because of his claim that he had been misled in these matters by a member of the Executive Committee, a feeling with which the committee concurred, Harvie's probationary period—during which his status was officially revoked—would be reduced from two years to one. As a result, his Amateur Championships of 1955 and 1956 would not be retroactively vacated, and he could apply for reinstatement of his amateur status on May 6, 1958, if he so desired.

Harvie indicated that he did so desire and would then apply for reinstatement. He was warned that if the committee decided to grant it to him, and he was ever found in violation of the Rules of Amateur Status a second time, no second reinstatement would be allowed. Asked if he had any further questions or comments, Harvie said that he had none. They then reviewed together the copy of the public statement earlier prepared by the committee. Harvie did not ask for or suggest any changes, and it was made public immediately after the meeting adjourned at 5:00.

That press release hit only a few days before the U.S. Open began, when golf was already front page news; the whole world learned that Harvie Ward was no longer an amateur golfer. Copies of the release were also sent to governing golf associations of Canada, Mexico, and

Great Britain, along with a letter expressing regret that a player from the United States in violation of these rules had competed in those countries' championships. And with that, in golf circles around the globe, the best amateur to emerge from North America for the last twenty years was now persona non grata.

From a distance it's clear the USGA had taken action out of duty and obligation to its charter, but had done so, at best, with a divided heart. Both Joe Dey and Richard Tufts had to excuse themselves from the room when Harvie's hearing ended, and both shed private tears over the result. Personal regrets notwithstanding, the next month, Executive Director Dey authored a lengthy essay that summed up the organization's view of the Ward case in the USGA's national journal. Although he declined to condemn Harvie's behavior in his own words, he quoted secondary sources—an executive and an academic—on the issue of sportsmanship with words that still sting fifty years later:

"The only way in which amateurism in sports can be defined is in the sportsman's own heart . . . To lie to yourself, and pretend to be an amateur, when you know in your heart you are lying, is just a ruinous habit. Schools that are supposed to train young men, yet warp their consciences by phony amateur standards, can't have much to brag about." (This came from the chairman of the board of Bethlehem Steel, at the time the best-paid executive officer in the country, who could well afford his own high-ceilinged standards.)

Dey then quoted Professor Charles W. Kennedy, a prominent English teacher from Princeton and vice president of the American Olympic Committee, who could invoke pious Anglophile clichés in the best ivory tower tradition: "Especially, you must not forget that the great victory of which you can never be robbed will be the ability to say, when the race is over and the struggle ended, that the flag you fought under was the shining flag of sportsmanship, never furled or hauled down, and that, in victory or defeat, you never lost that contempt for a breach of sportsmanship which will prevent your stooping to it anywhere, anyhow, any time."

The following week, Eddie Lowery received his own letter of rebuke from the USGA. They had deliberated long and hard about how to react to Eddie's leading role in all this, given his long and illustrious association with the game. They informed him that they could not accept his defense that he had played inside the rules by considering Harvie as his "guest," nor did they believe that enough business had been conducted on many of these trips to justify their being written off as a legitimate business expense.

"The Committee," the letter then concluded, "with deep regret, deplores this and the very awkward situation you have created in your relationship with the Association . . . You of course appreciate that there are substantial issues at stake—the welfare of the game of golf, and the future welfare of fine young men, of whom Harvie Ward is certainly one . . . The Committee is mindful of how deeply all these developments must have affected you. We sincerely hope that they will be of constructive value to you, to the end that your good influence in the game will again be established."

That letter was never made public, the whole matter kept in-house. Eddie Lowery did not contest the committee's conclusions and never served in any meaningful capacity within the USGA again.

From the distance of nearly half a century, two sad truths at the center of the scandal stand out: had Eddie Lowery decided to cover these expenses as part of Harvie's salary, an easy enough bookkeeping distinction, instead of writing them off to realize the tax benefits, none of this would have ever come to light. As Harvie had accurately stated, this practice of obeying the letter of the amateur status by-laws while loopholing around their intent had long been and would remain a common and all too human practice; the farcical state of the modern "amateur" Olympics is exhibit A. But once Eddie stood accused by the IRS of tax evasion, in the course of mounting his defense—charges of which he was soon to be completely acquitted—the evidence spilled into the public arena, and perhaps sensitized by the recent Deepdale scandal, the USGA saw no alternative but to take action. That the case involved the amateur game's best player and two-time current champion remained deeply regrettable, but if you intend to make a point to discourage future abuse, what better person to offer as a sacrificial lamb on the altar of sportsmanship to demonstrate one's dedication to the sacred standards?

Sadder still is the realization that Harvie could have avoided the entire disaster by simply turning professional once the story broke. That would in one swift stroke have removed him from the reach of the USGA's jurisdiction; the hearing would never have occurred. Just as Ken Venturi had done the previous fall, perhaps in part out of concern for what he sensed might be in the offing because of Eddie's predicament, Harvie could have been out on tour competing for its improving prize money unencumbered by scandal. Nor would that have prevented him from continuing to work at Van Etta Motors for as long as he wished; there were no rules that said golf pros couldn't also sell cars. Without ruining his lifestyle, he could have played as much or as little golf as he desired on the tour for years to come. Had Harvie Ward committed himself to that arena, he likely would have become the next great name in professional golf and be mentioned in the same breath today with Nicklaus and Palmer, as one of the greats of their generation.

But it was not to be. At the time Harvie felt turning pro would have amounted to an admission of guilt. The only reason he contested the charges with such conviction was because he truly, perhaps naively, believed he was innocent. He trusted Eddie Lowery, and he trusted the system. Now his name and reputation lay in ruins. The dismantling of the rest of his life soon followed.

Up until this moment Harvie had never faced a great test of real life adversity off the playing field; between his golf skills and his formidable charm, it had largely been smooth sailing. When he returned home to San Francisco—and later he was the first to say so—Harvie reacted disastrously. His personal and business relationships with Eddie Lowery had suffered a fatal wound, and he would leave the firm within a year; the five years he spent with Lowery would later disappear from his résumé. Harvie had always been a sensualist who struggled with temptation; now the fault lines within his character fractured seismically. Never a moderate drinker, he began to indulge heavily; that and his pursuit of women served as the twin prescriptions for the obliteration of his pain. His marriage to Suzanne, which now included their two adopted children, ended in less than three years. His plans for beginning his own auto leasing business took a backseat to his headlong escape from reality.

Golf, forever his guiding passion, now the painful reminder of his fallen state, lost its appeal. Those who had for so long championed Harvie were reluctant to voice their support in public. Bob Jones and Clifford Roberts, almost alone in the game's upper echelon, made their feelings about what the USGA had done crystal clear: while he was still serving his one-year suspension, the two men invited Harvie to play in the 1958 Masters, an invitational event over which the USGA has no jurisdiction. Harvie hoped to improve on his fourth-place finish from the year before—a victory would have been one of the great "I'll show you" moments in the history of sport. His close friend Byron Nelson, now anchoring the television broadcast of the Masters for a second year, was privately rooting for Harvie to shock the world. But this was real life, not the Hollywood version; Harvie played poorly and missed the cut. Instead he saw his friend Ken Venturi seize the spotlight, and then suffer another disappointment on that Masters Sunday, when a controversial ruling over an embedded ball of Arnold Palmer's at the twelfth hole ended in Palmer's favor and resulted in his first green jacket, and first major victory, and a second devastating Masters loss for Venturi.

Despite that disappointment, Venturi won four pro tournaments and finished third on the 1958 money list. Time and again Ken urged Harvie to join him out on tour and put the affair behind him, but Harvie stuck to his guns and sought reinstatement of his amateur status in May of 1958. The USGA Executive Committee granted it to him, as they had promised, and Harvie played in both their Open and Amateur Championships that year. At the Amateur at Olympic Club in San Francisco, before losing in the third round, Harvie narrowly defeated an eighteen-year-old freshman from Ohio State named Jack Nicklaus, Harvie's old putter coming to life just in time to neutralize the stocky, crew-cut youngster's jaw-dropping distance off the tee.

Harvie was only thirty-two and hadn't been away from the game for long, but two years can be close to a lifetime in any sport: Nicklaus was the next golden boy everyone, including Bob Jones, talked about now, and he would steamroll the competition during the rest of his collegiate career, winning the NCAA Championship and two National Amateur titles, just as Harvie had done. But Jack did it all before he turned twenty-one, and with his ascendance the focus of the sport shifted, and Harvie Ward discovered he had suddenly become old news. Privately shattered over the misfortune that haunted him, he would never completely recover his unvarnished love for the game. His last hurrah as an amateur would come in 1959, on his third Walker Cup team, when he once again went undefeated and, along with his young teammate and now fast friend Jack Nicklaus, led the American side to victory.

From that point on Harvie's playing appearances came fewer and farther between. He would partner with Ken in the Pro-Am at the Crosby Clambake in 1960, their first return visit as a team to Cypress Point. Ken won the pro side of that tournament, in the worst weather he'd ever played in, and the two men had a chance to win the Pro-Am as well, but Harvie casually tossed away a few strokes down the stretch, as if offering evidence for his lack of interest. Harvie himself said that during this time if he'd had a three-foot putt to win the Open and a girl in the gallery had winked at him, he might well have walked off with her and forgotten about the putt. Venturi had never seen his old friend behave that way on a golf course when it mattered; his anger gave way to concern that Harvie might be headed for the rocks. His concerns proved well founded. Although their lives appeared to be moving in opposite directions, with Ken climbing the ladder of the professional tour into public prominence while Harvie spiraled down and out of control, they were about to find themselves facing starkly similar ordeals.

A few months later, at the Masters in 1960, Ken appeared to at last have clinched his elusive first green jacket with a solid last round, holding the lead in the clubhouse. Then he watched with Byron and Louise Nelson as Arnold Palmer birdied the last two holes to catch and once again pass him for the win. This victory, coupled with his stirring come-from-behind charge in the last round of the U.S. Open at Cherry Hills two months later, would cement the Palmer legend as the game's new man-of-the-people champion. That 1960 Open, for a good part of the final two rounds, looked as if it might belong to forty-seven-year-old Ben Hogan, until he backed up a fifty-yard wedge shot off the green into a pond protecting the seventeenth hole and his chances found a watery grave.

Arnold Palmer shot 65 to win that memorable day at Cherry Hills, fending off a challenge not only from Hogan but also from twenty-year-old amateur Jack Nicklaus, whose cool performance under pressure established his presence on the game's biggest stage and set up a new marquee match-up whose battles would dominate the sport as it entered the television age. A few months later, after handily winning his second National Amateur title, Jack Nicklaus announced, to no one's surprise, that he was turning pro.

The economics of the PGA Tour had continued to improve so rapidly that there was no longer any reason to agonize over that decision, as there had been for Harvie Ward only four years earlier. Players possessing a champion's skills would from this point forward be considered crazy to turn down a chance at the kind of living professional golf now offered; to a man, the world's outstanding amateurs jumped to the PGA Tour without a backward glance. Exceptional players like Nicklaus and Palmer and Gary Player would soon follow Hogan's trailblazing footsteps off the course into entrepreneurial glory, brand-name tycoons presiding over diverse international kingdoms.

Harvie Ward's undefeated record in three Walker Cups has still never been matched, and his seventeen straight wins in the National Amateur would stand for thirty years until the arrival of Tiger Woods; but with his passing from the game, the last golden age of the gentle-man amateur champion—the aristocratic ideal sustained down the years from Ouimet to Jones and to, at the last, Harvie Ward—had been laid to rest in a gilded casket.

Ben Hogan's playing days effectively came to an end at the 1960 Open at Cherry Hills. His putting woes had grown so severe there were occasions when he couldn't make himself draw the club back from the ball. Never a man to indulge in wishful thinking about any-thing, Ben knew he had made his final run at a fifth Open or any other major title. His professional life now centered on his dynamic leadership of the Ben Hogan Company, where he crafted the most innovative and acclaimed mass-produced clubs in the history of the sport. One of the first pros Hogan offered an exclusive endorsement deal to was Ken Venturi, and they would remain devoted and loyal friends for the rest of Ben's life. In partnership with his friend Mar-vin Leonard, Hogan also created Shady Oaks Country Club in Fort Worth, which became his second home and refuge. When Hogan sold his company in the early 1960s to sports conglomerate AMF, agreeing to stay with it as a hands-on chairman of the board, he be-came one of the wealthiest men in Texas. His journey up from the caddie yard at Glen Garden was complete.

Byron Nelson joined ABC as their lead golf commentator in 1963, pairing with Chris Schenkel. Byron's greatest thrill behind the microphone came in 1964, at Congressional Country Club outside Washington, D.C., in crushing heat and humidity. Byron kept his private feelings out of his broadcast with consummate professional skill, but inwardly he was rooting as never before for his friend and student Ken Venturi, who stood six strokes out of the lead halfway through the U.S. Open.

Ken had suffered through four increasingly disappointing years on tour after his loss at the 1960 Masters. He had won ten events during his first four seasons, but none since. A back injury from a minor car accident had altered his swing, throwing it off for nearly two years, but his problems ran much deeper than the physical level. He had two young sons to support now; his marriage had begun to unravel, as had his health and finances; and in a deepening fog of depression he sought solace in the bottle, instead of from wiser friends like Byron Nelson and Ben Hogan. He plummeted toward the bottom of the money list in 1963, and all his corporate sponsors dropped him; he was perilously close to losing his tour card but seemed powerless to stop the slide. Even Eddie Lowery, no longer his boss but still a friend, and a man who was nothing if not upbeat and persistent, couldn't shake him out of his solitary doldrums.

Venturi appeared to be in danger of joining his old partner Harvie Ward on the skids; during this time, an acquaintance remembered seeing Harvie working a shift at a Fisherman's Wharf bar in downtown San Francisco, shucking oysters for pocket change and drinking money. This image of his fallen friend haunted Ken. Contemplating a return to selling cars for Eddie Lowery, he looked down the road beyond that humiliating retreat to what he knew would be eventual, inevitable self-destruction. When a bartender he'd befriended read him the riot act after yet another bender, telling him he was pissing his life away and letting down all the people who'd had such faith in him, Ken hit bottom, fell to his knees in his basement one desperate night, and prayed for guidance. The answer he found led him back to Byron Nelson, who agreed to help him with his game again, and to a San

Francisco priest who'd become a frequent playing partner, Father Francis Murray, from whom he sought pastoral counsel and who gave him in return sound, no-nonsense spiritual guidance. With the help of these two remarkable friends, Ken backed away from the abyss, stopped drinking and feeling sorry for himself, and determined to pick up the pieces of his life.

As a way to kick-start Venturi's comeback, Byron invited Ken to play as his partner in a televised match against Arnold Palmer and Gary Player, part of a series that Arnold, as the sport's reigning superstar, now hosted called *Challenge Golf*. Humbled and uncertain of himself, Ken began their match at Pebble Beach quietly, looking fidgety and ill at ease next to the sleek, world-beater cool of Palmer and Player. Byron, now in his early fifties but swinging as well as ever, and knowing how badly his young friend needed a boost, birdied four of the five first holes to help them jump out to a sizeable lead over their heavily favored opponents. Front and center in their gallery, leading the on-camera cheers that day, was none other than Eddie Lowery. Drawing from the well of Byron's early confidence, Ken's game came to life, and they ended up beating their champion hosts to end the match early, 3 & 2.

Nearly broke, too proud to borrow money from anyone, and playing on sponsors' exemptions, Ken eked out a couple of top ten tour event checks, which allowed him to compete in a local Open Qualifier. He squeaked in by two strokes at the local after a first-round 77 put him on the edge of elimination, then made it through the sectional and earned an invitation to play in his first U.S. Open in four years.

Keeping his expectations low, Ken worked himself into contention during the first two rounds of the Open through patient play and staying in the moment, qualities he'd seldom possessed in abundance. The final two rounds of the Open were still played on the same day—television was about to change that—making it the sternest ordeal in American championship golf. The night before,

Ken found a six-page letter in his locker from his friend Father Murray, offering practical and inspirational guidance. He then spent an hour in prayer and reflection at a nearby Catholic church before retiring early.

Venturi reached the course Saturday morning in a transcendent state of calm, ready to face his demons and accept whatever outcome lay in store. In his morning round, before the sun began to hammer down on Congressional, Ken shot the finest nine holes of his life, a five-under-par 30. By the time he finished his round that morning, with a scintillating 66 that left him only two strokes off the lead, the temperature had risen to well over a hundred degrees, with close to 100 percent humidity. Unaccustomed to such brutal weather on the West Coast, before he was even aware he had a problem, Ken staggered off the course suffering from serious heat prostration. He had been so focused on his round he hadn't had a single sip of water or taken a salt tablet for dehydration all morning. After treating his symptoms, doctors in the clubhouse urged him not to go back out for the afternoon round; in his present condition, there was a good chance the heat might kill him. Ken insisted he had to play his final round. In that moment, surveying the wreckage he'd made of his life, he decided he had nothing else to live for.

Afterward, Ken remembered nothing of what happened during the final round at Congressional that afternoon until the sixteenth hole. Attended by a doctor throughout, cold towels wrapped around his neck, wobbly on his feet, and constantly taking fluids, Ken drew on decades of instinct to keep the ball in the fairway, hit the middle of greens, and play for pars; the classic formula for contending in a U.S. Open. By the time he reached the ninth hole, Venturi had seized a share of the lead. He kept following his ball, avoided looking at leader boards, and, when he was clearheaded enough to do it, constantly thought back to the advice in Father Murray's letter, which steadied him during his hour of need. When he reached the eighteenth fairway, he regained focus long enough to ask his playing partner, twenty-year-old Raymond Floyd, where he stood. Floyd had known Ken for a while, knew he had lost his game and his status as an elite player, and had gone through qualifying with him to reach the Open.

"Stay on your feet," he said, "and you've got it."

Holding a two-stroke lead, Ken put his second shot at eighteen into a greenside bunker, then pitched out to ten feet. Almost unable to stand, he somehow persuaded that ball to drop for par and won the 1964 U.S. Open. Ken dropped his putter and nearly fell to his knees.

"My God, I've won the Open."

Ken looked over at Ray Floyd, who had tears in his eyes; Ken was so overcome by emotion he nearly passed out, and Floyd had to lift his ball out of the hole for him. The crowd went crazy and the ovation continued for minutes, as Floyd and some others stepped forward to help Ken stumble to the scorer's tent. "For the first time in my life," Floyd said, recalling the day, "I believed in something called destiny."

Ken remained so delirious as they went over his scorecard that he had no idea whether they had the right numbers written down for him or not, and he couldn't sort through whether he should sign the card and risk disqualification. Then he felt a friendly hand on his shoulder. It was USGA Executive Director Joe Dey, telling him he could sign his card; the numbers were correct.

The course of Ken Venturi's life turned on its axis that afternoon at Congressional. His career had been resurrected, and his personal life steered back toward longevity and fulfillment. Among the hundreds who called to congratulate him afterward was Bing Crosby, who cried when they got off the phone, one of the few times anyone could ever remember the self-possessed smoothie losing control. Ben Hogan and Harvie Ward and former President Eisenhower reached out to him as well. Ken was named the PGA's Player of the Year in 1964 and *Sports Illustrated*'s Sportsman of the Year. His endorsement money returned, far exceeding previous levels, and as a major winner he seemed at last to find the comfort and self-acceptance that had eluded him for his many years as a hungry, ambitious young man. He would win four more times on tour before being diagnosed with a severe case of carpal tunnel syndrome, brought on by years of hitting thousands of practice shots. Complications after a difficult surgery to correct the problem severely damaged the circulation to his hands, forced his game into decline, and prematurely ended his playing career in 1970. His troubled marriage to Conni finally came to end around that time, but he soon happily remarried and began working as an analyst for CBS Sports' coverage of the PGA Tour. He eventually became their senior analyst and held down his post as the voice of CBS golf for thirty-five years, the centerpiece of which continued to be their yearly coverage of the Masters.

After losing his amateur status, Harvie Ward spent the better part of twenty years, by his own admission, wandering in a wilderness of sorrow, confusion, and loss. Around the Bay Area, where he'd always been such a lively and popular presence, Harvie gradually disappeared from most of his friends' lives, but the fall from grace itself was swift and complete; his heart, and then his spirit, had broken. His business career faltered more than once, and he changed direction several times; without the game that had defined him since he was a boy, his life had lost its rudder. With the exception of appearing at the Masters, repaying a debt of gratitude he felt to Bob Jones and Clifford Roberts for their support, Harvie hardly played golf at all, and after his last Masters in 1966, he gave it up altogether. He taught tennis for a while, did public relations work for a Napa Valley resort, owned a piece of an auto-leasing business, then leased cars for someone else. A second marriage came and went, then a third, and his life continued to drift.

In 1974, at the age of forty-eight and in desperate need of a steady living, he had no other choice than to take the step he'd dreaded sixteen years earlier: Harvie declared himself a golf professional in order to play on the mini-tours that were then springing up around the country; but the competition with a whole new younger generation proved too tough a task. Three years later, he was living hand to mouth, reduced to giving golf lessons in a downtown San Francisco discount department store, when some friends from North Carolina invited him to work on the golf staff at a new resort called Foxfire, near Pinehurst. He left San Francisco and returned to North Carolina to live for the first time in twenty-seven years. Harvie was going home.

Slowly, very slowly, as a teacher humbly working with ordinary students on the range, Harvie began to find himself again. He spent ten years as head pro at Foxfire before accepting a position from a man who had remained a friend through the lean years, the next great amateur after Harvie who'd become a giant in the game, Jack Nicklaus. Harvie became director of golf at Nicklaus's brand-new Grand Cypress Club in Orlando, Florida. During that time he played for parts of two seasons on the fledgling PGA Senior Tour, finally making a few bucks playing against his peers. In his last hurrah, if only to show he still had it, Harvie won the 1980 Senior Open, the year before it became an official USGA championship. Despite his success, the grind of the itinerant tour player suited Harvie no better in later life than it had in his youth, and soon afterward he gave up playing competitive golf for good.

After three years at Grand Cypress, Harvie moved on to become director of golf at nearby Interlachen Golf Club. Two more marriages had come and gone before he found the woman in Orlando with whom he would finally forge a lasting connection, Joanne Dillon—whose father was one of Sam Snead's closest friends—and together they moved back to Pinehurst in the late 1980s. When they decided to marry, Joanne took Harvie home to the Midwest to introduce him to her parents in, of all places, Golf, Illinois, his first visit back to the town where his life had derailed nearly thirty years earlier. Harvie won over his skeptical, formidable new father-in-law in fifteen minutes, and bad memories of Golf were forever after tempered by the couple's newfound happiness.

Although he had long ago left the spotlight in his sport, Harvie remained friends through the years with all the men from The Match. He saw Byron frequently, Ben less so but they stayed in touch by phone and letter, Bing occasionally, and Kenny most of all, often at the Masters, which Harvie still loved to attend as an honored spectator and where Venturi had become a fixture for CBS. They were united again by a sharp sense of loss when Bing Crosby passed away in October of 1977, at the age of seventy-four. After shooting an 85 at La Moreleja Golf Club outside Madrid, Bing and his foursome were walking off the eighteenth green, when he said, "That was a great round of golf, fellas," took another step, and died instantly of a massive heart attack. A figure much larger than life, Crosby was mourned around the world, but in few places were there more mourners than in the world of golf.

Eddie Lowery followed Bing in death in 1984, at eighty-one. He remained a complex, fiery character and devoted friend to the game until the end. It's hard not to find fault with Eddie for leading Harvie down what looked like the garden path, but then Harvie was also a man more than a little willing to be led. Eddie had no way of anticipating that his financial life would be thrown open to the IRS, as a result of what turned out to be false and vindictive accusations of tax fraud. But if he was made an example for doing little in support of his amateurs that wasn't routinely being done around the country, as a member of the USGA's Executive Committee his advising Harvie that everything between them remained aboveboard appears as an act of bad faith. As a result his relationship with Harvie, and to a lesser extent with Ken, came to a terrible pass and caused considerable damage to the reputation of the amateur game. To his credit, Eddie would continue to support other players from the Bay Area, chief among them "Champagne" Tony Lema, former assistant caddie master at San Francisco Golf Club. Lema soon became a rising star on the PGA Tour, and won the 1964 British Open at St. Andrews before his life was cut tragically short in a plane crash at the age of thirty-two.

Eddie never again ran afoul of the USGA. He was a devoted father and family man, philanthropist, and an active player until the day he died, a fixture at both San Francisco Golf Club and Cypress Point. He had never been anything less than a force of nature, and if Eddie Lowery was a man about whom few of his peers failed to form a strong opinion, he was revered by the legions of caddies who had forever been the beneficiaries of his kindness and generosity over the years. This motley, colorful, vanishing culture of blue collar characters, exposed by the vagaries of the game to the weaker aspects of more successful men's natures, are famous for casting a jaded eye on their betters. For them, as the first of their lowly, forlorn caste to rise to great wealth and influence in the country's history, it's no exaggeration to say that to this day, Eddie Lowery remains their patron saint.

The word "saintly" can be more generally applied to the entirety of the life that Byron Nelson lived after his playing days ended in 1946. He continued to represent the game proudly in every possible respect—television commentator, author, Ryder Cup captain, elder statesman—all the while living the daily life of a modest, working rancher on his spread in Roanoke. He continued to teach and mentor some outstanding young players, no one more so than the great Tom Watson, whose personal and professional greatness lived up to Byron's early faith in him, winner of eight major championships and, after the decline of Arnold Palmer, principal rival to Jack Nicklaus in the autumn of his career. Beginning in 1968, only after learning that his doing so would enable a local charity organization called the Salesmanship Club to raise more funds, Byron lent his name to what had for many years been known as the Dallas Open. The Byron Nelson Classic quickly became one of the popular and successful stops on the PGA Tour and, with Byron volunteering hundreds of hours of his time every year, has since raised more money for charity than any other event in the sport's long history.

Byron never sought wealth for its own sake. His needs always remained as plain and unadorned as a gingham tablecloth, but through wise investment, solid counsel, and his own modest habits, wealth came to him nonetheless. And with that unexpected fortune, in quiet, everyday ways, never for show or to put his name in the papers, the good works he performed for people in need in his community of Fort Worth and the wider world are a human accomplishment of rare wonder. The number of people who benefited can hardly be calculated, nor did Byron ever want it to be. Suffice it to say that the nine-foot statue of him they eventually built at Los Colinas, where they play the Byron Nelson Classic, doesn't begin to represent the scope or size of his kindness, charity, and generosity of spirit. The quiet, resilient strength of character he had always displayed drew people in need to him like a beacon, and he made sure they knew where to find him; the Nelsons never moved from their simple two-story Roanoke ranch house. Modest to the end, they never even put in a dishwasher. "I'm the dishwasher around here," Byron used to say with a small amount of pride.

His beloved wife and companion, Louise, after forty-eight years of devoted marriage, suffered a severe stroke in 1983. Confined to a wheelchair, unable to speak, she lived a little longer than two years before a second stroke took her away. Byron cared for her lovingly at home throughout this tragic ordeal, losing his companion and best friend at the age of seventy-three. So profoundly did he feel her loss and so deep was his mourning that Byron's own life would have ended not long afterward, if he hadn't become reacquainted the following year with Peggy Simmons, an advertising writer thirty-three years his junior. A sprightly, joyful personality, Peggy became the main reason this "broken-down old pro"—as he called himself—regained his appetite for living, and they were married in late 1986. Byron, who deserved such an opportunity as much as few others, had been given a second chance at happiness.

On the other side of Fort Worth, Ben Hogan's life wound slowly down in an entirely different direction. The chronic pain he suffered in his legs, the lasting legacy of his catastrophic accident, worsened as the years went on, ending any enjoyment he could derive from playing even casual golf by the 1980s. As long as he was able, he would still repair to his office on the far right side of the driving range at Shady Oaks and hit golf balls with the same discipline, and for the same private satisfaction, that it had always given him. But during a time in their lives when Byron continued to travel the world, a friend to thousands as a beloved ambassador of their sport, Ben withdrew to the privacy of home and Shady Oaks, seldom venturing except by necessity outside those safe, familiar confines. He had had his fill of the world wanting a piece of him and seemed genuinely puzzled by its enduring interest; what he seemed to want, after all his time in the public eye, was to be left alone. After helping guide the Ben Hogan Company for over thirty years, he watched in dismay as the company that had bought it from him sold out to the same Japanese investors who would soon buy Pebble Beach. Their stewardship proved disastrous to Hogan's core business of innovative club design; it was sold twice more in quick succession, and Ben's active involvement came to an end.

Hogan lived in permanent horror at being thought of as a relic. The nostalgic, ceremonial roles that Gene Sarazen, Sam Snead, and Byron Nelson played in later life, hitting crowd-pleasing old-man drives on the first tee to open competition at the Masters each year, filled him with dread. Many honors and late-life tributes did deservedly come his way, but he agreed to participate in only a select few, one a memorable 1983 CBS Sports interview he gave to his old friend Ken Venturi, the most revealing glimpse Hogan ever allowed into his guarded past and impenetrable psyche, under Ken's patient and sympathetic questioning.

Hogan's intense need for privacy only served to amplify the world's insatiable curiosity about him. An almost mythic cult of personality developed during these years surrounding his extraordinary talents, with hints that he'd come into possession of tantalizing secrets no other man had ever wrested from the game, a bit of harmless prestidigitation he did little to discourage. His secrets, such as they were, in the end emerged as the concrete results of his life's work, an exhaustive distillation of the game's prime fundamentals, broken down and analyzed to an unprecedented degree, the result of his tireless labors and relentless pursuit of perfection. Hogan once had a dream that he'd played a round of golf in which he recorded seventeen holes in one, and woke up angry that he'd missed the last one. That perfectionism, and the legend it provoked, in the end created a different kind of burden for Hogan.

The enduring tragedies that drove him down his lonely path remained the only real secrets of Ben Hogan's extraordinary life. His legendary reticence, the product of not much more than innate shyness and stark childhood insecurity, assumed even more prominence as he aged, drawing inward and shrinking his social circle down to a select few. Not many ever knew him well, but those who did said they felt privileged and that he was vastly worth knowing. Ben Hogan was always and to the end a man of faultless loyalty, honor, and integrity, but seemed destined also to remain a solitary figure, profoundly alone, bearer of a deeply kind but cruelly wounded heart, in whose protection he had early on built walls that allowed him far less of the world's good grace and affections than he came to deserve. Those walls guarded secrets that had burdened his family across the better part of a century, and in fulfilling their purpose they denied Ben Hogan many of the simplest affections and trusts and bonds of companionship that enrich the pleasure of daily living. But even through all of those elaborate, reinforced, and involuntary defenses, toward the end a small mercy found its way to him.

During the last years of his life, as the strands of time came unstrung in memory, Ben referred often, sometimes puzzlingly, to an alternative version of himself he seemed to perceive, a person he called "Henny Bogan." Ken Venturi was one of the first to realize he was referring to the happy, carefree boy he had once been so long ago, until the age of nine, when his father catastrophically took his own life, and dragged "Henny Bogan" with him to the grave. But that poor misbegotten child hadn't perished for good; he'd simply gone to ground, exiled into some uncharted region of the soul, safe and free to emerge again only near the end of Ben's life. This phantom remnant of "Henny," perhaps even his lively inward presence, a little boy at long last safe within the shelter of the older man nearing the end of his journey, seemed to comfort and console him. Ben Hogan, who had suffered a great deal more than anyone's fair share of the harshest indignities of life and time, and stood his ground in a way that can only be described as genuinely heroic, died on July 25, 1997, at the age of eighty-four.

Ben's closest friend, George Coleman, had died only a few days earlier, in Florida, at the same age of eighty-four, recently retired after many years at the helm of Seminole Golf Club. George had divorced his first wife, Elizabeth, not long after The Match—she went on to remarry and become the duchess of Manchester—and lived out his life involved with many successful businesses, jetting between his homes around the world, happily married to his second wife, Dawn, for nearly forty years.

Ken Venturi served as one of Hogan's honorary pallbearers, along with Sam Snead. Byron Nelson did not receive an official invitation from Valerie Hogan, but attended anyway, with his wife, Peggy, sitting in the blazing midsummer heat with the thousands of other ordinary folks who felt compelled one last time to honor and pay their respects to the brave and stalwart champion who occupied such a special place in their memories.

Ken Venturi attended the services that day with an even heavier heart. He had suffered his own devastating blow earlier that year, when his beautiful second wife, Beau, the soul mate with whom he had shared twenty-five happy and successful years, was diagnosed with inoperable brain cancer. Beau died in his arms at home only three weeks before Ben Hogan's passing. As Ken sat alone in the back of the church in Fort Worth, the scenes of his life shifting through his mind, many cherished memories of Ben Hogan drifted back to him, prominent among them, and now forty years past, that glorious day they spent together at Cypress Point.

Harvie Ward had, with his new wife, Joanne, finally found his own redemptive peace by the 1990s, the couple a fixture now in Pinehurst, the classic idealized version of the small Carolina town in which he'd grown up. No community in America is more about golf, and Harvie represented the living history of the game better than any other citizen of Pinehurst, the place where it all began for him, at the North-South tournament in 1948. Teaching had become the center of his life, and the PGA named him their "Teacher of the Year" in 1990, an honor he came to value as much or more than any trophy he'd ever won in his prime. A cheerful, relaxed, and avuncular presence, holding court every morning from his own table in the local coffee shop, where photos of his playing days to this day adorn the walls, Harvie served as a kind of mayor without portfolio. He tooled around town in his shiny black Jaguar bearing the license plate "Ol' Harv," and he'd wave or stop to chat anytime you wanted to have a word, but he rarely talked about himself, unless it was some fantastic and funny yarn that ended at his own expense. If you were having an awful day, he'd find a way to cheer you up inside two minutes. Having seen the best and worst that life had to offer, Harvie had grown into a man supremely comfortable in his own skin, with depth, wisdom, and empathy to spare. His friends, even casual acquaintances, all felt the same way about him: that in his gracious company you never felt more recognized, more liked, or more richly entertained.

The sport of golf throughout the wider world began slowly to rediscover Harvie Ward around this time. His distinguished former teammate, fellow U.S. Amateur champion and formidable opponent during their prime Bill Campbell, while serving on the USGA's Executive Committee, took the extraordinary step of inviting Harvie to one of their committee meetings at the Country Club of North Carolina, in Pinehurst. With Harvie in the room, Bill recounted the full story of his great years, and the mitigating facts behind his fall from grace, to a new generation of officers who knew nothing about it: a remarkably kind and healing gesture that helped restore Harvie's faith in the game's governing organization, and Harvie Ward to his proper place in the canon of the game.

During regular golf trips he now began to take to Scotland, where, as far as fans of the sport were concerned, his greatness had never been forgotten, Harvie was welcomed like a prodigal son. He became a popular, sought-after presence at corporate golf outings, conducting clinics, working generously with teachers and schools. Among the dozens of talents he helped patiently to develop was the young Payne Stewart, who would soon go on to much greater things. In 1996 Harvie was paired with Sam Snead in a *Legends of Golf* event. That same year, at his tournament in Texas, Byron Nelson named Harvie Ward as the Classic's yearly honoree, making a point of having Harvie sit beside him on his viewing platform behind the eighteenth green, introducing a new generation of modern players to the man he called the greatest amateur to play the game since Bob Jones.

During one of his last trips to the Masters, just after the turn of the new century, Harvie spent a few minutes catching up with Ken Venturi in the Jones Cabin on the grounds at Augusta National. When Harvie left, a friend who'd been there with Ken asked him who that man was; he had a notion that it might have been an old amateur golfer named Harvie Ward.

"Let me tell you all you need to know about Harvie Ward," said Venturi, with his clipped, assured conviction. "Nicklaus in his prime, Harvie in his prime; I'll take Harvie."

Ken retired from his post at CBS Sports in 2002 after thirty-five years behind the microphone, the longest tenure of any network broadcaster in golf. Through tragedy and triumph, he had transformed from a brittle, vulnerable, stammering kid who nearly lost his early promise to one of the most respected and dignified men in all of sport. By the end of his television career, just as Byron Nelson had done before him, not only for the public but also the players, Ken Venturi had become the voice and face of American golf, a guardian of its traditions, a steward of its history, and a living example of its highest charitable values.

In 2004 Harvie Ward was diagnosed with advanced liver cancer. He was told any treatments would, at best, delay the inevitable, and that he should put his affairs in order. One of his closest friends from Pinehurst during the last decade of his life, Jeff Dawson, arranged a final trip to California and accompanied Harvie a few weeks after the Masters, recruiting another friend who owned a private plane to help Harvie cope with the travel. They flew in to Monterey and spent the next day playing a final round at Cypress Point. Harvie had hoped to renew his old friendship with the club's gracious longtime pro, the only man to hold the post after Henry Puget finally retired in 1961, Jim Langley, one of the game's great gentlemen, but Jim had been called out of town on business.

On the first hole, Harvie hit a superb drive, foozled his second about fifty yards, then hit his third to eight inches and tapped in for par. He winked at his partners, then promptly birdied the second hole. (Jeff warned them: "You're going to see a lot of that today.") As they played their way around the storied grounds, after a little cajoling Harvie opened up and regaled his foursome with stories about The Match. When news spread around the Monterey Peninsula that Harvie Ward was playing Cypress Point that day, the lightly trafficked course filled with people appearing from every direction, just to shake his hand. On the eighteenth green, with the hole cut in the same position as it had been that January day so many years before, Harvie challenged each of his partners to set a ball down on the spot from where Hogan had made his putt to clinch the match, and try to sink it himself. Not one of them could come anywhere near the cup.

"That was Hogan," said Harvie.

They spent the next day at San Francisco Golf Club, the first time Harvie had been back to his old club since he'd taken ill. Word had gotten around that this would be his last visit, but as he would have wanted, no one made a fuss. Harvie was welcomed as if he'd never been gone a day; the gruff old locker room attendant had a shined pair of his shoes and a line of old bantering insults, both ready for Harvie. Every employee and member on the grounds gathered at the first tee to watch them go off that morning.

"Harvie," asked Jeff, taking the tee, tongue firmly in cheek, "in case I play really well, what's the course record?"

"Sixty-three," said Harvie. Then with a grin: "Twice."

The crowd around them laughed, in on the joke. Harvie played well that day, as he did throughout their trip. A part of the course near the eighteenth fairway known as "Harvie's Hollow" still honors his fifty-year-old club scoring record at San Francisco Golf Club, and that record stands to this day.

Late that afternoon the group flew down to Palm Springs, to spend the next day and a half with Ken Venturi. The two friends greeted each other like old school chums; hugs, drinks, meals, a lot of laughs, concern for each other's health—Ken had recently gone through and survived his own battle with cancer. Harvie met Ken's lovely new wife, Kathleen, and charmed her, predictably, within minutes. Over dinner one night, among the stream of memories they shared was one final return to their match at Cypress Point, refreshed again in Harvie's mind after his recent round. The others sat spellbound around the table as Ken and Harvie relived the highlights of that incredible day. Both Ken and Harvie had told the story so many times over the years they could spin it like a platter on a jukebox, and the lore about it had by now slowly filtered out into the world and grown into legend, but they hadn't talked about it in thirty years in each other's company, and the immediacy of the experience came rushing back and filled them with wonder again.

"I still say we could have beat 'em if I'd had some sleep," said Harvie.

"We were kids," said Ken. "Who thought sleep was important?"

"Still, losing to a Ben Hogan birdie on the last hole? Not too shabby."

They were quiet for a while then.

"We had a hell of a time," said Harvie. "Out there on the coast."

"Yes we did, Harv."

The next day Ken drove them to the airport, parking beside the plane as they loaded in. The two old friends posed for pictures, there were hugs and kisses, and then it was time to say good-bye, for the last time, with tears in their eyes, and those of anyone else who was watching.

"Hey, I think I met your former wife last night," said Ken, teeing up one last old joke for him as Harvie climbed the stairs.

"Yeah?" said Harvie. "Which one?"

Harvie played his final round a few weeks later, at Forest Creek outside Pinehurst, where he often played and taught during his final years. He had trouble getting around by then, but he chipped in for birdie at the first, birdied the second, parred in from there, and called it a day. When he saw his companion's sadness that he was unable to continue at the turn, Harvie smiled, put an arm around his shoulder to console him, and said: "It doesn't matter. It's only golf."

Harvie died peacefully at home, with Joanne at his side, three months later, on September 4, 2004.

The whole community of Pinehurst turned out for his memorial service, and there was universal sorrow but also heartwarming reflection as friends and family paid tribute to Ol' Harv. Although he had captured far more than the average man's collection of trophies in his time, he prized his friends more highly. He hadn't become rich or unduly famous, the fate that had once seemed so indelibly written on the wind for him, but the winds had changed, and judging by the crowd that showed up for Harvie that day, he'd found something that in the end keeps a man much warmer when the nights turn cold. One of the best definitions of tragedy describes a man who suffers a fall from a high and favored place in life through the consequences of the actions of others and no fault of his own. That comes close to summing up what happened to Harvie Ward, but he never would have applied the word to his life; there was no bitterness or self-pity in him, and by virtue of his evolving character, at the end his life had become anything but tragic. When the crowd walked out of the memorial at Pinehurst Country Club that day, as it had for everyone he came to know throughout his eventful ramble, the memory of Harvie left them smiling through their tears. A close friend later offered a final word on Harvie's life, a passage of which he would have wholeheartedly approved:

"Life is not a journey to the grave with the intention of arriving safely in a pretty and well-preserved body. But rather, to skid in broadside, thoroughly used up, totally worn out, and loudly proclaiming . . . 'Wow, what a ride!'"

Above all else, Byron Nelson believed that in life a person must be useful to others: provide, contribute, share, love, and do no harm. As he moved into his nineties, forced by grudging infirmity to slow down his joyful embrace of an active, involved, and giving existence, he continued to find smaller ways to express that essence of his nature. Slowly, one by one and not by choice, he let go of the many human pursuits that had given him pure and simple satisfaction: riding a fine horse, mending fences, clearing trees, hitting a crisp golf shot, even walking, near the end. But nothing stopped him. He loved to work with wood, and built a clean, well-lit shop a few paces in back of his house; there are thousands of homes and offices and schools around the world that treasure the presence of a hand-crafted chair, or letter box, or pencil holder bearing his branded signature.

A competitive spark could still flare in his gentle gaze, whenever asked how he might do against the godlike modern champions: "I think I'd hold my own," he'd say, with the steely, confident understatement of a frontier sheriff. No doubt should remain on this question whatsoever; leaving the sport as early as he did may have deprived him of the lofty numbers we associate with some all-time greats, but few men have ever played or will ever play the game as well as Byron Nelson in his prime. If he no longer traveled as often as he used to, Byron welcomed a steady stream of visitors, well-wishers, and old friends to the ranch in Roanoke; what had begun fifty years earlier as six hundred isolated country acres was now an oasis in the developing suburban beltway of the Dallas–Fort Worth metroplex. His longevity and enduring physical energy were a testament to a clean life well lived, but living as long as he did, Byron also suffered the plentiful sorrows of watching so many companions and contemporaries pass before him. Despite which, with ever more time for reflection, Byron refused to live in the past, a model of kindness and decency keeping in close touch with the world and two new generations who found abundant reason to know and admire him.

Byron never talked much about Ben Hogan during his lifetime, and only with noticeable reluctance after Ben died. He recognized that, despite their similar origins and obstacles and many shared experiences, they were vastly different beings. Hogan truly puzzled him at some deep level, and he never came to fully understand why a man blessed with such great talent and so much to offer held himself apart from the world the way he did. Byron respected him, and refused to judge him, but he saw life first and foremost as a gift to be shared with others, and with regard to that crucial quality, they had finally parted ways. For nearly the last half century they'd known each other, Byron had never once been invited to Ben's house, or ever received a card or note or telephone call, when it was simply so fundamental to Byron's nature to reach out to people; he was as gregarious as a toddler. They were like brothers, estranged, joined at the start of life by circumstance and time, but finally separated by circumstances they couldn't control and their own mysteriously diverse natures. Neither was schooled or particularly interested in the modern fixation with the psychological. Byron didn't know the shameful secret that Ben had been forced to bear since he was a boy; no one outside the Hogan family ever did. Nor could he know the extent to which his father's tragic end had robbed Ben of feeling that the essence of who he was could be of any lasting value to another man. At peace with so much of life and who he was, there remained for Byron a small but tangible dissatisfaction that this gulf between them had never been fully reconciled.

As the shadows lengthened, Byron saw nothing there to fear. His faith, unwavering since boyhood, made deep rooted and unbreakable by time, only grew stronger. He remained active to his final days, making a set of his signature wooden keepsakes for the members of the 2006 American Ryder Cup Team. For all the honors and accolades the world bestowed upon him, few experiences on earth gave him deeper satisfaction than sitting near his wood shop, gazing out at the gently rolling ranch land he'd been so content to tend and care for all those years; and that's where Byron's life came to its end, quietly and in peace, on the morning of September 26, 2006. Peggy had left him at eight fifteen that morning to leave for a Bible study class. He kissed her tenderly and told her again, as he so often did, how proud he was of her. When she returned, shortly after noon, Byron was gone.

Even the frenzied headlong media-driven modern world seemed to stop spinning in place for a moment to take note. His turned out to be not just another obituary for a half-forgotten figure from a distant age long since passed. Because he'd touched so many lives for so many years, and remained so true to the basic principles by which he lived, Byron had remained timeless, standing outside of any particular memory or era. He'd stepped away from the glare of his sport's spotlight at thirty-four, and contributed far more of lasting value to the world around him, certainly as far as he was concerned, in the six decades that followed than he had during his thirteen professional years between the ropes. As an athlete, it's safe to say that there were few Americans who could rival him in any sport, and he established towering records that will never be broken. As a human being, Byron Nelson defined his own category, and in it stands alone.

Five speakers paid tribute to Byron's memory at his memorial service, held a few days later at the Nelsons' nearby church, Richland Hills Church of Christ. To reflect the proper perspective of the role the game played in his life, only one of them came from the world of golf, but he spoke first. Ken Venturi.

"This is a day that had to come, Peggy," he said, looking down at her from the podium. "But we never prepare for it."

He spoke fondly of his first meeting with Byron, as a teenager who'd pestered him with a camera in the middle of a tournament, how much he'd meant to him as a friend and mentor at the start of his career, and the many wonderful experiences they'd gone on to share during their fifty-year relationship.

"Some people come into our lives and quietly go away. Others stay for a while and leave footprints in our hearts and we're never the same because of it. He gave strength in times of weakness. He gave courage in times of fear. And he gave love in times of doubt. You could always turn to Byron when you were in need, he was always there, and he gave you the best he had.

"I once asked him how I could repay him for all he'd done for me. His answer was simple: 'Be good to the game and give back.'

"There is deep loss and sorrow in times like this. But there couldn't be a lot of sorrow unless there was a lot of happiness. Every time I think about Byron, I will smile . . .

"And to you, Byron, may God bless you and hold you in the palms of his hands. I will always thank God you passed my way. You've been like a father to me. Farewell, my friend. I will miss you, and I love you very much."

Ken Venturi is the last of that foursome who's still with us. Now entering his late seventies, confronting his own share of health challenges, Ken's life with Kathleen remains active and busy, filled with charitable works—among them a foundation he started in his name to help others who suffer from chronic stuttering—and hundreds of friends around the world in the game of golf, a legacy that would not disappoint either one of his mentors, Byron and Ben, or his best friend, Harvie.

Cypress Point, although perennially considered one of the world's greatest golf courses, is often said now to have been rendered somewhat obsolete as a stern test of the sport by today's cutting-edge technology in the hands of a new generation of powerful professionals. Although still a PGA Tour event, what used to be called the Crosby Clambake hasn't been played at Cypress Point for nearly twenty years; nor, regrettably, is the name Crosby any longer associated with the proceedings, and the broadcast now more often than not seems to serve as a vehicle to promote the antics of network sitcom clowns. The winner of the event takes home a check for just under a million dollars; more than double the combined career winnings of both Byron Nelson and Ben Hogan.

As a result of its departure from the PGA's calendar, aside from a few added yards and new tee boxes, the golf course at Cypress has resisted any fundamental "improvement" over the intervening decades, as so many of the classics have been compelled to do to keep the big boys interested. Cypress Point remains unfailingly true to the origins and genius of the extraordinary man and woman who originally brought it into being. Another thing about the course hasn't changed either; a round there remains one of the transporting experiences in sport, and no one, amateur and professional alike, who has a chance to play Cypress Point ever forgets it. In spite of all these modern, globe-trotting young guns armed with dangerously combustible golf balls and clubs forged with the latest futuristic R & D, only three players have since tied and no one has to this day yet broken Ben Hogan's course scoring record of 63 at the Cypress Point Golf Club.

The Match could never happen today. Not with all the money and handlers and media scrutiny swirling around the world of sports. It would end up on television, a hollow concoction cooked up by some calculating sharpie in a $2000 suit, bought and sold, and played, for cold, passionless cash. Nor could you any longer find two amateurs able to give golf's best pros anything close to a fight worth watching. The professional side's dominance of the game hasn't been in dispute for over forty years; the issue was settled not long after that day at Cypress Point when Ken Venturi turned pro and Harvie Ward lost his status. The career gentleman amateur like Bob Jones and these two men is officially an archaic figure, gone the way of the buffalo and the buggy whip. For two generations the game hasn't produced a player who could seriously contend in a major championship and was content to remain an amateur. There's an argument to be made that the loss of the once fierce competition at the amateur level has hurt the pro game as well, producing a steady stream of skilled but passionless corporate practitioners content with making their millions, who seem to lack the character, hearts, and fire of our greatest champions. There may be something to that; in the wake of Tiger

Woods, the last three-time U.S. Amateur champion—who learned how to focus and win at that level and whose stunning, unparalleled success has single-handedly shot the economics of the game into the stratosphere—not a single American player has won more than a handful of important events, or led his team to victory in the last great championship played for something other than money, the Ryder Cup. That's a sorrow, but facts are facts. Not enough of the meaningful prizes in life are contested solely for honor anymore, for the love of the thing itself, or the undiluted satisfaction of testing your mettle against the best you can find and, win or lose, walking away the better for it because of the truths it enabled you to face and find out about yourself.

No four men will ever play such a match again. No four men like these. The genuine way they lived their lives makes most of today's fast and frenzied sports and entertainment culture seem like so much packaged goods, a self-conscious, inauthentic hustle. In their best and worst hours alike each one of these four stood his ground, put all he had on the line, and for better or worse lived with the consequences of his actions and moved on. Some green, untested souls might be tempted to wonder why one should still care, but none of us are here forever, we're not even here for long; and if it's true that our collective past exists inside all of us, unless we take time to bear witness to the best of those who strived before us, our chance to learn from their lives will be lost forever, and we will be the poorer for it.

APPENDIX

MONTEREY AND CYPRESS POINT

It has been called the most sublime collision of land and sea anywhere in the world. A blunt headland jutting out from the coast, viewed in outline from above, the Monterey Peninsula looks like nothing so much as the head of a sturdy Scottish terrier staring resolutely west into hostile waters. A geologic remnant of violent tectonic activity, its twenty square miles encompass a remarkable diversity of terrain, flora, and fauna. The rocky granite coastline dotted by picturesque cypress gives way to a belt of sandy dunes that quickly rise into steep, craggy hills blanketed by dense pine forests. A microclimate of marine-layer fog often blankets the headland to the peak of the hills; on the eastern, drier slope the land transitions over to California oak and chaparral. The deep-water bays that bracket the Peninsula host a bounty of fish and shellfish, seals and sea otters. Various Native American tribes of hunter-fisher-gatherers found everything they needed to sustain human life in the area as long ago as 4000 B.C. They would exist there undisturbed until Portuguese mariner Juan Rodríguez Cabrillo sailed by in the sixteenth century, only fifty years after Columbus, mapping the coastline. An expedition headed by Spanish explorer Sebastián Vizcaino finally made landfall, laid claim to the land in 1602, and named it after his patron, the Count of Monterey.

Spanish priests and soldiers arrived in force to colonize the region in 1769, in a race against Russian fur trappers, working their way south from their Alaskan territory. The Spaniards established two towns at opposite ends of the Peninsula's neckline: Monterey to the north, where they built a port and presidio to guard it, and Carmel to the south, named after the mission that Father Junipero Serra built there for his patron saint, San Carlos de Borremeo de Carmelo. From this beachhead, the missionaries spread inland and in both directions, and Monterey soon became the capital of the Spanish colony of California. Fifty years later, in 1821, the Mexican flag was raised over the governor's hacienda when that nation won independence from Spain. Twenty-five years after that, during the Mexican-American War, three American gunboats full of marines sailed into Monterey, captured the city without incident, and claimed six hundred thousand square miles of California for the United States. The capital stayed in Monterey, but when statehood followed eight years later, it was moved to San Jose and then Sacramento, closer to the action of the 1849 gold rush that ignited migration to California.

Soon afterward most of the land on and around the Peninsula passed into the hands of a Scottish immigrant, David Jacks—he bought thirty thousand acres for a grand total of $1000—who said it reminded him of home. (He's remembered today for a local cheese he favored that was eventually named after him: Monterey Jack.) The whaling industry flourished in and around Monterey through its brief heyday in the mid-nineteenth century, and attracted a wave of settlers to the area. Throughout these early decades, in slow, sad, predictable fashion, the Peninsula's native Neolithic Ohlone tribe, pressed into servitude by various occupiers, lost their land, their culture, and eventually their lives.

The lush fisheries in Monterey Bay—schools of sardines, halibut, mackerel, and shellfish—allowed modern life on the north end of the Peninsula to flourish in the early twentieth century. Over twenty canneries soon lined the wharves, and attracted waves of working-class Sicilian fishermen, who tripled the population of Monterey in twenty years. To the northwest, near Point Pinos, a group of Methodists from San Francisco established a summer retreat on land granted to them by David Jacks in 1875. They pitched their camp tents on tidy $50 lots, and once they were connected by light rail to Monterey, their colony developed into the conservative, blue collar town of Pacific Grove.

To the south, in sharp contrast, Carmel-by-the-Sea gradually blossomed as a writers' and artists' colony; many of its new residents relocated there after the devastating San Francisco earthquake of 1906. That theatrical bohemian community gave rise to a popular school of Western American landscape painting, became home to the first outdoor playhouse west of the Rockies, and nurtured the early career of nature photographers Ansel Adams and Edward Weston. Authors as diverse as Jack London, Robert Louis Stevenson, Ernest Hemingway, Henry Miller, Gertrude Stein, Sinclair Lewis, and John Steinbeck all drew inspiration from the Peninsula's magnificent isolation, stunning landscapes, exotic social mix, and moody climate.

As the emerging American middle class began to develop a taste for leisure activities and vacations in exotic locales, tourism emerged as a marketable commodity that at least one of the region's farsighted business leaders saw as the future. In 1879 most of the Peninsula's undeveloped real estate had been sold for $35,000 by David Jacks to the Pacific Improvement Company, an entity owned by the four horsemen of Northern California's Gilded Age: railroad barons Charles Crocker, Leland Stanford, Collis Huntington, and Mark Hopkins. They erected a massive resort in 1880 called the Del Monte Hotel, with accompanying racetrack, tennis courts, botanical garden, and polo field, just north of Monterey, to attract tourists to the area. A complex of swimming and reflecting pools was added, and they installed hot sea baths—a current fad—for those "suffering from rheumatic complaint." An old horse trail that meandered south to Carmel was upgraded, dubbed the Seventeen Mile Drive—the length of the round trip from the hotel to Pebble Beach—and advertised, not inaccurately, as the most scenic drive on the West Coast. The hotel sent guests out to experience the drive by carriage and, soon afterward, chauffeured cars. The nine-hole golf course they added in 1897, and later expanded to eighteen holes, is now the oldest in the country west of the Mississippi.

The Del Monte resort thrived for a generation, but by 1915 the Victorian flagship was limping along at less than half capacity, tired and out of step with changing times. The tycoons of Pacific Improvement ordered their company's new manager to liquidate all their holdings in what was known as the Del Monte Forest, fifty-two hundred heavily wooded acres between Monterey and Carmel. That manager was a man named Samuel Finley Brown Morse, namesake and distant cousin of the nineteenth-century Yankee genius who invented the telegraph. Based on what he did after taking a long look at the Peninsula, it seemed that Samuel Morse had inherited a spark of the same visionary instinct.

Only thirty-two at the time, the ambitious, Massachusetts-born Morse saw exploitable assets where his aging employers saw liability. Within four years he secured his own financial backing, bought the property himself, and created Del Monte Properties Company to manage it. But the old Victorian-era resort and its primitive links would not serve as the centerpiece of his dream; Morse, former captain of the Yale football team but not yet a golfer, was satisfied with neither of them. The declining hotel had been built at a chilly remove from the spectacular coastline, while the golf course offered little challenge to the serious golfer and nowhere near enough scenery for the casual vacationing player. Convinced of the emerging sport's potential to attract the upscale American consumer—exactly as he had

seen it do in Pinehurst, North Carolina—Morse laid out a master plan
to develop Monterey Peninsula into a world-class destination that
would include another hotel and at least five additional golf courses.

He called his initial effort "The Second Course," but Morse soon
changed the name of the course he ordered in 1916 to the Pebble
Beach Golf Links. Codesigned by two talented amateur golfers
named Jack Neville and Douglas Grant, the creation followed a
unique figure-eight routing through the upland pines, with eight
holes that hugged the rugged coastline. Although not a links in the
strict definition of the word, Pebble Beach was the first American resort course that so vividly recalled the Scottish origins of the game.
Morse replaced a rustic log cabin near the golf course that had
served as a traveler's way station with a grand hotel he called the
New Del Monte Lodge. With its completion on a bluff above the
course's eighteenth green for a cost of $75,000, Morse's Pebble
Beach resort opened for business in 1919.

Pebble Beach soon became a favored destination for the well-
heeled from the booming communities of Los Angeles and San Francisco, but Morse's ambitions for the Peninsula were just beginning.
He possessed a developer's hunger to bring civilization to the area
and a conservationist's zeal about preserving its natural grandeur.
Next to open in 1926 would be a private club and real estate complex north of Pebble Beach, called Monterey Peninsula Country
Club, designed to serve the influx of wealthy residents who Morse
thought would want to build homes in this unique environment.
While that club was in the planning stages in 1923, Morse made his
next smartest decision: he hired a thirty-year-old woman named
Marion Hollins as the athletic director of the Pebble Beach Resort.

On December 3, 1892, in East Islip, New York, Marion Hollins
had been born into a cloistered Gilded Age world of unimaginable
wealth and privilege. Her father owned a Wall Street brokerage firm
and had for years been an investing partner with his closest friends,
William Vanderbilt and J. P. Morgan. Gliding between their Man-

hattan mansion and a six-hundred-acre estate on Long Island, Harry and Evalina Hollins were leading figures in Eastern society. In these last decades before income tax, America's superrich lived like Old World royalty. When one of his sons complained their estate didn't have a proper beach for swimming, Harry Hollins bought a fifty-acre island in Long Island Sound.

Spending summers chasing four older brothers around their estate, Marion developed a tomboy's interest in sports. Haunting the family stables, she could ride almost before she could walk; in childhood photos of her on horseback she looks as joined to the animal as a Pony Express rider. As a teenager Marion enjoyed an odd kind of fame as a driver of a "coach and four," a huge four-horse carriage, one of the most demanding tasks in horsemanship. During World War One Marion made all the front pages on the East Coast when she drove one of these rigs from Buffalo to New York, raising money for the war effort. She became the most accomplished female polo player in the country—the *only* one who played regularly in men's leagues—and also made headlines as the first woman to ever drive a race car in mixed company. But more lasting fame would come to Marion Hollins because she was also an extraordinarily talented golfer.

After discovering golf during trips to Europe, Harry Hollins took up the game in its American infancy before the turn of the century. When his daughter showed interest, Harry commissioned a young Scotsman named Willie Dunn, who had just finished his first course nearby, called Shinnecock Hills, to build a private course on the Hollins estate. At the age of six Marion began taking lessons; by the time she was ten she was beating her older brothers. At fourteen she entered the U.S. Women's Amateur and won the title at the age of twenty-nine. Marion's game was astonishingly different from other women's of her era; a tall, strapping blonde, she smashed every shot with full-bodied fury, routinely driving over 250 yards. But, a feminine grace note to her power, she paused at the top of every backswing and silently recited the word "poise."

Nicknamed "The Golden Girl" after her win at the 1921 Amateur, Marion was often called the female counterpart to Bobby Jones. Not long after her championship, Bobby and Marion played an exhibition in Atlanta, and Bobby confided in a friend that he was fortunate Hollins hadn't been born a man, because he was fairly certain he'd never have beaten her. But Marion Hollins was a lot more than a premier athlete. She had come of age in the company of greatness and from the outset possessed a magnetic, vital personality, a gift for social interaction, and what was often described as a "man's mind." Even as a teenager, Hollins was filled with restless purpose and a hunger to achieve, along with the energy, intelligence, and drive to bring her visions into being. Her motto, which she quoted freely to anyone who questioned her chances, was "Failure is impossible."

But after her Amateur win Marion hit the ceiling of where golf could take her; there would be nothing like a pro tour for women for another two decades. A lesser person might have complained that in an age dominated by men she was denied opportunities, but Marion was an early suffragette and took equality between the sexes as a given. Her first effort as an entrepreneur grew from an unheard-of conviction that women deserved a course of their own. After winning the Amateur, Hollins toured the classic courses of Britain and returned home to organize the first women's private golf club in the world, Women's National in Glen Head, New York. She hired Devereaux Emmet, one of America's few established architects, helped him design the course, and recruited the membership. Women's National became an immediate success.

When Harry Hollins lost his fortune in a bank failure before Marion could inherit, she set out to make her own living. During her first trip to the West Coast and Monterey, Hollins made such an impression on developer Samuel Morse that he offered her the job of athletic director at Pebble Beach. The resort's untapped potential made such a powerful impression that Marion accepted on the spot. She went to work organizing tournaments to draw golfers to the area, and dominated the first two women's events. Since she knew every net-worth millionaire on the East Coast, she began helping Morse sell real estate, set up an office in New York, and over the next two years became one of the first "bi-coastal" commuters. In 1924, attracted by the mild winters and relaxed lifestyle, Marion moved full-time to the Peninsula. California now seemed the only place big enough to contain Marion Hollins and her oversized dreams.

Hollins's first assignment was to help Morse plan the other golf courses he had in mind. Marion identified a 150-acre parcel a mile north of Pebble Beach that early Spanish settlers had named "*La Punta de Cipreses.*" Here, at Cypress Point, all the geologic themes of the peninsula came together in a stunning fusion of dunes, coves, tide pools, rolling hills, and towering pine. The gnarled, angular silhouettes of wind-bent cypress trees lined rugged cliffs over a tempestuous slate gray sea. When the sun burned through the overcast in late afternoon and bathed the coast in golden light, the wind relented, and the waves let up their perpetual assault against the cliffs of the Point, Marion Hollins felt a transcendent charge light up her senses. Cypress Point, she told Morse, was *the* place to build the most glorious golf club on the planet. Not a family resort catering to the general public like Pebble Beach; an ultra-private course for discriminating captains of industry. Less sure that the profits he had in mind could be wrought from such uncompromising land, Morse needed more convincing. So certain was Hollins about her instinct that she decided to option the parcel from Morse—at $1000 an acre—and create Cypress Point Golf Club herself.

Hollins hired established architect Seth Raynor to design Monterey Peninsula Country Club—for Morse—and then bring to life her vision of Cypress Point. Raynor, a Princeton graduate and civil engineer by trade, had apprenticed under the tyrannical Charles Blair McDonald during his creation of America's first great golf course on Long Island, the National Golf Links. After creating his own firm, and over sixty courses around the country during the game's first great expansion, Raynor remained an oddity among his peers: a golf architect who never played the game. He had nearly finished Monterey Peninsula Country Club and was drawing up plans for Cypress Point when, exhausted by the demands of success, he died suddenly of pneumonia at the age of fifty-one.

Within months, Marion Hollins found Raynor's replacement. If Raynor had approached his profession with the mind of a technician, Dr. Alister MacKenzie possessed the soul of a poet. Born in northern England to industrious Scottish parents, MacKenzie followed his father into medicine, earning degrees in chemistry and natural science at Cambridge. After serving as a surgeon in the army for three years during the Boer War in South Africa, he settled into private practice in his home city of Leeds, a manufacturing center in north central England. During his years under fire in field hospitals, MacKenzie developed a strong interest in the strategic use of camouflage, a battlefield art with which the underdog Boers—at the cost of thousands of British lives—excelled at in concealing defensive emplacements. MacKenzie carried this unique interest home with him, where after a chance encounter it merged with the pursuit that was about to become the sustaining interest of his life: the game of golf.

The first man to earn his living in Great Britain as a golf course architect possessed one of the most professionally prophetic names of all time: Harry *Shapeland* Colt. In 1906 Colt was invited to Leeds to submit ideas for the redesign of Dr. MacKenzie's home course, the Alwoodley Club. That invitation may not have been brokered by Dr. MacKenzie, who chaired the greens committee, but he welcomed Colt's arrival. A hearty outdoorsman, MacKenzie was a latecomer to the game but quickly discovered an affinity for it not only as a player; he had strong opinions, some of them downright revolutionary, about golf course design. Once Colt arrived and the two men recognized their shared obsession with the fledging art form, MacKenzie insisted Colt stay in the doctor's guest room during the remainder of his visit.

After weeks of discussions about how to improve the mid-dling course at Alwoodley, MacKenzie experienced a life-changing epiphany: he wasn't a talented amateur with some passable ideas; he was a passionate, aspiring artist in the wrong line of work. His col-laboration with Colt was judged an unqualified success. Over the next seven years, in his spare time, MacKenzie designed a dozen courses, until in 1914 he announced he was giving up medicine to pursue golf architecture full-time. Later that year, he won an inter-national write-in contest for *Country Life* magazine, contributing a design for the home hole of a new course on Long Island called the Lido. In a life often beset by bad timing, MacKenzie's winning entry was announced on the day that World War One erupted in Europe.

The forty-seven-year-old MacKenzie rejoined the British Army to again serve as a front-line surgeon. Witnessing the unprece-dented brutalities that came close to destroying civilized Europe, Dr. MacKenzie finally persuaded his traditional superiors to con-sider his experimental theories about defensive camouflage on the battlefield. He resigned his commission as a major in the Medical Corps and took a lieutenant's rank in the Royal Engineers in order to try to implement them. The hidebound military bureaucracy re-sisted most innovations, so the number of lives saved as a result re-mains uncertain, but MacKenzie emerged as one of the world's leading authorities on the subject.

After the war ended, MacKenzie resumed his career in Great Britain as a golf architect, publishing the first definitive book on the subject. This led to his first important professional commission, in 1923, as a consultant on St. Andrews's fabled Old Course for the Royal & Ancient Golf Club, where he developed a system for champi-onship pin positions that is still in use today. His intense months-long scrutiny of the evolving miracle that had served as the cradle of his game immensely enriched the doctor's appreciation for the history, art, and science of his adopted practice. He was ready to fulfill what he clearly saw as his life's destiny: to be a creator of classic golf courses.

Eager to expand his horizons, but restricted by postwar economic doldrums in Britain, the fifty-five-year-old MacKenzie embarked on his first trip to pursue American employment in early 1926. The doctor crossed paths just after his arrival with a wealthy author, teacher, and philanthropist named Robert Hunter. Hunter was a study in contrasts: a committed Midwestern middle-class Socialist who'd authored a best-selling book about sources of poverty in capitalist America—placing the blame entirely on the rich—while living on the vast estate of the rich family into which he had recently married. Hunter ran unsuccessfully for governor of Connecticut on the Socialist ticket and eventually became a professor of English and economics at the University of California in Berkeley. A lifelong interest in golf helped mitigate his bias against the upper class. A talented player himself, Hunter moved his family to Pebble Beach just after Samuel Morse opened his resort, and had begun work on his own book about the emerging arts and principles of golf architecture when he met Alister MacKenzie.

Hunter directed MacKenzie to his home in Northern California, and a job to redesign a country club in Claremont, across the Bay in nearby Oakland. That led to MacKenzie's second local commission, at the Meadow Club in Marin County. Both of these projects were built by a construction company owned by Robert Hunter. During their collaboration, the socially connected Hunter introduced MacKenzie to Marion Hollins. Immediately after that meeting of like minds, Marion Hollins tapped MacKenzie to carry the torch after the death of Seth Raynor. Cypress Point picked up momentum again.

MacKenzie knew that in Cypress Point he had been handed the most magnificent canvas on which to create a course any architect had ever known. His only concern was that the holes suggested by the existing landscape would be so inherently difficult not even accomplished players could ever hope to master them. But backed by the unqualified support of Hollins—thousands of miles from the restricting traditions of home—the radical artist in MacKenzie for the first time felt free to give full expression to the cutting-edge theories he'd nurtured during his long apprenticeship.

MacKenzie walked the Cypress property throughout February of 1926, often with Marion Hollins at his side, in every kind of weather. The land varied wildly, quickly sloping up from the coastal cliffs, banked by ancient dunes all along the northern edge, skirting up into the forested foothills of the Santa Lucia Mountains, where herds of black-tailed deer and elk ran free. Knowing that all the consensus "great" courses in the world rested on consistent, unvarying terrain, MacKenzie decided he would instead make a bold virtue of this shortcoming. He orchestrated a route through these different zones that would create not only a rising physical challenge and a dramatic progression of mood but, by its climax along the rocky, windswept coast, provoke a spiritual journey for the soul. MacKenzie submitted his initial plan for Cypress Point to Marion Hollins, in the form of a magnificent God's-eye-view painting, in early March, and then returned home to England, where, under a variety of pressures, his marriage was coming to an end.

With MacKenzie's design as a powerful selling tool, Marion Hollins went to work selling memberships. Her goal was to recruit two hundred members at $2500 apiece, to underwrite costs of constructing the course and clubhouse. When she netted a hundred members in less than a year, Hollins called in her option and completed the purchase of the land from Morse. She hired the famous Olmsted Brothers—responsible for New York's Central Park—to create a landscape plan integrating the club into the Peninsula's surroundings. By the time MacKenzie returned in 1927 to modify the final placement of tees and greens, all the financial goals had been reached, which allowed Robert Hunter and company to begin construction of the golf course in late November.

MacKenzie's plans called for a vast transformation of the existing landscape; over forty-five acres of Monterey pine were dynamited to widen playing areas and open up vistas to the ocean. Thirty more usable acres were created along the rocky coastline by trucking in tons of topsoil to cover them and in which to plant hardy, seaside turf. They consulted chemists to balance and perfect the composition of soil, and expert botanists helped select their grass seeds. To ensure that the integrity of the doctor's designs would be realized intact, Hunter brought over two foremen who had worked with MacKenzie in England. Their mule teams spent months reshaping the towering sand dunes and crafting new bunkers to perfect MacKenzie's vision of an utterly natural, "found" look. They uncovered countless layers of pottery, arrowheads, and other archaeological artifacts, broken remnants of the Ohlone tribe's centuries of existence on the Peninsula. Although the project was budgeted at $150,000, Robert Hunter's team would bring it in at less than two thirds of that price and two months ahead of schedule. MacKenzie, whose deal called for a fee of 10 percent of the finished price, ended up being paid $8800 for his contribution. The course opened to members for play in August of 1928; the club's gracious colonial clubhouse, designed by another famed architect, George Washington Smith, opened in 1930.

MacKenzie's concerns that the members of Cypress Point would find his golf course too difficult proved unfounded. Unable to be present at the opening—and used to having what he considered his best work savaged by the average duffer—he was alarmed when Hunter cabled him that not a single discouraging word had been uttered. From the moment the opening drive was struck, critics raved that Cypress Point was the greatest golf course ever built in the United States. It wasn't until he returned to tweak the finished product himself in November of 1928 that MacKenzie realized why: people were too busy gasping in astonishment at its beauty to care how they played. The hand of man had so artfully improved on the raw materials of nature that no one could tell where the work of one ended and the other began, and it took everyone's breath away.

But MacKenzie knew it was more than just the incomparable picture postcard panoramas his players were reacting to. He had always maintained that no other course in the world could ever possibly compete with or surpass St. Andrews for its inherent greatness, the eternal interest of its strategic challenges, and the sheer excitement it generated for golfers of every ability. As he wrote that November just after his visit, "the completion of Cypress Point has made me change my mind."

Marion Hollins and Alister MacKenzie had created a masterpiece. With the support of his rich and generous patron, a bold, revolutionary artist had been recognized in his lifetime. In the flush of that unqualified success, the future suddenly seemed limitless, and other opportunities began to flood their way. For both of them, but for one more brief, shared moment in the sun, it would be all downhill from there. In the high wake of success at Cypress Point in 1928, Marion Hollins, newly rich again because of her oil investments, bought a promising 570-acre parcel of rolling hills fifty miles to the north, near Santa Cruz. She hired Dr. Alister MacKenzie to create another golf course for her, the centerpiece of a massive, all-in-one resort she built there called Pasatiempo, Spanish for "passing time." Hollins envisioned a master planned community, designed to compete with Pebble Beach: real estate, schools, roads, marina, polo fields, racetrack, grand hotel, the works. With her deep pockets, mad energy, and connections in high society and Hollywood, she brought it to fruition in less than two years. For opening day of her new golf course in 1929, Marion played a ceremonial foursome with British Amateur champion Cyril Tolley, three-time U.S. Women's Open champion Glenna Collett Vare, and the game's immaculate avatar, Bobby Jones. The opening was a smash success, and Pasatiempo appeared destined for the same sort of greatness and worldwide popularity already enjoyed at Pebble Beach.

A few weeks later, the American stock market crashed and the national mood turned on its heel. Marion plunged ahead with her ambitious plans, laughing at forecasts of gloom and doom; she'd seen markets tailspin a dozen times since her gilded childhood and saw no reason to give up pursuit of a permanent good time. She was also instrumental in founding the Curtis Cup, the distaff version of the Walker Cup competition between American and British amateurs, and captained the first American team in 1931. Throughout the early grim years of the Depression she continued spending and expanding Pasatiempo, against everyone's advice, always confident the sun would rise the next day on a better world. To her credit, as the financial picture darkened, hotel guests vanished, and her expensive real estate parcels didn't sell, she refused to cut her payroll during hard times or stop caring for indigent or wayward family and friends.

Her friend and business partner Dr. Alister MacKenzie had, since the opening of Cypress Point, enjoyed a career renaissance, traveling around the globe designing courses that are still regarded among the finest in the world: Crystal Downs, Royal Melbourne, the Valley Club, Lahinch, and his work with Marion Hollins at Pasatiempo. Then, during that memorable opening weekend at Pasatiempo, Marion introduced Dr. MacKenzie to Bob Jones, who greatly admired both that course and Cypress Point. Impressed in every way by the older man, Jones hired MacKenzie to design the ambitious new course he was planning in his native Georgia, Augusta National. MacKenzie completed his work on Augusta in 1932, but in the darkening shadows of the Depression, he never visited the finished version of what would eventually become the most celebrated golf course in North America. In the end, keeping company with Marion Hollins and her wealthy circle during those desperate times had cost him dearly; MacKenzie's own finances were by now in ruin; he was living hand to mouth with his new wife in a small home near Pasatiempo. After sending a series of panicked telegrams to Clifford Roberts, trying to collect the last installment of his commission for Augusta, on New Year's Eve, 1933, MacKenzie died of a massive heart attack at the age of sixty-three. A few days later his ashes were scattered over the fairways of Pasatiempo. The appreciation of Augusta National prompted by the advance of the Masters aside, not for nearly half a century afterward, when the reawakening of interest in early golf course design began in earnest in the 1980s, was the body of MacKenzie's gigantic contribution to the soul of the game given its full and just recognition.

Nearly out of money herself, the end for Marion Hollins and Pasatiempo began on the night of December 2, 1937. Winding its way on the narrow roads near the resort, Marion's sports car was struck head-on by a drunk driver. She suffered severe head injuries and remained bedridden for six months. Lingering effects of her concussion triggered a worsening set of neurological and behavioral symptoms that poisoned Hollins's sunny optimism into a venomous hash of paranoia, depression, and delusion. No longer willing or able to face harsh reality, by 1940 Marion was forced to sign over Pasatiempo in its entirety to her creditors; a few months later she lost her beautiful home there as well. She was now nearly penniless, caring for her alcoholic brother, and barely able to care for herself. Her spirit, after so many decades of titanic effort, ambitions realized and thwarted, had broken. Of all the wealthy and privileged friends around the world she'd treated with such generosity and warmth throughout her life, only her former employer at Pebble Beach, Samuel Morse, stepped forward to help. He saw to it that Marion was moved back down to Pebble Beach and gave her a house, rent-free, and a face-saving title, with no actual responsibilities, with his Del Monte Properties Company.

On her good days, increasingly fewer and farther between, Marion played golf with friends or hotel guests, and she could still pull her formidable skills together on the course. In 1942 she won the Pebble Beach Women's Championship, the tournament she'd started to promote the resort twenty years earlier, for the eighth and final time. Shortly after that Marion beat the reigning U.S. Amateur champion, Marion Hicks, in an exhibition match at Pebble. Hicks was twenty-one at the time, Marion forty-nine. She never played another competitive round of golf. Marion Hollins died two years later, on August 28, 1944, alone and forgotten in a nursing home in nearby Pacific Grove, at the age of fifty-two, a few miles from her beloved Cypress Point.

NOTES ON WRITING

After hearing a shorthand version of The Match years back, I began two years ago to make inquiries about it and eventually, in an extended series of conversations with a warm and generous Ken Venturi, and an unforgettable day with Byron Nelson, pieced together the story. Although Harvie Ward passed away before I could spend time with him, his widow, Joanne, and close friend Jeff Dawson helped me come to feel as if I'd known Harvie for years; soon afterward I had a vivid dream about playing golf with Harvie, and, eerily, the very next night, he appeared to Joanne in a dream to say how much he had enjoyed meeting me. (Make of that what you will.) Jim Langley and Joey Solis at Cypress Point were invaluable in helping me re-create the day, and to experience and appreciate the golf course. Eddie Lowery's daughter, Cynthia Wilcox, who played such an important part in my coming to understand her father during the writing of *The Greatest Game Ever Played,* generously shared Eddie's voluminous correspondence from this period in his life. Many others, acknowledged below, contributed various pieces of this mosaic, so that this retelling is exclusively drawn from the memories, memoirs, and recollections of the six primary figures involved, and surviving witnesses. The dialogue herein is either verbatim or re-constructed from their various accounts. When the accounts varied, as in oral histories they inevitably do, the differences have been weighed and the results offered along whichever way the preponderance of opinion directed.

ACKNOWLEDGMENTS

This undertaking would not have been possible without the broad and generous cooperation of many people, most particularly Ken Venturi and Byron Nelson, two gentlemen one counts oneself most fortunate indeed to have met or known. I am also deeply and particularly indebted to Joanne Ward, Jeff Dawson, Jon Bradley, Peggy Nelson, Cynthia Wilcox, Eddie Merrins, Jim Langley, Joey Solis, and Dawn Coleman for their invaluable contributions.

Many others to thank for their insights: Sandy Tatum, Bill Campbell, Nathaniel Crosby, Jack Burke, Ben Crenshaw, Jim Vickers, Raymond Floyd, Rayburn Tucker, Suzanne Tindale, Patty Moran, Rand Jerris, Peter Kessler, Bob Donovan, Bill Stitt, Gary Laughlin, Ric Kayne, John Keller, Casey Reamer, Sid Matthew, Jack Frazee, Scott Nye, John Marin, Andy and Margaret Paige, John Campanionette, Catherine Lewis, Jack Whittaker, Gary Lieberthal, Todd Yoshitake, Mike Yamaki, Joe Patterson, Terry Quinn, Selwyn Herson, Ron Cherney, Don Bisplinghof, Jim Ferree, John Sklvara, Tom MacLean, and Brian Wynbrandt.

As always, enduring gratitude to my great friend and agent, Ed Victor; to my wonderful editor, Gretchen Young; and my favorite publishers, Will Schwalbe, Ellen Archer, and Bob Miller.

INDEX